The Humanity of Jesus in Matthew

The Humanity
of Jesus in Matthew

MATT JONES

☙PICKWICK *Publications* · Eugene, Oregon

THE HUMANITY OF JESUS IN MATTHEW

Pickwick Publications
An Imprint of Wipf and Stock Publishers
199 W. 8th Ave., Suite 3
Eugene, OR 97401

www.wipfandstock.com

PAPERBACK ISBN: 978-1-7252-8658-0
HARDCOVER ISBN: 978-1-7252-8659-7
EBOOK ISBN: 978-1-7252-8660-3

Cataloguing-in-Publication data:

Names: Jones, Matt, author.

Title: The humanity of Jesus in Matthew / by Matt Jones.

Description: Eugene, OR: Pickwick Publications, 2021 | Includes bibliographical references and index.

Identifiers: ISBN 978-1-7252-8658-0 (paperback) | ISBN 978-1-7252-8659-7 (hardcover) | ISBN 978-1-7252-8660-3 (ebook)

Subjects: LCSH: Jesus Christ—Humanity | Bible. Matthew—Criticism, interpretation, etc.

Classification: BS2575 2021 (paperback) | BS2575 (ebook)

04/30/21

This project is dedicated to the Triune God.
May he be glorified in light of this study of the Gospel of Matthew.

Contents

Acknowledgments

THERE IS NO WAY to acknowledge every single person the Triune God used to make it possible for me to complete this project, but here are a few that came immediately to my heart and mind when I reflect on this process.

To Duane Geib who taught me to love the Scriptures.

To Dennis Ingolfsland who gave me the freedom to ask any question I wanted to ask about the human Jesus.

To Timberline and Bear Valley who prayed, supported, listened, encouraged, and believed.

To Graham Twelftree who pushed me to write, to think, and to accomplish more than I thought I could.

To Mom who prayed that I would still love Jesus at the end of this project. Mom, I still do.

To Dad who sacrificed by doing whatever I asked to help me throughout the work on this project.

To Kenzie who helped correct this book.

To Tyler who asked how the project was going.

To Hannah who believed I could complete a book.

To Cat who loved in light of and in spite of me throughout this project. Without you, no project exists.

Preface

SINCE MY TIME IN undergraduate studies, I have been interested in the humanity of Jesus. Belief in his transcendence was reinforced regularly, especially as I read the Gospels, but I found myself asking questions that emphasized how Jesus was human like us so we could be like him. My fascination with his humanity and its pragmatic implications far outweighed the assumed belief in Jesus's transcendence which led to this book.

This project contributes to the understanding of Matthean Christology through a study of Matthew's portrayal of the humanity of Jesus. Interchanging narrative and discourse to tell the Jesus story, Matthew portrays the human story to provide evidence for and belief in Jesus as the Christ. However, Matthew uses Jesus's humanity for more than simply deepening the faith of his reader. To establish the significance of Christ's humanity, Matthew divides the human story into three parts with the use of the transitional phrase ἀπὸτότεἤρξατο ("from that time he began," Matt 4:17; 16:21). These structural markers, in conjunction with redaction and narrative criticisms, assist to draw out Matthew's interest in the portrait of Jesus's human beginning (1:1—4:16), human life with transcendent status (4:17—16:20), and human end (16:21—28:20).

Working with traditional undergraduate students for over fifteen years, I have found that some deem humanity incapable of modeling Jesus because he was God-incarnate. That mentality causes me to ponder whether we are really asking too much of people to pursue imitating Jesus because of his transcendent status. This in-depth examination of Matthew's interest in and connections between Jesus's human story and the rest of humanity leads us to conclude that Matthew wrote so that humankind can imitate Jesus, the exemplar.

As the first narrative critical examination of the humanity of Jesus in Matthew's Gospel, this project examines Matthew's Gospel et seriatim. As a result, the evidence suggests three primary considerations regarding

Matthew's use of the human portrait of his main character. First, how does Matthew prioritize his interest in Jesus's humanity in comparison to the other Gospels? Second, how does Matthew approach the human and transcendent identities of Jesus to encourage belief in his main character? Third, how and why does Matthew preserve and develop the human story of Jesus? Answering these questions in this book will demonstrate the priorities that guide Matthew's portrayal of the human Jesus.

Believing in the humanity of Jesus gives people hope. Hope not only that Jesus's character and priorities can be imitated but also hope that imitating him affects the world around us. His teachings, example, and power through the Holy Spirit should inspire humankind to make this world a place where people work together to help humanity flourish. While study and research are vital to a proper understanding and imitation of Christ, scholars need to care just as deeply about the pragmatic nature of academic findings. Taking the human story of Jesus seriously should not end without a reminder of the pragmatic nature of what it means to reflect Jesus's character and priorities. He was the greatest human who ever lived for God's glory and for the flourishing of human existence.

Abbreviations

1QM	Milḥamahor War Scroll
1 Chr	1 Chronicles
1 Esd	1 Esdras
1 Tim	1 Timothy
1–2 Cor	1–2 Corinthians
1–2 Kgs	1–2 Kings
1–4 Macc	1–4 Maccabees
1–2 Pet	1–2 Peter
1–2 Sam	1–2 Samuel
1–2 Thess	1–2 Thessalonians
AB	Anchor Bible
ABD	*Anchor Bible Dictionary*
ABRL	Anchor Bible Reference Library
Ag. Ap.	*Against Apion*
AnBib	Analecta Biblica
ANRW	*Aufstieg und Niedergang der römischen Welt: Geschichte und Kultur Romsim Spiegel der neueren Forschung.* Part 2, *Principat.*
Ant.	*Jewish Antiquities*
BA	*Biblical Archaeologist*
Barn.	Barnabas
BDAG	W. Basuer, F. W. Danker, W. F. Arndt, and F. W. Gingrich, *Greek-English Lexicon of the NT* (2000)
BECNT	Baker Exegetical Commentary on the New Testament
BETL	Bibliotheca Ephemeridum Theologicarum Lovaniensium
BEvT	Beiträgezurevangelischen Theologie

BHT	Beiträgezur historischen Theologie
BJS	Brown Judaic Studies
BNTC	Black's New Testament Commentaries
BR	*Biblical Research*
b. Šabb.	Babylonian Talmud tractate *Šabbat*
b. Sanh.	Babylonian Talmud tractate *Sanhedrin*
BZ	*Biblische Zeitschrift*
CBQ	*Catholic Biblical Quarterly*
CD	Cairo (Genizah text of the) *Damascus (Document)*
Cels.	*Contra Apion = Against Apion*, by Josephus
Colloq	*Colloquium*
ConBNT	Coniectanea Neotestamentica or Coniectanea Biblica: New Testament Series
CSHJ	Chicago Studies in the History of Judaism
CurTM	*Currents in Theology and Mission*
Dan	Daniel
DBI	*Dictionary of Biblical Interpretation.*
Deut	Deuteronomy
Di	*Dialog*
DJG	*Dictionary of Jesus and the Gospels.*
EDB	*Eerdmans Dictionary of the Bible.*
Eph	Ephesians
ETL	*Ephemerides Theologicae Lovanienses*
ExAud	*Ex Auditu*
Exod	Exodus
Ezek	Ezekiel
FF	Foundations and Facets
Gen	Genesis
Geogr.	*Geographica= Geography*
Hab	Habbakkuk
Hag	Haggai
Haer.	*Dehaereses= Heresies*
HBT	*Horizons in Biblical Theology*
HHBS	History of Biblical Studies
Heb	Hebrews

Hist.	*Historiae = Histories*
Hist. eccl.	*Historia ecclesiastica= Ecclesiastical History*
Hos	Hosea
HTR	*Harvard Theological Review*
HvTSt	*Hervormdeteologiese studies*
IBC	Interpretation: A Bible Commentary for Teaching and Preaching
IBS	*Irish Biblical Studies*
ICC	International Critical Commentary
IDS	*In die Skriflig*
Int	*Interpretation*
Isa	Isaiah
JBL	*Journal of Biblical Literature*
JECS	*Journal of Early Christian Studies*
Jer	Jeremiah
Josh	Joshua
JRT	*Journal of Religious Thought*
JSNT	*Journal for the Study of the New Testament*
JSNTSup	Journal for the Study of the New Testament Supplement Series
Judg	Judges
J.W.	Jewish War
LEC	Library of Early Christianity
Lev	Levitcus
LNTS	The Library of New Testament Studies
LXX	Septuagint (the Greek OT)
Mal	Malachi
Marc.	*Contra Marecellum= Against Marcellus*
Matt	Matthew
Mic	Micah
Menah.	Menahot
NAC	New American Commentary
NIBCOT	New International Biblical Commentary on the Old Testament
NICNT	New International Commentary on the New Testament

NICOT	New International Commentary on the Old Testament
NovT	*Novum Testamentum*
NovTSup	Supplements to Novum Testamentum
NT	New Testament
NTL	New Testament Library
NTM	New Testament Message
NTS	*New Testament Studies*
Num	Numbers
OT	Old Testament
Pesiq. RabKah.	*Pesiqta de RabKahana = Pesiqta of RabKahana*
PG	Patrologiagraeca = Patrologiae cursus completus: Series graeca. Edited by J.-P. Migne. 162 vols. Paris, 1857–1886
Phil	Philippians
PL	Patrologia Latina =Patrologiae cursus completus: Series latina. Edited by J.-P. Migne. 217 vols. Paris, 1844–1864
ProEccl	*Pro Ecclesia*
Prov	Proverbs
PRSt	*Perspectives in Religious Studies*
Ps/Pss	Psalms
Pss. Sol.	Psalms of Solomon
Q	Quelle, a hypothetical document used by Matthew and Luke
Rev	Revelation
Rom	Romans
SBT	Studies in Biblical Theology
ScrC	*Scripture in Church*
SHBC	Smyth & Helwys Bible Commentary
Sir	Sirach/Ecclesiasticus
SNTSMS	Society for New Testament Studies Monograph Series
SNTW	Studies of the New Testament and Its World
SP	Sacra Pagina
TDNT	G. Kittel and G. Friedrich (eds.), *Theological Dictionary of the New Testament*
T. Gad	Testament of Gad
T. Naph.	Testament of Naphtali

TynBul	*Tyndale Bulletin*
WBC	Word Biblical Commentary
Wis	Wisdom of Solomon
WTJ	*Westminster Theological Journal*
WUNT	Wissenschaftliche Untersuchungenzum Neuen Testament
Zech	Zechariah
Zeph	Zephaniah
ZNW	*Zeitschriftfür die neutestamentliche Wissenschaft und die Kunde der älteren Kirche*

1

The Humanity of Jesus in Matthew

BIBLICAL SCHOLARS NOTE THAT each of the Gospels portray Jesus as similar to the rest of humankind. If Jesus is one of us, then study of his humanity has significant implications for life. Raymond Brown argues that the Jesus of the Gospels is like other humans because he is "tired, testy, indistinguishable in a crowd, treated as a fanatic and a rabble-rouser."[1] Describing Jesus as a first-century exorcist, John P. Meier resolves that "Jesus was a man and a Jew of his times."[2] John Knox proposes that the "humanity [of Jesus] is both more sure and more important than the pre-existence."[3] Additionally, Dale C. Allison Jr. explains that several "texts present [Jesus] as a human being like the rest of us, a person of flesh and blood and of human psychology."[4] Providing examples, Allison states: "He admits that he does not know when the end will come (Mark 13:32). He prays to God, and in the face of death he must wrestle to annul his desire before the divine will (Mark 14:32–42). And, at the end, he dies, feeling that God has forsaken him (Mark 15:34)."[5] Allison relies on Mark's text to develop the idea that Jesus is a human like us, but the question is whether Matthew presents Jesus as a human like the rest of us and what he attempts to accomplish through his portrait of Jesus.

1. Brown, *Introduction*, 27.

2. Meier, *Mentor, Message, and Miracles*, 406–7, argues that exorcisms do not separate Jesus from other humans because of the existence of other exorcists (Mark 9:38–40; Matt 12:27 // Luke 11:19; Acts 19:11–17). See also Vermes, *Jesus the Jew*, 19–41.

3. Knox, *Humanity and Divinity of Christ*, 74.

4. Allison, *Historical Christ*, 80.

5. Allison, *Historical Christ*, 80. Harrington, "Jesus Our Brother," 118–28, underscores other human characteristics such as faith, prayer, anger, and fear in the NT.

Matthew's portrayal of Jesus's humanity not only reflects his sources, Mark and Q,[6] but also deviates from them.[7] Notably, Matthew removes Jesus's failure to heal a blind man on his initial attempt (Mark 8:22–25). In a scene by the Sea of Galilee, only Mark's Jesus desires to have a boat ready to leave the crowd in case θλίβωσιν ("they might crush") him (Mark 3:9 // Matt 12:15 // Luke 6:17–19). In other instances, Matthew chooses to maintain,[8] change,[9] and transpose[10] from one pericope to another human qualities of Jesus. Matthew adds human features to the Jesus story, such as a genealogy (Matt 1:1–17), needing protection from Herod (Matt 2:13–23), and paying temple taxes (17:24–27). Examples like these lead us to question whether Matthew possesses a different emphasis than Mark regarding Jesus's human existence.[11]

Even though scholars such as Allison and W. D. Davies indicate Matthew possesses a "higher Christology" than Mark,[12] the previous examples cause one to reconsider that idea.[13] Matthew's reliance on, yet deviation

6. For the purposes of this project the Two Source hypothesis solution to the synoptic problem will be accepted not only due to NT scholar general acceptance but also due to comparing the internal evidence within the Synoptics. See ch. 1, n11 below. For further discussion on the synoptic problem, see Goodacre, *Synoptic Problem*; Stein, *Studying the Synoptic Gospels*; Edwards, *Hebrew Gospel*; Baltes, *Hebräisches Evangelium und synoptische Überlieferung*; Porter and Dyer, *Synoptic Problem*.

7. Goodacre, "Criticizing the Criterion," 167, states: "Matthew's and Luke's reluctance to relate Markan material that limits Jesus's power illustrates the possibility that the same kind of thing happened in the earliest decades."

8. In the Garden of Gethsemane, Jesus is described as ἀδημονεῖν ("to be troubled") and περίλυπός ("very sorrowful," Matt 26:37–38 // Mark 14:33–34).

9. Also in the Garden of Gethsemane, Matthew shifts Jesus's emotion from ἐκθαυβεῖσθαι ("to be greatly distressed") to λυπεῖσθαι ("to be sorrowful," Mark 14:33 // Matt 26:37). Moreover, in Matthew's text, a crowd (Matt 9:33), the disciples (8:27, 21:20), and Jesus (8:10) all θαυμάζω ("marvel") at one time or another in the Matthean narrative. However, Matthew removes that very emotion from the scene in Nazareth where Jesus faces rejection (Mark 6:6 // Matt 13:58).

10. Matthew and Luke remove Jesus's ἐμβριμησάμενος ("sternly charged") command to the leper to say nothing (Matt 8:4 // Luke 5:14 // Mark 1:43), yet, apart from Mark and Luke, Matthew adds an ἐνεβριμήθη ("sternly charged") command to the two blind men to remain silent after their healing (Matt 9:30 // Mark 10:52 // Luke 18:43).

11. Davies and Allison, *Matthew 1–7*, 1:104–5, also suggest that Christology evolves from lesser to greater as "there was an enhancing of feeling: of reverence, an increase in Jesus's position and status. Hence, because Matthew possesses a higher Christology than Mark, and because he lacks certain details which make Jesus more human, all presumption is against Matthean priority."

12. Davies and Allison, *Matthew 1–7*, 1:104–5.

13. Davies and Allison, *Matthew 1–7*, 1:104–5, provide examples which remove Jesus's emotions, such as ἐμβριμησάμενος ("sternly charged," Matt 8:4 // Mark 1:43 // Luke 5:14) and ἐθαύμαζεν ("marveled," Matt 13:58 // Mark 6:6). However, both of these later

from his sources, shows that he prioritizes the humanity of Jesus due to his own purpose for and perspective on Jesus's humanity. This project will explore whether Matthew's portrayal of the humanity of Jesus differs from the other Gospels in order to propose the priority for, purpose of, and perspective on Matthew's portrait of the human Jesus.

1.1 A DEFINITION

Before addressing the priority, purpose, and perspective the humanity of Jesus play in Matthew's Christology,[14] the definition of "human" requires attention. Any understanding of Jesus's identity begins with the human aspects of life that he has in common with all humankind.[15] It is clear that the humanity of Jesus plays an important role in each Gospel story.[16] Jesus experiences aspects of humanity such as birth, hunger, temptation, family, ignorance, suffering, and physical death. A closer comparative reading of the Synoptics not only demonstrates that the stories highlight different elements of Jesus's human existence but also raises the question of whether the authors view his humanity in the same way.

In a study of the humanity of Jesus in John's Gospel, Marianne Meye Thompson defines "human" as one who is "differentiated from animals on the one hand and God on the other; accordingly, certain elements—birth, family, life activities, death—constitute the outline of what we expect to be told about any human being."[17] This definition serves as the means to evaluate Matthew's perspective on Jesus's humanity. While Matthew includes

appear in Matthew's narrative. See ch. 1, n9 and n10 above. These examples suggest Matthew's inconsistent use of sources to portray Jesus's human emotions.

14. The earliest patristic testimonies attribute the author of the first Gospel to the apostle Matthew. Although modern scholarship treats the patristic testimony with suspicion, Papias identifies the author of the Gospel as the disciple Matthew in Eusebius: *Hist. eccl.*, 3.39.16. Due to church history, external evidence attributing the Gospel to the disciple, and no other viable authorial candidate, this project will work from the perspective that the disciple Matthew is the author. Also see Wilson, *When Will These Things Happen?*, 63–64; Gundry, *Old Is Better*, 49–73; France, *Gospel of Matthew*, 15.

15. Macquarrie, "Humanity of Christ," 245.

16. Voorwinde, *Jesus' Emotions*, summarizes the emotional focus of the four Gospel authors. He presents Matthew's Jesus as "The Compassionate King," Mark's as "The 'Man of Sorrows," Luke's as "The Sympathetic Son," and John's as "The Loving Lord." Grün, *Jesus*, provides a portrait of Jesus's humanity by following Luke's narrative theology through the earthly life and deeds of Christ. Thompson, *Humanity of Jesus*, 10, primarily using Bultmann and Käsemann as conversation partners, advances four topics that serve as evidence that John had an interest in the portrayal of the humanity of Jesus through observing "Jesus' origins, incarnation and flesh, signs, and death."

17. Thompson, *Humanity of Jesus in the Fourth Gospel*, 7.

each of the aforementioned aspects of the life and activity of Jesus, the question remains whether Matthew makes similar distinctions between animal, human, and God in his portrayal of Jesus.[18]

An exegete's goal is to define "human" in light of an author's understanding. While each Synoptic maintains the perception that Jesus is a man,[19] none of the Synoptics defines "human" or how the term applies to Jesus.[20] However, other early Christian literature contrasts Jesus to Adam (Rom 5:14–15; 1 Cor 15:21) and identifies him with the rest of humankind (1 Tim 2:5; Heb 2:6).[21] Peter's sermon in Acts designates Jesus as ἄνδρα ("a man") attested by God (Acts 2:22), but the book of Acts never offers a definition of human. The lack of definition for human suggests that early Christian authors neither need to define nor describe what it means to be human since the readers know what is necessary to classify a creature as human.

1.2 A DISTINCTION

Raymond Brown correctly states that "human beings are by nature limited."[22] Jacob Neusner defines God as wholly other or transcendent at "the point at which humanity cannot imitate God but must relate to God in an attitude of profound humility and obedience."[23] While Matthew's portrayal offers a doctrine of two natures, human and transcendent, that is reflective of the early church,[24] his portrayal also depicts Jesus as distinct from God because he experiences human limitations. For example, in the OT, God is a timeless being (Ps 90:2; Job 36:26), yet Matthew's Jesus dies on the cross (Matt 27:45–54). The Father knows the hour of the return of the Son of Man, but Jesus fails to know that hour (24:36). At the scene in Gethsemane, the Father has a will, and Matthew portrays Jesus as a humble, obedient son to that will (26:36–46). The obedient, humble son, who possesses limitations to his

---

18. While it is clear that Matthew does not consider Jesus an animal, Matthean redactions and portrayal demonstrate that Jesus has a human lineage (Matt 1:1–17), is born to a human mother (1:18—2:1), and has a human family with brothers and sisters (12:46–50; 13:54–58).

19. Matt 8:27; 9:8; 11:19; 12:23–24; 13:56; 26:61, 72; 27:24, 47. Mark 2:7; 14:71; 15:39. Luke 7:34, 39, 49; 23:4, 6, 14, 18, 41, 47.

20. Thompson, *Humanity of Jesus*, 7.

21. Bauer, "ἄνθρωπος," BDAG, 81.

22. Brown, *Introduction*, 25.

23. Menah. 29b III.5. Neusner, *Questions and Answers*, 109, comments on the Aggadah of Rabbinic Judaism.

24. Luz, *Studies in Matthew*, 96.

knowledge and dies, demonstrates that Matthew recognizes and maintains a human portrayal of Jesus that is distinct from God.

The Jesus of Matthew experiences other aspects of life similar to other human beings in his portrayal. For example, Jesus and the disciples experience hunger (Matt 4:2; 12:1; 21:18). They travel by boat (8:23–27). Both John the Baptist and Jesus die (14:10–12; 27:50). Unique to Matthew, an unspecified number of people and Jesus experience a bodily resurrection (27:52; 28:6). Sharing those experiences reminds us of Thompson's definition of human: "certain elements—birth, family, life activities, death, constitute the outline of what we expect to be told about any human being."[25] Not only does Matthew's main character experience each of these events,[26] Jesus shares them with other humans in Matthew's story. It is clear that Matthew's portrayal of Jesus fits within the parameters of human existence.

Yet, in several cases, Matthew redacts his sources on one hand to portray the humanity of Jesus and on the other to build an argument for Jesus's transcendent status. One example is Jesus asleep on the boat at the first storm calming (Matt 8:23–27). At least once in Matthew's Gospel, Jesus sleeps (8:24). After being awakened and stilling the storm, the disciples ask ποταπός ἐστιν οὗτος ("what sort of man is this," 8:27). Bernard Batto suggests that this pericope should be understood in light of an "epiphanic context" because this is the only time ἐκάθευδεν ("[Jesus] was asleep," 8:24) in the NT.[27] Two difficulties arise with an epiphanic understanding of καθεύδω ("sleep," 8:24). First, Matthew uses forms of καθεύδω ("sleep") to describe others sleeping. One instance is the men in the parable of the wheat among the weeds and the other is the disciples in the garden (13:25; 26:26). Second, the Jewish perspective in Genesis Rabbah implies that one distinguishing characteristic between humanity and transcendence is that humankind sleeps and God does not.[28] While God does not sleep (Ps 121:4), there are OT passages depicting people who seek to wake God from sleep,[29] but these examples are metaphors.[30] In the pericope of Jesus calming the seas, Jesus

---

25. Thompson, *Humanity of Jesus*, 7.

26. Matt 2:1; 13:55–56; 21:18; 27:50.

27. Batto, "Sleeping God," 174.

28. Genesis Rabbah VIII: X: Neusner, *Genesis Rabbah the Judaic Commentary*, 1:ix, 83, indicates that "Genesis Rabbah presents the first complete and systematic Judaic commentary on the book of Genesis. In normative and classical Judaism, that is, the Judaism that reached its original expression in the Mishnah, ca. A.D. 200."

29. Pss 35:23; 44:23–24; 59:4; Isa 51:9. Davies and Allison, *Matthew 8–18*, 2:72.

30. Dahood, *Psalms I*, 268, explains that God cannot and does not sleep and the passage symbolizes that the perception of God's inattentiveness to prayer gives the idea that God is asleep.

sleeps like other humans. The disciples wake the human Jesus at the first stilling of the sea (Matt 8:25), but then Jesus demonstrates his transcendent power over the winds and the sea causing the disciples to question his identity (8:26–27). Matthew changes the disciples' question in Mark and Luke from τίς ἄρα οὗτός ἐστιν ("who then is this," Mark 4:41 // Luke 8:25) to ποταπός ἐστιν οὗτος ("what sort of man is this," Matt 8:27). Why does Matthew modify the question and ask "what sort of man is this?" It will be seen that, as Matthew's portrayal builds the argument for Jesus's transcendence, he does not do so at the expense of Jesus's humanity. Matthew intentionally depicts Jesus as distinct from a solely transcendent figure.

As the First Evangelist builds the argument for Jesus's transcendent status, a key title Matthew applies to Jesus is "Son of God."[31] In the ancient world within Judaism, Son of God is commonly used for human beings,[32] however, the meaning of Son of God is in development during the first-century. According to James D. G. Dunn, those watching and participating in the life of Jesus assume and understand Jesus to be a human who shares in "the divine mind" or is "specially favored by God or pleasing to God."[33] Matthew portrays Jesus as more than a human through a Spirit-conceived virgin birth (Matt 1:18–25). He also provides multiple applications of the title Son of God[34] and modifies Peter's confession to include a description that Jesus is the Son of the living God (Matt 16:16 // Mark 8:29). It will be seen that Matthew's story assists to establish Jesus as a human in whom God is fully present.[35]

Matthew's interest in the humanity of Jesus is recognized very early in the church's history. Irenaeus points out that Matthew's Gospel "is the Gospel of [h]is humanity; for which reason it is, too, that a humble and meek man is kept up through the whole Gospel."[36] The irony is that the early church debate centers on defining the divinity of Jesus at the Council of Nicaea (325 CE). The Nicene Creed describes Jesus as "conceived of the Holy

---

31. Matt 4:3, 6; 8:29; 14:33; 16:16; 26:63; 27:40, 43, 54. Luz, *Studies in Matthew*, 85–96, demonstrates three titles, Son of God, Son of David, and Son of Man, as the most important titles for Matthew. Although Kingsbury, *Matthew*, 122, lists several additional christological titles, he specifies that Son of Man and Son of God are of "paramount importance" to Matthew.

32. Dunn, *Christology in the Making*, 14. Kirk, *Man Attested by God*, connects divine sonship to figures other than Jesus throughout his text (2 Sam 7:14; Ps 2:7; 89:26; Hos 1:10).

33. Dunn, *Christology in the Making*, 16.

34. Matt 4:3, 6; 8:29; 14:33; 16:16; 26:63; 27:40, 43, 54.

35. Harrington, "Jesus Our Brother," 118.

36. Irenaeus, *Haer.* 3.11.8.

Spirit, born of the virgin Mary, suffered under Pontius Pilate, was crucified, died and was buried." Examination of this declaration stresses rather than diminishes the humanity of Jesus.[37] He is born and suffers. He is crucified and dies. The only transcendent portion of the Creed is a conception within a virgin by the Holy Spirit.[38] At the Council of Chalcedon (451 CE), the description of Jesus's existence as a human includes everything but sin.[39] Matthew and church history recognize and emphasize the importance of Jesus's humanity.

In spite of Matthew's portrayal of Jesus surpassing normal, ordinary human experience, to ignore the humanity of Jesus fails to recognize a crucial distinction for Matthew's main character. Drawing attention to several human dynamics of Jesus's humanity,[40] Matthew not only develops the human story of Jesus as distinct from God but also carefully crafts a character who is, by definition, human. The question is whether scholarship from the time of redaction criticism until now has maintained the interest in developing the understanding of the humanity of Christ as the church once had.

1.3 FROM REDACTION CRITICISM TO RECENT STUDIES

As has been suggested, the humanity of Jesus plays a role in Matthew's Gospel story. While publications that focus on the topic of Jesus's humanity continue to increase,[41] J. R. Daniel Kirk uses the term "thin" to describe the limited amount of work done on the humanity of Jesus in the Gospels.[42] In order to increase our understanding, this book endeavors to expand the conversation concerning Jesus's humanity.

One tool to identify Matthew's christological interests is redaction criticism, and Günther Bornkamm's 1948 article, "*Die Sturmstillung im Matthäusevangelium*" began the redaction critical era.[43] This serves as the

37. Johnson, *Jesus Controversy*, 62.

38. Johnson, *Jesus Controversy*, 62.

39. For an overview on the state of the two-nature discussion prior to the Council of Chalcedon between the theological centers of Alexandria and Antioch, see Crisp, *Divinity and Humanity*, 34–71. For an example of a summary of Cyril and Nestorius and their comprehension of the divine sufferings, see Hallman, "Seed of Fire," 369–91.

40. Kirk, *Man Attested by God*, 387.

41. Thompson, *Humanity of Jesus*; Grün, *Jesus, The Image of Humanity*; Voorwinde, *Jesus' Emotions*; Keith, *Complete Humanity in Jesus*; Ware, *Man Christ Jesus*; Bock and Simpson, *Jesus the God-Man*; and Kirk, *Man Attested by God*.

42. Kirk, *Man Attested by God*, 16.

43. Stanton, *Gospel for a New People*, 24–25. Osborne, "Redaction Criticism,"

era in which we begin to examine the level of interest in Jesus's humanity within christological and Matthean studies. A review of the literature will demonstrate that Matthew's perspective of Jesus's humanity deserves attention because of the priority, purpose, and perspective it plays in the First Gospel.

1.3.1 Christological Studies

A review of christological studies will show the need for an investigation into the humanity of Jesus, and when we combine that with Matthean studies, we will see the importance of this project. In the wake of redaction criticism, Oscar Cullmann, known for challenging his contemporaries to honor the underpinning documents of the Christian faith,[44] defines Christology as the "science whose object is Christ."[45] He divides *The Christology of the New Testament* into the pre-existent, earthly, present, and future work of Christ. For each division, Cullmann provides christological titles to summarize Jesus's identity. For the earthly period, he summarizes Jesus's identity with the titles "Jesus the Prophet," "Jesus the Suffering Servant of God," and "Jesus the High Priest," yet Jesus's existence as a human makes the functions of prophet, servant, and high priest possible. Cullmann does not develop the humanity of Jesus because Jesus's human existence is not a question of nature but of function. This opens the door to address the nature of the humanity of Jesus in Matthean Christology.[46]

In 1967 Raymond Brown examines the extent of Jesus's knowledge with the publication of *Jesus God and Man: Modern Biblical Reflections*.[47] Asking how much Jesus knew, Brown contrasts texts that indicate Jesus's "ignorance" (Mark 5:30–33; 13:32; Luke 2:46)[48] with a text that suggests

663–66, reinforces Bornkamm's place in redaction criticism. His work is followed by Conzelmann, *Die Mitte der Zeit*. The first use of the term *Redaktionsgeschichte* ("history of redaction") appears in Marxsen, *Der Evangelist Marcus*.

44. Dorman, "Oscar Cullman (1902–1999)," 334.

45. Cullmann, *Christology of the New Testament*, 1.

46. As Cullmann, *Christology of the New Testament*, 3–4, attempts to explain that christological controversies deal with the person or nature of Christ, he concludes, "[The controversies] refer on the one hand to the relation between his nature and that of God; on the other hand, to the relation which exists in Christ himself between his divine and his human nature. If we are to avoid the danger of seeing the christological problem of the New Testament in a false perspective from the very beginning, we must attempt first of all to disregard these later discussions." His rationale is that Christology is not a question of nature, but rather of function.

47. Brown, *Jesus God and Man*.

48. Brown, *Jesus God and Man*, 45–46.

Jesus's superhuman knowledge (Mark 2:6–8). Matthew preserves Jesus's knowledge limitations (Matt 24:36 // Mark 13:32), yet Luke removes the explicit unawareness of the time of the Son of Man's return (Luke 21:33–34).[49] Even though Brown's work demonstrates the differences between the transcendent and human knowledge of Jesus, his work raises two unanswered questions. First, what is Matthew's view of Jesus's knowledge? Second, what other elements of Jesus's humanity does Matthew adjust?

Soon after, in 1968, Wolfhart Pannenberg noted how Jesus lives as "The True Man" in *Jesus-God and Man*.[50] As a true man, Jesus exists as a prophet and representative priest for humankind before God.[51] Pannenberg states that as "the Son, Jesus is in a prototypal way what all men ought to be: the reality of the sonship that is intended for all in trusting obedience to the Father."[52] Instead of examining the nature of Jesus as a true man, Pannenberg views Jesus as an exemplar of humankind's obedience to the Father as a function of the humanity of Jesus. This project endeavors to explore Jesus's existence as a true man in order to clarify Matthean Christology.

In 1981 James D. G. Dunn suggests that the Matthean and Lukan birth narratives are comparable to the "modern historical novel."[53] It will be seen that he correctly argues that approaching the narrative in this way can assist the interpreter to understand that the Gospels allow "freedom in detail to make a claim in terms which the intended readers would understand and whose character they would appreciate."[54] Matthew demonstrates an attention to detail in portraying the birth of Jesus, and this project will apply the principle of narrative criticism to discern further the significance of the human portrait throughout Matthew's Gospel.

Akin to Dunn's "modern historical novel" method,[55] Ulrich Luz's *The Theology of the Gospel of Matthew* approaches Matthew's Gospel as a story (1995).[56] Two of Luz's findings bear on this project. First, using narrative criticism, Luz concludes that for Matthew the "story of the earthly Jesus is already an elementary expression of the *lasting* presence of God."[57] Just as

49. Other possible passages that suggest the ignorance of Jesus are Matt 13:51–52; 14:12–13; 27:34, 46. For a fuller discussion, see Brown, "How Much Did Jesus Know," 315–45.

50. Pannenberg, *Jesus-God and Man*, 191–211.

51. Pannenberg, *Jesus-God and Man*, 195, 208–11.

52. Pannenberg, *Jesus-God and Man*, 198–99.

53. Dunn and Mackey, *New Testament Theology in Dialogue*, 67.

54. Dunn and Mackey, *New Testament Theology in Dialogue*, 68.

55. Dunn and Mackey, *New Testament Theology in Dialogue*, 67.

56. Luz, *Theology of the Gospel of Matthew*, xi.

57. Luz, *Theology of the Gospel of Matthew*, 33, (emphasis original). Kupp, *Matthew's*

God was with Jesus, God is with the Matthean community in the present.[58] Second, Luz observes the importance of prophetic fulfillment through the human Jesus for the Matthean community.[59] Luz's observation raises the question of how Matthew prioritizes the humanity of Jesus to meet the expectations of his readers.

Rather than exploring Matthew's interest in the human Jesus, Luz provides a macroscopic view of the temporal role of Jesus's existence. He argues that Matthew's use of "Son of Man" arouses within his audience thoughts of Jesus's journey both temporal and eternal.[60] Instead of dealing with both elements of the journey, Luz focuses on the eternal, eschatological nature of Jesus as the Son of Man, which leaves the temporal, suffering side of Jesus's human identity relatively unexplored. This project searches for a deeper understanding of Jesus's humanity in the First Gospel. We will see that Jesus's suffering not only reminds the reader of the human element but also serves as an example of the suffering that his audience will face.

In 1999 Birger Gerhardsson maintains that Matthew presents Jesus as a *"strongly didactic character."*[61] From the beginning of the Gospel, Matthew establishes that Jesus works as God's servant in Israel.[62] As God's servant, Jesus lives what he teaches and functions as the model for ethics. Living life according to the scriptures, Jesus models life in a Jewish social milieu,[63] yet Gerhardsson lacks the in-depth examination of the humanity of Jesus from Matthew's perspective to strengthen the intentionality of the didactic function.

Viewing the Gospel of Matthew through the lens of narrative criticism, Terence Donaldson observes that Matthew's chief title for Jesus is Son of God,[64] even though Son of Man, a designation for a human being, is numerically dominant.[65] According to Donaldson, Jesus is portrayed as God's

---

Emmanuel, 49–108, develops the theme of divine presence among his people by identifying God's past, immediate, and future active presence.

58. Luz, *Theology of the Gospel of Matthew*, 33.

59. Luz, *Theology of the Gospel of Matthew*, 39.

60. Luz, *Theology of the Gospel of Matthew*, 114.

61. Gerhardsson, "Christology of Matthew," 21, (emphasis original).

62. Gerhardsson, "Christology of Matthew," 22.

63. Gerhardsson, "Christology of Matthew," 26.

64. Donaldson, "Vindicated Son," 101.

65. Matthew uses the title "Son of Man" thirty times (Matt 8:20; 9:6; 10:23; 11:19; 12:8; 12:32, 40; 13:37, 41; 16:13, 27–28; 17:9, 12, 22; 19:28; 20:18, 28; 24:27, 30, 37, 39, 44; 25:31; 26:2, 24, 45, 64); "Son of God" ten times (4:3, 5; 5:9; 8:29; 14:33; 16:16; 26:63; 27:40, 45, 54); and "Son of David" ten times (1:1, 20; 9:27; 12:23; 15:22; 20:30–31; 21:9, 15; 22:42).

Son, as a Davidic king of the Jews, yet Matthew depicts Jesus in a "humble, obedient, servant role that was to characterize Israel."[66] Donaldson demonstrates how the baptism and temptation scenes exemplify Jesus's role as Son in light of the father-son relationship, yet ignores the role the humanity of Jesus plays in that relationship. The portrayal of Jesus's identity deserves clarification, and that clarification becomes possible through balancing a transcendent status with a humble, human existence. That balance will be demonstrated as we point out Matthew's apparent inconsistent use of the humanity of Jesus.

The inconsistent use of Jesus's humanity by Matthew suggests that the priority of a Gospel author is theological, not historical.[67] In 2009, Dale C. Allison Jr. rightly proposes there is more than one Jesus to be observed in these Gospel stories.[68] Allison indicates that Jesus exists as a "man" and interacts with other humans in the first-century in the Gospels.[69] He also proposes that Jesus's humanity is a "doctrine to be believed, not a fact to be felt,"[70] yet Allison does not develop Jesus's human story as a reality to be experienced. Pragmatically, for Jesus to endure as a tangible moral exemplar,[71] his humanity should not only be a doctrine to be believed but also a reality to be experienced. With more than one Jesus to be observed, Allison's comments provide an impetus to consider Matthew's depiction of Jesus's humanity.

In 2014 Richard A. Burridge's *Four Gospels, One Jesus?* argues the symbol associated with Matthew's depiction of Jesus is the human face from the vision of Ezekiel (Ezek 1:10).[72] Burridge says the symbol of the human face reflects Matthew's design to provide "the revelation of God in the presence of Jesus."[73] That revelation for Matthew occurs through Jesus's earthly life. Asserting that Matthew's portrayal of Jesus can be likened to ancient biographies,[74] Burridge notices that Matthew handles the identity of Jesus

---

66. Donaldson, "Vindicated Son," 118.

67. Allison, *Historical Christ*, 43.

68. Allison, *Historical Christ*, 45.

69. Allison, *Historical Christ*, 45, 80. Allison humanizes Jesus even more as he states: "Jesus was, as Acts 2:22 plainly states, 'a man' (ἀνήρ), a human being who struggled and doubted and knew some things, not others."

70. Allison, *Historical Christ*, 82.

71. Allison, *Studies in Matthew*, 149, describes Jesus as "a real human being" and "a real ethical model."

72. Burridge, *Four Gospels, One Jesus?*, 67.

73. Burridge, *Four Gospels, One Jesus?*, 67.

74. Burridge, *Four Gospels, One Jesus?*, 68.

cleverly due to the character he is attempting to portray.[75] Supporting his case, Burridge picks up on Matthew's tendency to omit Mark's references to human feelings to remind the readers that Jesus is "nothing less than the Son of God."[76] However, Burridge fails to address examples of Matthew adding human emotions to his narrative, and attributing them to Jesus. This project will expose these inconsistencies and propose that while Jesus is the Son of God, that singular description insufficiently reflects Matthean Christology because of Matthew's priority for, purpose in, and perspective on Jesus's humanity.

More recently, in *A Man Attested by God: The Human Jesus of the Synoptic Gospels* (2016), J. R. Daniel Kirk suggests Jesus is an idealized human figure for readers in the first-century.[77] Relying on Peter's language in Acts (Acts 2:22), Kirk encourages his readers to reimagine Jesus's identity as an "idealized human being."[78] Attempting to provide a third way to envision Christ as more than "a mere human being" yet less than "the God of Israel," Kirk's approach to describe Jesus as a human idealized figure does not remove the possibility that either Jesus is divine or is being depicted as divine.[79] Kirk admits that "divine and preexistence Christology is attested in other early Christian literature,"[80] and his admission allows us to challenge the assumption that the title "idealized human being" sufficiently describes the Jesus of the Gospels.

While Kirk rightly states that each writer reflects a "peculiar theology,"[81] we will see that even the humanity of Jesus is portrayed differently by the Synoptic authors. Kirk concedes that "it will be Matthew, in particular, whose exalted human Christology at times takes turns that might step beyond the category of idealized human figure."[82] In light of this, Kirk reinforces a tension felt when reading Matthew's portrayal of the identity of Jesus as human and transcendent. As "an idealized human,"[83] the portrayal

---

75. Burridge, *Four Gospels, One Jesus?*, 77–78.

76. Burridge, *Four Gospels, One Jesus?*, 78.

77. Kirk, *Man Attested by God*, 44–176, defines "idealized human figure" and provides extensive support within and outside the canon that one can classify Jesus as an idealized human figure in the first-century.

78. Kirk, *Man Attested by God*, 1, credits McCartney, "*Ecce Homo*," 1–21, for planting the seed for his work.

79. Kirk, *Man Attested by God*, 3.

80. Kirk, *Man Attested by God*, 4.

81. Kirk, *Man Attested by God*, 7.

82. Kirk, *Man Attested by God*, 7.

83. Kirk, *Man Attested by God*, 12.

of the humanity of Jesus deserves attention, which leads to the question, what role does the humanity of Jesus play in Matthew?

When the motif of Jesus's humanity has been discussed in the texts reviewed, the human portrayal is not a primary topic of concern even though the Gospel authors portray Jesus as a human. As will be seen, for Matthew and his Jewish Christian audience, the humanity of Jesus is a reality in the late first-century. Therefore, the intent of this project is to detect Matthew's priority for, purpose in, and perspective on the humanity of Jesus to determine the role it plays in his Christology. As we shift to a review of Matthean studies, it will also expose the need for an exploration of Matthew's portrait of the human Jesus.

1.3.2 Matthean Studies

In 1980 Graham Stanton wrote an overview of "The Origin and Purpose of Matthew's Gospel: Matthean Scholarship from 1945 to 1980."[84] Using Bornkamm's work, "*Die Sturmstillung im Matthäusevangelium*," to mark a new era in Matthean studies,[85] Stanton identifies topics such as redaction criticism, authorship, Christology, ecclesiology, purpose, setting, audience, and Matthew's relationship to contemporary Judaism as central to Matthean scholarship from 1945 to 1980. However, as early as 1925, W. C. Allen identifies that Matthew changes the emotions of Jesus apart from Mark's Gospel,[86] yet Matthew's specific interest in the humanity of Jesus is absent from the topics Stanton considers central to Matthean studies. Prima facie, understanding Matthean Christology is impossible without taking into consideration Jesus's humanity.

Stanton's overview appears between two publications by Jack Dean Kingsbury.[87] In 1986, with the publication of *Matthew as Story*, Kingsbury establishes himself as the first narrative critic of Matthew's Gospel.[88] Prior to this in 1975, Kingsbury's *Matthew: Structure, Christology, Kingdom* presents his understanding of the structure of Matthew.[89] As Kingsbury argues for a three-part structure, he relies on the transitional phrase ἀπὸ τότε ἤρξατο

---

84. Stanton, "Origin and Purpose," 1889–951.

85. Stanton, *Gospel for a New People*, 24.

86. Allen, *Critical and Exegetical*, xxxi.

87. Kingsbury, *Matthew*; Kingsbury, *Matthew as Story*.

88. Powell, "Narrative Criticism," 240, provides evidence that narrative criticism became a biblical discipline in the early 1980s.

89. Kingsbury, *Matthew*, 8.

("from that time he began," Matt 4:17; 16:21).[90] The three-part structure consists of "The Person of Jesus Messiah" (1:1—4:16), "The Proclamation of Jesus Messiah" (4:17—16:20), and "The Suffering, Death, and Resurrection of Jesus Messiah" (16:21—28:20).[91] In light of Kingsbury's attention to Jesus's self-designation υἱὸς τοῦ ἀνθρώπου ("Son of Man"),[92] parts one through three lend themselves to consider Matthew's portrayal of the humanity of Jesus and the role Jesus's primary self-designation plays.[93]

In 1982 Robert Gundry describes Matthean interests in *Matthew: A Commentary on His Literary and Theological Art*.[94] Those interests include Jesus as the Son of God, Son of Man, Son of David, the one who fulfills the scriptures, the miraculous, the role of the law, discipleship, false prophets, a righteousness that surpasses that of the scribes and Pharisees, the law, the law of Christ, Christ's authority, and the widespread fear of persecution.[95] As one can observe, missing is the humanity of Christ and this project demonstrates whether that omission is warranted.

In 1989 R. T. France proposed that Matthew's christological portrait presents Jesus as a teacher and as an evangelist for a Jewish Christian community.[96] To accomplish this, France relies on Matthew's use of christological titles and his *Sitz im Leben* ("setting in life"). In spite of this approach, France posits that Matthew's Jesus "fits no formula"[97] because Matthew's goal was not to provide "a systematic doctrinal statement."[98] As has been seen from Gundry, Matthew's interests vary, and a solely title-based reconstruction of Jesus's identity lacks credibility.[99] In light of Matthew's multiple

90. Kingsbury, *Matthew*, 8.

91. Kingsbury, *Matthew*, 9.

92. In English, Jesus's self-designation can be rendered "'the man,' or 'the (this) human being.'" Kingsbury, *Matthew as Story*, 103. For additional research on Son of Man, see Muller, *Der Ausdruck "Menschensohn,"*; Burkett, *Son of Man Debate*; Allison, *Constructing Jesus*, 293–303; Hurtado and Owen, *'Who Is This Son of Man?'*; Moloney, "Constructing Jesus," 719–38.

93. Matt 8:20; 9:6; 10:23; 11:19; 12:8; 12:32, 40; 13:37, 41; 16:13, 27–28; 17:9, 12, 22; 19:28; 20:18, 28; 24:27, 30, 37, 39, 44; 25:31; 26:2, 24, 45, 64.

94. Gundry, *Matthew*, 5–10.

95. Gundry, *Matthew*, 5–10.

96. France, *Matthew*, 97.

97. France, *Matthew*, 306–8.

98. France, *Matthew*, 279.

99. Novakovic, "Jesus as the Davidic Messiah," 149, argues that while titles assist in analyzing Matthew's Christology, they remain insufficient for obtaining the entire picture. Even though analysis of the titles is helpful, the context of its use, the activities associated with the title, and the way Matthew narrates Jesus's life all contribute to the portrait Matthew attempts to depict.

interests and the evidence of his attention to the human story, this project emphasizes Matthew's concern for the human element of his story's main character.

Understanding Matthew's Gospel as a story,[100] Luz published a collection of essays entitled *Studies in Matthew*. The essays ranging from 1971 to 2003 cover the story, provenance, ecclesiology, ethics, and Christology of Matthew. A section on Matthean Christology titled, "The Son of Man in Matthew: Heavenly Judge or Human Christ?,"[101] alludes to,[102] but falls short of, developing the role the humanity of Jesus plays. Although attention is drawn to the Son of Man motif, Luz's limited focus on the "horizontal dimension" of that motif leaves room to engage in Matthew's view of Jesus's humanity.[103]

Dale C. Allison Jr. demonstrates Matthew's "fundamental interest" in Jesus as a person with his *Studies in Matthew* (2005).[104] According to Allison, Matthew's work reflects a period before Docetism and Nicaea that made it possible for readers to consider Jesus "a real human being" and "a real ethical model."[105] Just as Matthew's Jesus pursues righteousness, the Jewish Christian community can pursue righteousness (Matt 3:15; 5:17). As will be seen, Matthew's *imitatio Christi* motif should be understood in light of his human portrayal of Jesus, a topic this project explores.

More recently, David C. Sim published, "Matthew: The Current State of Research" (2011).[106] He explains that the previous twenty years have focused on the social setting of Matthew and the role community plays in the composition of Matthew's narrative.[107] That setting includes Matthew's relationship to the Hebrew, gentile, and Roman worlds. Even though the focus has been the social setting of Matthew, Sim specifies that there is a desperate need for an advanced study of Matthean theology somewhat akin to multiple studies of Pauline theology.[108] In light of Sim's observation of the need to advance Matthean theology, this project will advance Matthew's portrait of the human Christ.

100. Luz, *Studies in Matthew*, 370.

101. Luz, *Studies in Matthew*, 97–114.

102. Luz, *Studies in Matthew*, 97–98.

103. Luz, *Studies in Matthew*, 91–93.

104. According to Allison, *Studies in Matthew*, 142–49, the canonical Gospels can be considered biographical if understood in light of the Greco-Roman genre.

105. Allison, *Studies in Matthew*, 149.

106. Sim, "Matthew," 33–54.

107. Sim, "Matthew," 35–36.

108. Sim, "Matthew," 34–35.

This literature review has demonstrated that the conversations regarding the humanity of Jesus within christological and Matthean studies are limited and need development. The instances of emphasis on Jesus's humanity are insufficient and deserve greater insight. This project endeavors to demonstrate Matthew's priority, purpose, and perspective in order to advance the importance of the humanity of Jesus in Matthean Christology.

1.4 METHODOLOGY

In order to understand Matthew's portrait of the humanity of Jesus and its role, two primary tools will be used. These tools help identify the nature, extent, and function of the human motif in Matthew's Christology. These approaches have been used to discuss Matthew's interest in multiple subjects, for example, Jesus, the Son of God, the one who fulfills the scriptures, the miraculous, the role of the law, and discipleship.[109] Applying redaction[110] and narrative criticisms[111] to Matthew's Gospel will help to see that Matthew intentionally portrays Jesus's humanity. His priority, purpose, and perspective benefit a Jewish Christian audience situated in a particular *Sitz im Leben*[112] during the last quarter of the first-century.[113]

109. Gundry, *Matthew*, 5–10. Luz, *Studies in Matthew*, 115–242, and Allison, *Studies in Matthew*, 147–54, 163–236, demonstrate that the various themes of interest for Matthew also include discipleship, the law, miracles, divorce, the Passion, and the *imitatio Christi*.

110. For an introduction to redaction criticism, see Perrin, *What is Redaction Criticism?*; Carson, "Redaction Criticism," 119–46; Law, "Redaction Criticism," 181–215.

111. For an introduction to narrative criticism, see Powell, *What is Narrative Criticism?*; Resseguie, *Narrative Criticism*.

112. Kilpatrick, *Origins of the Gospel*, 2, discusses the relationship between Matthew and Judaism which greatly influences Matthean studies. His key contribution is "that the context or '*Sitz im Leben*' of a new Gospel was as important a feature in its production as it was in the shaping and carrying on of unwritten tradition."

113. Sim, *Gospel of Matthew*, 2, states: "Most scholars would argue that the Gospel of Matthew was written in the period following the first Jewish revolt against Rome, and reflects a bitter conflict between the evangelist's community and the leading figures in emergent formative Judaism." Also, Davies and Allison, *Matthew 1–7*, 1:128, state: "The majority opinion is that the First Gospel was composed in the final quarter of the first century A.D."

1.4.1 Redaction Criticism[114]

Derived from the word *Redaktionsgeschichte*, meaning "editorial history," redaction criticism has become a useful tool in the study of the Synoptics. According to Grant Osborne, redaction criticism "is a literary discipline that studies the way a biblical author/editor altered his sources to develop his unique theological message."[115] While dependent on source and form criticisms,[116] redaction criticism's objectives are to understand why items from tradition, oral and written, are edited in order to identify theological motifs and elucidate the theological point of view of the author. Comparing the Gospels demonstrates that editorial comments emerge as early as the time between the life of Jesus and the authorship of the Gospels. As the traditions of Jesus's life on earth, his message, and his mission are transmitted orally, they are written and copied. They are collected and utilized by Gospel authors who further edit the material for their anticipated audience, *Sitz im Leben*, exposure to the traditions, and theological viewpoints.

Although redaction criticism helps to identify theological interests of the Gospel authors, weaknesses exist.[117] Clifton Black says, "in order to discern the earliest Evangelist's redactional (= authorial) activity, every investigator is compelled to engage in often highly speculative conjectures about the history of traditions *behind* the Evangelist."[118] The application of redaction criticism is speculative because its credibility rests on the selection from the various solutions to the synoptic problem.[119]

The synoptic problem causes us to question the relationship between the Synoptics on a literary level.[120] Providing a solution to the problem involves attempting to explain the similarities and differences between the Synoptics. According to Stanley Porter and Bryan Dyer, the primary solutions include the Two Source, Farrer, Two Gospel, and Orality and Memory

---

114. For examples of implementing redaction criticism specifically in Matthean studies, see Stanton, *Gospel for a New People*; Allison, *New Moses*.

115. Osborne, "Redaction Criticism," 663.

116. Redaction criticism distinguishes itself from form and source criticism by focusing on the author of the completed narrative. Law, *Historical-Critical Method*, 182.

117. For further evaluation of redaction criticism weaknesses, such as equating the meaning of a text with an author's meaning, acknowledging the Gospels as "*literary creations*," and recognizing a lack of methodological consensus, see Law, *Historical-Critical Method*, 211–15, (emphasis original).

118. Black, "Quest," 19–39, (emphasis original).

119. See ch. 1, n6 above.

120. Porter and Dyer, *Synoptic Problem*, 13.

hypotheses.[121] While these hypotheses have varying degrees of support and probability, the selected solution by the investigator has a direct impact on the conclusions regarding an author's theological intention. This project will adopt the Two Source Hypothesis. This hypothesis argues that Matthew and Luke primarily use two sources, Mark and Q, in the composition of their Gospel.[122] Applying the Two Source Hypothesis in conjunction with redaction criticism will provide insight into understanding Matthew's priority for, purpose in, and perspective on the humanity of Jesus.

1.4.2 Narrative Criticism[123]

One purpose of literature is to tell a story,[124] and scripture is full of stories. Stories are designed to convey information in order to provoke a response from the audience. The composers of the Gospel stories rely on their sources not only to provide a portrayal of events in light of their *Sitz im Leben* but also to offer a theological message through story.[125] Narrative criticism views and analyzes the Bible as literature.[126] The goal of narrative criticism is "to determine the effects that the stories are expected to have on their audience."[127] Consequently, the narrative critic observes the literary techniques that contribute to the meaning of the narrative within the text by examining its literary rhetoric, plot, point of view, and character development or lack thereof.[128]

121. Porter and Dyer, *Synoptic Problem*, vii.

122. According to Porter and Dyer, *Synoptic Problem*, 15–16, this theory recognizes that Luke and Matthew include material from independent sources and effectively synthesizes the Two and Four Document theories. Proponents of the Two Source Hypothesis generally agree that the number of sources typically include more than two or four sources.

123. For a specific application of narrative criticism to Matthew and Mark, see Kingsbury, *Matthew as Story* and Rhoads et al., *Mark as Story*.

124. Bressler, *Literary Criticism*, 11, provides a brief explanation of the difficulties associated with defining literature.

125. Parry, "Narrative Criticism," 528–31.

126. This project does not intend to address the level of influence the Holy Spirit had on the authorship of scriptures. The purpose of this section is to define and explore the nature and value of narrative criticism. In spite of this, a level of caution should be expressed in treating the Bible solely as a work of literature.

127. Powell, "Narrative Criticism," 240.

128. Resseguie, *Narrative Criticism*, 12.

The narrative critic identifies the effects of the techniques within the stories through the eyes of the implied author and the implied reader.[129] Mark Allen Powell states: "By 'implied author,' narrative critics mean the perspective from which the work appears to have been written, a perspective that must be reconstructed by readers on the basis of what they find in the narrative."[130] Application of narrative criticism enables the critic to discern the values, beliefs, and perception of the implied author from solely within the text.[131] For example, whether the author of the Gospel of Matthew is a Jewish tax collector or not has no bearing on the narrative critic's literary analysis. The role of the narrative critic is to attempt to reconstruct the perspective of the implied author from which the work was written.

Because the narrative critic attempts, in part, to determine the beliefs or values the narrator of the story wants the implied reader to adopt,[132] properly understanding the implied reader remains important. Powell states that "[i]mplied readers are those who actualize the potential for meaning in texts, who respond to text in ways consistent with the expectations ascribed to their implied authors."[133] The value of narrative criticism is that it can clarify the distinction between the responses of the actual reader and its implied reader.[134]

Projecting the possible effects of the text on the implied reader is tempered by three principles. First, the critic reads the text sequentially[135] and in its entirety.[136] For example, the narrative critic does not read the parable of the seed and the sower in Matthew as an isolated parable (Matt 13:1–6). The narrative critic assumes the parable is written with the entire Gospel narrative in mind, and the emphasis on the location of the story reveals the causal links between events.

---

129. Powell, *What is Narrative Criticism?*, 10.

130. Powell, "Narrative Criticism," 202.

131. As Powell, "Narrative Criticism," in *Hearing the New Testament*, 242, points out, "Biographical information concerning the author's agenda or personality should not be imposed on the story." While this list does not incorporate all literary analysis tools, it does provide several important means used to analyze the text. For a brief explanation of these terms, see Powell, "Narrative Criticism," in *Hearing the New Testament*, 245–49. For a fuller explanation, see Resseguie, *Narrative Criticism*, chs. 2–6.

132. Resseguie, *Narrative Criticism*, 21.

133. Powell, "Narrative Criticism," 242.

134. Powell, "Narrative Criticism," 202–3.

135. Longman, *Literary Approaches*, 60.

136. Resseguie, *Narrative Criticism*, 19.

The second principle adopted is that the implied reader comprehends certain aspects of reading and does not realize others.[137] The reader either knows information or is ignorant of information. This influences the ability to discern the expected effect on the reader. For example, an implied reader of Matthew's Gospel should be able to connect the meaning of Χριστός ("Christ") and υἱοῦ Δαυὶδ υἱοῦ Ἀβραάμ ("son of David, son of Abraham," Matt 1:1) without explanation. Predicting the effect the implied author desires the implied reader to experience requires an assumption that the reader will be able to fill in the gaps to understand the full effect of the story.

The third principle is that the narrative critic accepts and interprets the stories from the perspective of the author's beliefs and values that undergird the narrative.[138] If the narrative indicates animals can talk, paralytics are healed, or angels and demons actively participate in the realm of human affairs, then the narrative critic believes those components are real or true in the narrative. The narrative critic suspends questions of reliability or credibility in order to discern the meaning the narrative aims to communicate by the implied author to the implied reader.

Matthew relies on narrative to portray the story of his primary character, Jesus Christ. Although narrative critical approaches have been applied to Matthew,[139] his portrayal of the human Jesus deserves further exploration.[140] This opens up the opportunity to address the implied author's desired effect on the implied reader when reading about the human Jesus. As this study transitions to considering the audience of Matthew's Gospel, examination of the narrative of Matthew's Gospel will show that the identity of Jesus as a human is intentionally portrayed by the implied author and is intended to be useful for the implied reader.[141]

---

137. Powell, "Narrative Criticism," 203.

138. Powell, "Narrative Criticism," 203.

139. E.g., Kingsbury, *Matthew as Story*; Luz, *Studies in Matthew*.

140. Focusing on the miracle stories, Luz, *Studies in Matthew*, 240, states: "There is much work still to be done here in the fields of literary criticism, hermeneutics, and theology."

141. Johnson, *Jesus Controversy*, 72.

1.5 MATTHEW'S AUDIENCE

The message of the Gospel of Matthew is written with an audience in mind.[142] Known as the "Jewish Gospel,"[143] the provenance, internal Jewish Christian identity,[144] and influence of Matthew's Gospel are best understood in light of a primarily Jewish Christian audience.[145] Several factors contribute to this view. Unlike Mark,[146] Matthew uses a genealogy to link Jesus to the physical descent of Israelite patriarchs associated with covenants that promise a deliverer (Matt 1:1–17).[147] His first line, Βίβλος γενέσεως Ἰησοῦ Χριστοῦ

---

142. Bauckham, *Gospels for All Christians*, 1, challenges the assumption that the Gospels are written with a particular audience or community in mind. In response, Klink, *Audience of the Gospels*, 1–26, 153–66 (166), provides a discussion on the current debate. He concludes that due to the numerous approaches and sub-disciplines involved, a question like audience and origin may be unanswerable yet advocates that the audience affects how one reads the Gospels. Vine, *Audience of Matthew*, 10, 202, concludes that due to the nature of the debate, the audience question "remains open and in need of further consideration." In light of this, he concludes that selecting a specific community results in an "inadequate reading of the Gospel." In spite of this, he does not exclude the possibility that Matthew is aware of the audience component of composition. This project, based on the evidence mentioned above, has selected a Jewish Christian audience with the awareness that there are other early audiences which Matthew engages.

143. Clarke, *Gospel of Matthew*, xx.

144. For a discussion on the history of "Christian Jews" and "Jewish Christians" in English literature, see Myllykoski, "'Christian Jews' and 'Jewish Christians,'" 3–44. Jewish Christian and Christian Jew were used throughout the seventeenth century, however, Myllykoski suggests that John Toland introduced Jewish Christian in *Nazarenus* (1718). Myllykoski, "'Christian Jews' and 'Jewish Christians,'" 18, specifies using "Jewish Christian" allows authors to refer to the earliest Jewish converts to Christianity. Toland, *Nazarenus*, 43–44, indicates that use of Jewish Christian emphasizes that the conversion to Christianity by Jews does not require them to disregard Mosaic Law. In light of Matthew's additions in the Sermon on the Mount that warn those who may teach laxity toward the law, Toland's emphasis and title, Jewish Christian, will be adopted.

145. Luz, *Studies in Matthew*, 9–11. In addition, France, *Gospel of Matthew*, 15, states: "Most scholars would now agree that the Gospel derives from a largely Jewish-Christian community." Overman and Saldarini both emphasize the Jewishness of the Matthean community and the role the law and its observance play in Matthew's Gospel. See Overman, *Matthew's Gospel*; Saldarini, *Matthew's Christian-Jewish Community*.

146. According to Bock and Simpson, *Jesus According to Scripture*, 159, although different from Matthew, Luke's portrayal also includes a genealogy that connects Jesus as the Messiah especially because of the messianic emphasis in the birth narratives. Unlike Matthew who initiates the Gospel with Jesus's Messianic status, Luke neither introduces his Gospel nor emphasizes in the same manner Jesus as the descendant of David or Abraham in the genealogies. Instead, Luke traces Jesus's genealogy back to his existence as Son of God (Luke 3:23–38).

147. For a fuller discussion of χριστός ("Christ") and its significance, see Grundmann, "χρίω," *TDNT*, 9:495; 527–28; 531–32.

υἱοῦ Δαυὶδ υἱοῦ Ἀβραάμ ("The book of the genealogy of Jesus Christ, son of David, son of Abraham," 1:1), demonstrates an interest in Jesus as χριστός ("Christ"). Χριστός signifies for a Jewish Christian audience that Jesus is an individual who fulfills Israel's hopes of a deliverer.[148] Other significant evidence includes Matthew's preoccupation with the OT fulfillment motif,[149] transliteration of Aramaic words (5:22; 6:24; 27:6),[150] and references to Jewish customs.[151] Each reinforces the presupposition that Matthew's Gospel was intended for a Jewish Christian audience. Establishing Matthew's audience assists in clarifying what Matthew desires the reader to understand regarding the humanity of Jesus.

Modern scholarship primarily locates the provenance of the Gospel in Antioch of Syria.[152] According to Luke, Antioch is the capital of a Roman province where Jesus's disciples are called Christians for the first time (Acts 11:26). Ignatius, a bishop of Antioch, refers to Matthew and only Matthew mentions Syria as a location where the fame of Jesus spreads (Matt 4:24).[153] Antioch of Syria is a logical location for Matthean authorship due to similarities between the Gospel and Jewish Haggadah and the large Jewish population.[154] While tentative, the provenance of Matthew's Gospel is Antioch of Syria and is accepted in this project.[155]

As Jewish Christians in Antioch, the readers of Matthew's Gospel would have already come to believe in Jesus, yet not every Jew believed (Matt 28:11–17). Richard Longenecker postulates that Jesus's identity as a

148. Bauer, "χριστός," BDAG, 1091.

149. Matt 1:22–23; 2:5–6, 15, 17–18, 23; 4:14–16; 8:17; 12:17–20; 13:14–15, 35; 21:4–5; 27:9–10. Gerhardsson, "Christology of Matthew," 28, claims that "practically every page of the New Testament witnesses to the early Christians' eagerness to show that the ministry of Jesus took place 'according to the scriptures' . . . The efforts are most strikingly evident in the Gospel of Matthew, especially in the eleven so-called formula quotations." This project adopts Gerhardsson's limitation of the number of Matthean fulfillment prophecies to eleven.

150. France, *Matthew*, 97.

151. France, *Matthew*, 97, provides examples. In comparison to Mark and Luke, only Matthew mentions tassels and phylacteries (Matt 23:5); Jewish customs for burial (23:27); and issues with an escape on a particular day, the Sabbath (24:20). Each of these suggest a concern for and interest in Jewish sensibilities in the first-century.

152. For a summary of multiple views on the provenance of Matthew, see Davies and Allison, *Matthew 1–7*, 1:138–39. For background on Antioch, see Brown and Meier, *Antioch and Rome*, 11–86.

153. Clarke, *Gospel of Matthew*, xxii. Streeter, *Four Gospels*, 500–523, suggests an Antiochene origin by citing evidence such as Ignatius's writings and quotations in the Didache.

154. Davies and Allison, *Matthew 1–7*, 1:145–46.

155. Davies and Allison, *Matthew 1–7*, 1:145–46.

descendant of David is embedded in Christian belief at an early date.[156] To demonstrate this, he claims that the "fact" that God raises Jesus from the dead solidifies Jesus as the Messiah (Acts 2:22–36),[157] yet it will be seen that Matthew provides a different approach for belief in Jesus's identity.[158] While his identity is in a state of development during the time of authorship,[159] comparing the Synoptics, Matthew's Gospel develops and argues for a Messianic portrait using Jesus's humanity.

As belief and understanding developed, the Jewish Christians of Antioch received information. Whether through oral tradition, eyewitness accounts, Mark's Gospel, Q, or other sources, Jesus was worthy of their belief and trust. Matthew's redactions attempt to answer questions of who Jesus was (Matt 16:13–20 // Mark 8:27–30 // Luke 9:18–21) and whether he fulfilled OT prophecy.[160] The answers had implications for living as a Jewish Christian in a first-century context.[161] Matthew's narrative is an attempt to solidify Jesus's identity among the Jewish Christian community. As Christianity develops as a fulfillment of Jewish Messianic hopes, Matthew answers questions regarding Jesus's identity in the Gospel narrative.[162]

1.6 MATTHEW'S ROLE FOR JESUS'S HUMAN IDENTITY

A cursory reading of Matthew's portrait demonstrates that Jesus's earthly life closely aligns with other humans. For example, just as human beings have a lineage, Matthew provides an earthly genealogy for Jesus (Matt 1:1–17). Matthew depicts Jesus as born of a human mother with human brothers and sisters (1:18—2:1; 13:55).[163] Matthew's Jesus needs protection

156. Longenecker, *Christology*, 109, bases this understanding on Paul's common confession in the letter to the church in Rome (Rom 1:3).

157. Longenecker, *Christology*, 80.

158. Matt 1:1–25; 3:13–17; 8:23–34; 9:32–34; 11:2–6, 25–30; 12:22–32; 13:53–58; 14:22–33; 16:13–20; 17:1–13; 21:1–11, 23–46; 22:41–46; 26:57–65; 27:11–14, 32–54; 28:1–20.

159. Brown, *Jesus God and Man*, 87, demonstrates the development by stating that "under the necessity of giving proper honor to Jesus, especially in the liturgy, it was understood that 'God' was a broader term that could include both the Father and Jesus. This designation became more frequent for Jesus in the last third of the first century, as far as our evidence permits us to determine."

160. Matt 1:22–23; 2:5–6, 15, 17–18, 23; 4:14–16; 8:17; 12:17–20; 13:14–15, 35; 21:4–5; 27:9–10.

161. Matt 5:2—7:27; 10:5–42; 13:3–52; 18:1–35; 23:1—25:46.

162. Matt 7:28–29; 8:23–27; 9:1–7; 11:2–6; 12:22–32; 16:13–20; 17:1–8; 22:41–46; 26:57–68; 27:11–14, 32–54.

163. Luz, *Matthew 8–20*, 302, adds, "Of course, 'brothers' and 'sisters' must be

(2:13–23), faces temptations (4:1–11; 16:21–23),[164] experiences hunger (4:2, 21:18), expresses emotions,[165] displays a lack of knowledge (24:36; 27:46), endures suffering,[166] exhibits dependence,[167] and dies (27:45–54).

Expanding the human story, Matthew tells an origin story describing Jesus's backstory prior to depicting his baptism, temptation, and ministry initiation (Matt 1:1—2:23). Due to the nature of the origin story, Matthew's Jesus is not simply an "idealized human figure," as Kirk puts it.[168] As will be seen, Matthew's portrayal of his main character develops Jesus's human identity while providing a miraculous explanation for Jesus's transcendence. Matthew specifies that Jesus's conception ἐκ πνεύματός ἐστιν ἁγίου ("is of the Holy Spirit," 1:20), expressly without prior sexual contact between Mary and Joseph (1:25). Framed as a fulfillment of prophecy, Matthew calls Jesus Ἐμμανουήλ ("Emmanuel"), which means μεθ᾽ ἡμῶν ὁ θεός ("God with us," 1:23). With a description of Jesus's existence occurring as a result of a transcendent conception in conjunction with the human genealogy, Matthew structures the opening narrative to introduce a dual identity of Jesus.[169] As Matthew portrays the dual identity of Jesus, it raises the question why Matthew wishes to integrate Jesus's human and transcendent identity.

---

understood in keeping with the simplest meaning to refer to physical siblings of Jesus, there is nothing in the text that would lead the readers to understand the terms any other way."

164. Brown, *Introduction*, 27–28, provides insight into the Jewish understanding of the "resemblance" between Jesus and human beings. Relying on the Epistle to the Hebrews, both human beings and Jesus were tempted to sin, but the only human exception made between Jesus and human beings was that Jesus faced temptation and did so without sin (Heb 2:18; 4:15).

165. Ἐθαύμασεν ("He marveled," Matt 8:10); ἐνεβριμήθη ("he sternly charged," 9:30); forms of σπλαγχνίζομαι ("have compassion," Matt 9:36; 14:14; 15:32; 20:34); λυπεῖσθαι ("to be grieved") and ἀδημονεῖν (" to be troubled," 26:37); περίλυπός ("very sorrowful," 26:38).

166. Matthew not only constructs his narrative to anticipate the suffering of Jesus (Matt 16:21; 17:12) but also provides the most descriptive activities of the authorities, Roman and Jewish, who cause Jesus's sufferings (Matt 26:67–68 // Mark 14:65 // Luke 22:63–65; Matt 27:26 // Mark 15:15; Matt 27:27–31 // Mark 15:17–20 // Luke 19:1–3).

167. Matthew's Christology suggests a dependence on God to raise Jesus from the dead as Matthew intentionally changes Mark's ἀναστήσεται ("will rise") to ἐγερθήσεται ("will be raised"), even though Luke retains Mark's descriptor (Matt 17:23 // Mark 9:31; Matt 20:19 // Mark 10:34 // Luke 18:33). See chapter 4, n21 below.

168. Kirk, *Man Attested by God*, 3.

169. Matthew also draws attention to the dual identity of Jesus's existence as early as the first and second chapters of Matthew. Matthew isolates Mary as τῆς μητρὸς αὐτοῦ ("his mother," Matt 1:18; 2:11, 13, 14, 20, 21), but does not refer to Joseph as his father in the birth narrative.

Is Matthew's Jesus transcendent, human, or something other? Matthew maintains not only human characteristics of Jesus but also the portrait of Jesus's existence as a man. His disciples (Matt 8:27), his hometown (13:56), the crowds (9:8), and Pilate (27:24), are portrayed as having this perception.[170] For Matthew, describing Jesus as a human is a correct identification, but does that term sufficiently describe Matthew's perspective of Jesus's identity?

For Matthew, the title "Son of God" is a central christological title.[171] First-century Judaism applies the title not only to Jewish people in terms of being sons of God,[172] but also to anointed kings as sons of God.[173] However, Matthew's portrayal suggests that the title Son of God is meant for more than a solely human understanding of Jesus. In Matthew's account, Jesus is born of the virgin Mary through a transcendent conception (Matt 1:18–25). Twice, a voice from heaven calls out, οὗτός ἐστιν ὁ υἱός μου ὁ ἀγαπητός ("this is my beloved Son," 3:17; 17:5). Jesus is referenced as "the Son" (11:27; 24:36; 28:19) and the "Son of God" (8:29). Matthew is the only Gospel author to add to Peter's confession of Jesus's identity, ὁ υἱὸς τοῦ θεοῦ τοῦ ζῶντος ("the Son of the living God," Matt 16:16 // Mark 8:29 // Luke 9:20). Due to this evidence, to describe Jesus as solely human remains inadequate. Matthew's portrayal suggests there is more to Jesus's identity. On the other hand, as will become clearer as a result of this project, to describe Jesus as solely transcendent would also inadequately describe Matthew's Christology. This raises the question of whether it is more appropriate to say that Jesus is the human person in whom God is wholly present.[174] This question encourages us to pay attention and to explore the human Christology in Matthew's Gospel.

As Matthew heightens Jesus's distinction from other human beings through miracle accounts, fulfillment motifs, and community titles, such as Christ, Son of God, Son of David, and Son of Man,[175] a question remains. What is he attempting to accomplish through the human element of the

170. Luz, *Studies in Matthew*, 106, points out that the outsiders understand Jesus as merely a "man."

171. Kingsbury, *Matthew*, 41.

172. Exod 4:22; Hos 11:1; Isa 1:2; 30:1; 63:16; Jer 3:19–22; Sir 4:10; Pss. Sol. 13:9; 17:27–30; 18:4; Jub. 1:24. Longenecker, *Christology*, 97.

173. 2 Sam 7:14; Pss 2:7; 89:26; 110:3.

174. Harrington, "Jesus Our Brother," 118.

175. Luz, *Studies in Matthew*, 85–96, demonstrates three titles, Son of God, Son of David, and Son of Man, as the most important titles for Matthew. Although Kingsbury, *Matthew*, 122, lists several christological titles, he indicates that Son of Man and Son of God are of "paramount importance" to Matthew.

portrayal?[176] This project will argue that Matthew possesses a priority for, purpose in, and perspective on the role of the portrayal of the humanity of Jesus.

Matthew elaborates on the life activities of the human Jesus to establish him as the one who fulfills OT prophecy. As Matthew selectively maintains and even strengthens the essence of the human Jesus, he also develops the narrative to build a case for Jesus's transcendent status. Matthew's portrayal purposely connects the horizontal and vertical aspects of Jesus's identity.[177] According to Benedict Thomas Viviano, Matthew's Jesus is the "presence of the Transcendent in our world in a human way, horizontally."[178] As Luz points out, connecting the vertical activity as Son of God with the horizontal activity as Son of Man "anticipates remarkably closely the doctrine of two natures in the later church."[179] For Matthew, Jesus's identity includes both the transcendent and the human. While the Matthean portrayal surpasses the normal, ordinary human experience, we will see that to describe Jesus as solely transcendent ignores the human story that Matthew purposely maintains.

Matthew maintains, changes, adds to, and transposes from his sources to tell a biographical story of Jesus. The form and function of Matthew's narrative is comparable to the Greco-Roman biography.[180] According to David E. Aune, Greco-Roman biographies consist of three major features: 1) Men prominent in public life. Jesus gathered crowds and held the attention of the public (Matt 4:23–25; 7:28; 13:2). 2) External factors contribute to the chronology. For example, Matthew includes historical settings (2:1; 16:13; 21:1), social settings (13:53–58; 21:9–11), and biographical data (1:1–25; 11:2–6; 27:45–50). 3) Rhetorical purpose portrays the subject as a moral

---

176. For example, Matthew says that Jesus, as fulfillment of prophecy, will be called Ἐμμανουήλ ("Emmanuel"), which means μεθ' ἡμῶν ὁ θεός ("God with us," 1:23). In addition, only Matthew adds that Jesus is ὁ υἱὸς τοῦ θεοῦ τοῦ ζῶντος ("the Son of the living God") to Peter's confession (Matt 16:16 // Mark 8:29 // Luke 9:20).

177. Luz, *Studies in Matthew*, 96.

178. Viviano, "God in the Gospel," 34.

179. Luz, *Studies in Matthew*, 96.

180. Aune, "Greco-Roman Biography," 107–26. Prior to the twentieth century, numerous readers considered the Gospel of Matthew biographical in nature. Burridge, *What are the Gospels?*, 3, reintroduces a biographical view of the Gospels. For the internal and external comparison of the features of the Gospels that reflect a Greco-Roman biography, see Burridge, *What are the Gospels?*, 185–212. Allison, *Studies in Matthew*, 142, claims that even though many scholars of the twentieth century reject this view, there is a growing sense that the Gospels are biographies if understood in light of ancient usage. For a review of ancient biographies see also Cox, *Biography in Late Antiquity*. Witherington, *Matthew*, 43, classifies Matthew as an ancient Jewish biography that apologetically explains how Jesus can be in the Davidic line but not the son of Joseph.

model.[181] Also, Burridge states: "Ancient biographies held together both words and deeds in portraying their central subject. Many were written explicitly to give an example to others to emulate."[182] For example, Jesus is the primary character in the Gospel of Matthew and only Matthew portrays Jesus as desiring to fulfill all righteousness (3:15). As Jesus's first words in Matthew's Gospel, Luz uses this redaction to suggest that Jesus is the "prototype and model" for the Christian.[183] In addition, Paul, Origen, and other early Christian authors consider Jesus a model for emulation.[184] As Matthew portrays Jesus, the question is whether a purpose in the portrayal of Jesus's human story is the *imitatio Christi*.[185]

From oral tradition,[186] Q, and Mark, Matthew inherits a view of the human and transcendent identity of Jesus. His resulting narrative offers a portrait of Jesus that ultimately corresponds to, yet remains distinct from, not only the Synoptics but also the rest of humanity. In spite of those distinctions, Matthew prioritizes the human story of Jesus with perspective and purpose. His interest in the humanity of Jesus plays a role in the story and that interest will be explored in order to contribute to our understanding of Matthean Christology.

---

181. Aune, *New Testament*, 62, (emphasis original), remarks that Matthew and Luke "do not explicitly emphasize the *imitation* of Jesus" because the exemplar status is "implicitly understood."

182. Burridge, *What are the Gospels?*, 305–6, provides examples from Scripture that indicate the importance of the imitation of an individual (1 Cor 11:1; Phil 3:17; 1 Thess 1:6; 2 Thess 3:7, 9).

183. Luz, *Matthew 1–7*, 142. As Jesus preaches to Israel, the disciples are sent to Israel (Matt 10:5–6). As Jesus possesses the power to heal diseases, the disciples heal (4:24; 9:35; 10:1, 8). Just as Jesus suffers persecution, the disciples will also suffer (10:17, 23; 26:57–68; 27:1–2, 11–44).

184. Allison, *Studies in Matthew*, 148–49, nn43–45. Sim, "Pacifist Jesus," 2, emphasizes that Jesus as "the definitive role model whose example was to be emulated" was a matter of importance to Matthew, Paul, and other early Christians (1 Cor 11:1; Rom 15:1–7).

185. Allison, *Studies in Matthew*, 135–57, devotes a chapter to the *imitatio Christi* in light of Matthew's structure and biographical emphases.

186. Longenecker, "Christological Materials," 47–48, states that "most scholars are convinced (1) that there existed among early believers in Jesus various oral and written Christological materials, (2) that these materials were first formed and used in the contexts of worship, preaching, and teaching, (3) that these materials gave guidance to the authors of the New Testament in their presentations and arguments, and (4) that it is possible to identify some of these early materials and to describe some of their essential features."

CONCLUSION

It has been seen that Matthew's use of his sources and the resulting narrative shows he chooses not only to maintain, change, and transpose from one pericope to another human characteristics of the life of Jesus, but also elects to add to the human story. The question is why? This question becomes even more relevant as we show the level of Matthew's interest in the humanity of Jesus in spite of the lack of interest in Matthean and christological studies. I will continue to demonstrate that Matthew integrates tradition, source materials, and community expectations to encourage his audience's belief in Jesus's dual identity as both human and transcendent. What would be the consequences of such an approach to his primary character? Would the human portrayal remain consistent or would a tension between the humanity and transcendence from Matthew's sources result in a portrayal that creates a balance as he integrates Jesus's dual identity? Application of narrative and redaction criticisms will assist to answer these questions.

Matthew's christological assertions regarding Jesus's identity are designed to alleviate the confusion that exists within the community. As will be seen, Matthew uses the humanity of Jesus to emphasize the human story more than the other Gospel authors. A question is how he uses the human story in relationship to OT prophecy.[187] In the midst of the reader's new moral milieu,[188] does Matthew rely on the humanity of Jesus to present him as a moral exemplar akin to other Greco-Roman biographies of the time? Matthew clearly builds a case for the transcendent status of Jesus, but to what extent does Matthew reinforce the humanity of Jesus? Does he abdicate the human aspect of his main character or does Matthew emphasize the human portrayal more than the other Synoptic authors? Answering these questions will assist to discern the priority for, purpose in, and perspective on the role the humanity of Jesus plays in Matthew's christological portrait.

---

187. Matt 1:22–23; 2:5–6, 15, 17–18, 23; 4:14–16; 8:17; 12:17–20; 13:14–15, 35; 21:4–5; 27:9–10. According to Meeks and Wilken, *Jews and Christians in Antioch*, 18, if the Gospel was written in Antioch, Judaism was an "active influence" on Christianity until the Jews were driven out in the seventh century.

188. Matt 5:17–48; 9:14–17; 11:25–30; 12:1–21; 15:1–39; 23:1–39. Allison, *Studies in Matthew*, 148, points out that Jesus becomes the new model of how to live life.

2

Portrait of the Human Beginning
(Matthew 1:1—4:16)

MATTHEW DRAWS ATTENTION TO Jesus's humanity at the outset of and throughout his Gospel. The human portrait of Jesus's pre-ministry life reflects Matthew's christological interests. As he writes to a Jewish Christian audience struggling to make the transition from Judaism to Christianity,[1] he draws attention to details of Jesus's human existence. Matthew's portrait of the beginning of Jesus's life includes building the case for his transcendence as well.[2] However, as Irenaeus pointed out, Matthew is the Gospel of Jesus's humanity.[3]

In a gospel, which was chosen as a fitting vehicle to communicate his Christology,[4] Matthew addresses Jesus's origin, baptism, temptation, and ministry initiation (Matt 1:1—4:16). This chapter explores various elements within these stories that illustrate Matthew's interest in and perspective on the humanity of Jesus. First, we will see that Matthew uses the human story of Jesus to fulfill Jewish Messianic expectations.[5] This use of the human

---

1. Matt 5:17–48; 9:14–17; 11:25–30; 12:1–21; 15:1–14; 23:1–39. Williams, "Gospel of Matthew," 81, points out that Matthew's position at the start of the New Testament is the "most excellent segue from God's law to God's Messiah."

2. Matt 1:18–25; 2:15; 3:17; 4:3. Blomberg, *Matthew*, 58, emphasizes the importance of both the transcendent and human nature of Jesus. As transcendent, Jesus saves people from their sin (Matt 1:21), and as human, Jesus serves as humankind's representative and sacrifices himself as our substitute.

3. Irenaeus, *Haer.*, 3.11.8.

4. Brown, *Birth of the Messiah*, 38.

5. Abegg and Evans, "Messianic Passages in the Dead Sea Scrolls," 191–203, provide

portrayal serves as an apologetic for its reader.[6] Matthew develops the life activities of the human story to provide justification for confidence in Jesus as the Messiah. Oral tradition, sources such as Mark and Q, and personal experiences of the original hearers require Matthew to portray Jesus's humanity in a manner that reflects the audience's perception of reality.[7] Second, we will see that Matthew balances Jesus's transcendent and human identity. Matthew begins with, maintains, and expands the human element in conjunction with building his case for Jesus's transcendence. Third, it will become clear that Matthew's Jesus serves as a model. To achieve these objectives, Matthew describes the human identity of his main character in the origin story (1:1—2:23), baptism (3:1–17), temptation (4:1–11), and ministry initiation of Jesus (4:12–16).

2.1 AN ORIGIN STORY (MATT 1:1—2:23)

As a Greco-Roman biography,[8] Matthew's work prefaces the ministry career of Jesus with an origin story that includes a genealogy and birth narrative (Matt 1:1—2:23). The origin story provides biographical background

---

Second Temple Judaism terms used in reference to messianic figures. The key terms include משיח ("anointed one"), שיא ("prince"), שבט ("scepter" or "rod"), צמח דויד ("branch of David"), בן ("son"), מבשר ("herald"), and בחיר אלהא ("elect one of God"). A review of each of these key terms demonstrates that the Jews of the Second Temple period assume a human messianic figure. Although the use of בן ("son") signifies the tradition of "divine sonship" of the king of Israel, its meaning is disputed. Abegg and Evans state: "It has been argued that the son of God figure is an evil person, perhaps even an antichrist figure . . . It has been argued that this figure is the son of a Jewish king, but that the son of God language is not messianic. And, of course, it has been argued that this figure is indeed a messianic figure, as the parallels with Luke 1:32–35 and 2 Samuel 7 would seem to suggest." In spite of these disputed understandings, there remains evidence for a human Messianic figure. Disregarding the humanity of Jesus inaccurately represents Jesus and undermines Jewish Christian belief in him as the expected Messiah. Lichtenberger, "Messianic Expectations," 9–20, reviews the "Saviour Figures in the Expectation of the Community of Qumran," "Messianic Expectations and Figures in the Pseudepigrapha," and "Messianic Expectations in the Diaspora." Lichtenberger's research reinforces that even though the expectations were quite high for this figure, the Messiah dies (4 Ezra 7:26–44), just as the rest of humankind dies.

6. Brown, *Birth of the Messiah*, 47, rightly suggests that while apologetics do not dominate Matthew's Gospel, the Gospels provide "instruction and exhortation" for the community that confirms their faith.

7. In terms of the infancy stories, Brown, *Birth of the Messiah*, 29, suggests that the events may be derived from "Christian memory of events that happened." For a discussion on the value of and confidence in eyewitness memory, see Bauckham, *Jesus and the Eyewitnesses*, 319–58.

8. Aune, "Greco-Roman Biography," 107–26. See ch. 1, n180 above.

that sets up and explains the significance of its main character, Jesus. The first two chapters are devoid of any words from Christ, yet Matthew's portrayal of Jesus as the Messiah demonstrates a fundamental concern for this character.[9]

A comparison of the opening statements of each Gospel demonstrates Matthew's interest in and prioritization of Jesus's humanity. John's Gospel begins with the deity of Jesus: Ἐν ἀρχῇ ἦν ὁ λόγος, καὶ ὁ λόγος ἦν πρὸς τὸν θεόν, καὶ θεός ἦν ὁ λόγος, ("In the beginning was the Word, and the Word was with God, and the Word was God," John 1:1). Luke's introduction, more concerned with an ἀκριβῶς καθεξῆς ("orderly account") for Theophilus, initiates his Gospel with John the Baptist (Luke 1:1–25). Mark opens his Gospel with Ἀρχὴ τοῦ εὐαγγελίου Ἰησοῦ Χριστοῦ [υἱοῦ θεοῦ] ("The beginning of the good news of Jesus Christ, [Son of God]," Mark 1:1).[10] In order to establish a series of events, Mark selects ἀρχὴ ("beginning") to summarize the Gospel's content of how and with whom the good news spread.[11] Matthew opens his Gospel with Βίβλος γενέσεως Ἰησοῦ Χριστοῦ υἱοῦ Δαυὶδ υἱοῦ Ἀβραάμ ("The book of the genealogy of Jesus Christ, son of David, son of Abraham," Matt 1:1).[12] Portraying Jesus as a human descendant of David and Abraham not only authenticates him as a Jew,[13] but also as a covenantal, royal descendant.[14] The initiation of Matthew's Gospel clearly marks Jesus as a human figure who undoubtedly is born physically. As the only Gospel to initiate and structure the story with Jesus's genealogy and birth at the outset,[15] it is clear that Matthew's Gospel prioritizes the human element of the origin story.

To set up Jesus's biography, Matthew opens his Gospel with the γενέσεως Ἰησοῦ Χριστοῦ ("genealogy of Jesus Christ," Matt 1:1). With Jesus's origin story being the primary focus of Matthew's introduction,[16] the use of Βίβλος γενέσεως ("book of genealogy") purposely alludes to a formulaic

---

9. Allison, *Studies in Matthew*, 146.

10. The reading of υἱοῦ θεοῦ ("Son of God") is likely to be secondary due to the lack of early manuscript attestation. In addition, omitting the opening sentence of a work in those early manuscripts is unlikely. See Collins, "Establishing the Text," 111–27.

11. As a non-generic term, Becker, *Das Markus-Evangelium*, 112, argues for the polyvalence of the term ἀρχὴ ("beginning") as a beginning, title, and description of the Gospel.

12. Viviano, "God in the Gospel," 341–42, describes the divinity of Jesus as "de-centered" in the introduction to Matthew because the "focus is on the humanity of Christ."

13. Luz, *Matthew 1–7*, 81–82.

14. Bock and Simpson, *Jesus According to Scripture*, 123–24.

15. See ch. 1, n146 above.

16. Luz, *Matthew 1–7*, 70; Turner, *Matthew*, 56.

designation used in the LXX to initiate genealogies (Gen 2:4; 5:1).[17] A human lineage assumes a human birth, and the term γένεσις ("birth") has a nuance of "'what has come into being as distinct from the Creator."[18] Even though Matthew connects Jesus's birth to the transcendent through a conception made possible by the Holy Spirit (Matt 1:20), Jesus's existence is both connected to,[19] yet distinct from a transcendent Creator. Raymond Brown states that a physical birth "underlined the true humanity of Jesus' origins."[20] This can be seen through the use of γενέσεως ("genealogy of," 1:1), the reference to the γένεσις ("birth," 1:18), and choosing the verb form of γεννάω ("give birth to," 2:1). Even though Matthew offers an explanation for the transcendence of Jesus through a Spirit conception and virgin birth in the origin story (1:18–25), he initially focuses on a human origin of Jesus as distinct from the Creator.

Matthew's distinction between human and Creator in the infancy narrative is even more pronounced through observing the description of the relationships between Joseph and Mary, Mary and Jesus, and Jesus and Joseph. Descriptions of the relationships differ, yet remain consistent. Matthew uses possessive personal pronouns to describe the relationship between Joseph and Mary: ὁ ἀνὴρ αὐτῆς ("her husband," Matt 1:19), τὴν γυναῖκά σου ("your wife," 1:20), and τὴν γυναῖκά αὐτοῦ ("his wife," 1:24). Mary is referred to as the mother of Jesus in the phrases τῆς μητρὸς αὐτοῦ Μαρίας ("his mother Mary," 1:18) and Μαρίας τῆς μητρὸς αὐτοῦ ("Mary his mother," 2:11). Four times Matthew describes the relationship between Jesus and his mother with the phrase τὸ παιδίον καὶ τὴν μητέρα αὐτοῦ ("the child and his mother").[21] To end the genealogy, Matthew selects a feminine singular pronoun ἧς ("whom," 1:16) to indicate that Mary is the human mother of Jesus.

To accentuate the different familial descriptors, nowhere in the birth narrative does Matthew refer to Joseph as the father of Jesus (Matt 1:1—2:23).[22] Luke's Gospel refers to Joseph as ὁ πατὴρ αὐτοῦ ("[Jesus's] father," Luke 2:33) at the presentation of Jesus at the temple, eight days into Jesus's life.[23] Matthew's birth narrative, unlike Luke, ignores opportunities

---

17. Hagner, *Matthew 1–13*, 9. According to Milton, "Structure of the Prologue," 176, "The Matthean genealogy reiterates this faith in even more ringing tones as it is united with the declaration that Jesus is the fulfillment of the scriptural hopes and promises."

18. Büchsel, "γένεσις," *TDNT* 1:682.

19. Matt 1:18–25; 2:15; 3:17; 4:3.

20. Brown, *Birth of the Messiah*, 25.

21. Matt 2:13, 14, 20, 21.

22. Jesus is referred to as the carpenter's son by the crowd (Matt 13:55).

23. Matthew waits until the middle of Jesus's ministry to suggest a father-son

to identify Joseph as the father of Jesus. Matthew's omission is intentional due to a desire to avoid the implication that Joseph is the biological father of Jesus.[24] If that is the case, why consistently omit that connection in spite of the consistent reference to Mary as his mother?[25]

Matthew desires to ensure the audience perceives the unique, Spirit-conceived, nature of Jesus's conception and birth as including both the human and transcendent (Matt 1:18–25). Even though Joshua Leim focuses on the theological grammar of Matthew to conclude that Jesus Christ and the identity of God are undividedly connected,[26] Matthew's theological grammar accomplishes more than connecting the identity of Jesus and God. His story also makes a distinction between Jesus and God, the Father.[27] Matthew repeatedly connects Jesus to an earthly mother,[28] uses γένεσις ("birth," 1:18), and omits opportunities to connect Joseph as the father. Matthew prioritizes the humanity, yet purposely balances Jesus's human and transcendent identity throughout the origin narrative and, as will be seen, the rest of the Gospel.

One way Matthew establishes Jesus's transcendent identity is through a Spirit-conceived virgin birth in the origin story (Matt 1:18–25), yet the Jewish community would view the Christ as a human figure.[29] Matthew reinforces Jewish belief that Jesus is the Χριστοῦ ("Christ") through linking prophetic fulfillments to the humanity of Jesus all while establishing his transcendent identity. The question is how Matthew portrays the origin story of Jesus to demonstrate him as the fulfillment of the Jewish Christian Messiah? One way is the humanity and life activities of Jesus. Matthew uses the human story of Jesus to show that Jesus meets the qualifications to be the fulfillment of prophetic utterances.[30]

---

relationship between Joseph and Jesus (13:55).

24. Brown, *Birth of the Messiah*, 62. This is also further evidenced by Matthew's addition that Joseph kept Mary a virgin until the birth of Jesus (Matt 1:25).

25. Matt 1:18; 2:11, 13, 14, 20, 21.

26. Leim, *Matthew's Theological Grammar*, 245. Leim effectively demonstrates the theological and grammatical relationship of Matthew's use of προσκυνέω ("worship") to argue for the connection between the divine-filial identity connecting the Father and the Son.

27. Matt 1:1–17; 2:11; 3:17; 11:25–30; 16:16; 17:5; 24:36; 26:38–44, 63–64.

28. Matt 1:18; 2:11, 13, 14, 20, 21.

29. See ch. 2, n5 above.

30. Gundry, *Use of the Old Testament*, 5, argues that Matthew's references are similar with other Synoptic forms and generally reflect the LXX parallel passages used in Mark.

There are five *Erfüllungszitate* ("fulfillment quotations") within the origin story. Four of the five repeat the same fulfillment formula.[31] Georg Strecker notes that Matthew's interests lay in verifying Jesus's *historisch-biographische Faktizität* ("historical-biographical facticity").[32] For audience belief, this becomes possible through the use of prophetic fulfillment quotations.[33] For the reader of Matthew, a connection between the human existence of Jesus and the Messianic prophecies is clear.[34]

The first prophetic fulfillment quotation in the origin story explains the transcendent nature of Jesus, yet Matthew's portrayal of the event maintains his humanity. Matthew depicts a virgin will conceive and bear a son who will be called Emmanuel (Matt 1:18, 22–23). Even though the child in Isaiah's prophecy will be Emmanuel through solely natural means (Isa 7:14; 8:3–4), Matthew's use of Isaiah's prophecy for his own christological purposes communicates that in Jesus, "God is with us" (Matt 1:23).

The expression of "God with us" accomplishes two primary motifs. First, God's presence with his people is observable in Jesus (Matt 1:23), and second, that presence shifts from Jesus to his followers (18:20; 28:20). As we will see with the portrayal of Jesus's life, just as the audience reads and observes how "God with us" expresses itself in the human life of Jesus,[35] Jesus is with his people after the resurrection (28:19–20).[36] According to Luz, "It is fundamental to his story that the Jesus of *then* is at the same time Emmanuel, that is, the form of God's presence *now*."[37] Jesus's human life illustrates for the reader how God's presence expresses itself.[38] This marks a

---

31. Matt 1:22–23; 2:15, 17–18, 23.

32. Strecker, *Der Weg der Gerechtigkeit*, 85.

33. Matthew's use of the OT is a topic of interest in Matthean studies due to the prominent use of formula quotations. Matthew relies on prophetic fulfillment more than any other Gospel author. See Gundry, *Use of the Old Testament*; Stanton, *Gospel for a New People*, 346–63; Strecker, *Der Weg der Gerechtigkeit*, 49–85.

34. As previously noted, the Jews expect the Messiah to be a human figure. See ch. 2, n5 above. In light of this, Matthew portrays how Jesus fulfills prophecy in human form. For example, the logic of the human Jesus being called out of Egypt is made possible by the danger Herod presents to Jesus's safety (Matt 2:13–15). Being raised as a human in Nazareth makes it possible for Jesus to be called a Nazarene (2:23).

35. In the second discourse, Jesus commands the disciples not only to be like their master and teacher (Matt 10:24–25), but also expects them to perform similar miraculous works (10:1, 8).

36. Novakovic, "Jesus as the Davidic Messiah," 148, frames Matthew's Gospel as an inclusio. He opens with Jesus being Emmanuel, God with us, and closes with Jesus's promise to the disciples that he will always be with them (Matt 1:23; 28:20).

37. Luz, *Studies in Matthew*, 28, (emphasis original).

38. Heil, *Death and Resurrection of Jesus*, 9.

new approach to what a life of obedience can be for one who understands that God is with them.[39]

As a result, Matthew not only implies that Jesus's conception combines the transcendent and human (Matt 1:18, 22–23),[40] but he also explains how this child can be considered "God with us" in a way that differs from Isaiah's prophecy because a human father is not involved (Isa 8:3–4; Matt 1:25).[41] Matthew portrays a fulfillment that God is with humanity in Jesus which does not occur without the virgin giving birth to a physical, human son in an earthly, physical location.

Specifying the physical location for Jesus's birth (Matt 2:1), Matthew continues to use the humanity of Jesus for a second prophetic fulfillment. Human beings have a birthplace, and Bethlehem, the birthplace of Jesus, provides a geographical fulfillment (2:1, 5–6).[42] The information regarding the birthplace of the Christ comes to Herod through the chief priests and scribes. By Matthew citing a prophecy from Micah, he reinforces the belief that the Christ γεννηθέντος ἐν βηθλέεμ ("was born in Bethlehem," Mic 5:2; Matt 2:1). Two additional elements of this fulfillment deserve attention in light of Matthew's use of the humanity of Jesus.

First, while the same geographical birthplace of Jesus is portrayed by Matthew and Luke (Matt 2:1 // Luke 2:15), Bethlehem's location in the region of Judea is key for Matthew. Repeating Judea twice (Matt 2:1, 5–6),[43] the connection communicates to the Jewish Christian audience that Jesus is born in the city of David.[44] Second, Matthew uses Jesus's humanity to illustrate that there is nothing transcendent about the physical birth of the Messiah. Just as Matthew applies ἐγεννήθη ("had been born," 26:24) to Judas, Matthew also applies γεννηθέντος ("was born," 2:1) to Jesus. Through

---

39. Blomberg, *Matthew*, 60.

40. Brown, *Birth of the Messiah*, 161, uses the language human and divine to communicate that the relationship between "Davidic sonship and divine sonship had become complementary."

41. Oswalt, *Book of Isaiah 40–66*, 222, argues קרב ("draw near") is a euphemism to describe intercourse (Gen 20:4; Lev 18:6, 14, 19; 20:16; Deut 22:14; Ezek 18:6).

42. Matthew does not follow his traditional pattern of *Erfüllungszitate* ("fulfillment quotations") with this fulfillment prophecy. Luz, *Studies in Matthew*, 247, rightly suggests that due to Matthew's negative presentation of the Jewish religious leaders throughout his Gospel, it is illogical to initiate a fulfillment utterance from their mouths (Matt 23:1–36). Therefore, Matthew avoids the ἵνα πληρωθῇ ("in order to fulfill") clause and uses the narrative to imply that the chief priests and scribes confirm the birthplace to be Bethlehem.

43. This may have been necessary because of the Bethlehem in Zebulun from Joshua (Josh 19:15–16).

44. Turner, *Matthew*, 78.

using passive forms of γεννάω ("give birth to") in both instances, Matthew describes the birth of Jesus and the birth of Jesus's betrayer with the same language. While the conception demonstrates Jesus is Emmanuel, there is nothing suprahuman about the birth itself. As the human birth is narrated, the geographical birthplace serves as a second fulfillment passage to confirm Jesus's humanity as the Christ.

The third OT fulfillment that reinforces the role the humanity of Jesus plays in the portrayal is the call out of Egypt.[45] Matthew holds the balance of the transcendent and human nature of Christ before the reader. This is clearly seen within the third fulfillment quotation from Hosea that God's Son will be called out of Egypt (Hos 11:1; Matt 2:15). The movement of the narrative precipitates the need for Joseph to take the child and his mother to Egypt. Herod seeks the child ἀπολέσαι αὐτό ("to destroy him," Matt 2:13), which assumes the limitations of a human life for the main character. If Matthew's concern was solely to present Jesus as transcendent, why flee to Egypt for protection from Herod? Matthew's description of the humanity of Jesus makes it possible for the audience to believe that danger exists to the child in the story. With Jesus exposed to danger, Joseph's move with the child and his mother makes narrative sense. The realization of the call out of Egypt fits as a third OT fulfillment due to the possibility that Jesus can be killed (Matt 2:13).

Prior to the third OT fulfillment, only Matthew adds Magi coming from the East (Matt 2:1–12). Jesus is presented gifts of gold, frankincense, and myrrh (2:11). Early church father writings connect the gifts with Jesus's humanity and divinity,[46] yet a stronger association exists between the gifts and a prophecy in Isaiah (Isa 60:6). In Isaiah's context, the nations would come to Israel because the glory of the Lord had come to the people. They would bring offerings of gold and frankincense.[47] In the OT, frankincense was for burning in worship at the temple to Israel's God (Lev 2:1–2, 15–16). The irony is that if Matthew is solely concerned with the transcendent nature of Jesus, why fear destruction of the Christ child and have the Magi give the gift of myrrh, a traditional burial spice?[48] In light of this evidence, Luz, correctly describing the significance of gifts, states: "Jesus receives gold as a king, frankincense as God, and myrrh as a human being."[49] Matthew's

---

45. Witherington, *Matthew*, 69, specifies Jewish traditions exist to suggest that Jesus and his family spent time in Egypt. Also see b. Sanh. 107b; b. Sabb. 104b.

46. See PG 56:641–42. PL 94:541CD.

47. Leim, "Worshiping the Father," 75–76.

48. *Haer.* 3.9.2; *Cels.* 1.60. Van Beek, "Frankincense and Myrrh," 85–86.

49. Luz, *Matthew 1–7*, 107. Brown, *Birth of the Messiah*, 199.

unique inclusion of the gifts themselves holds the identity of Jesus in balance for the reader. These gifts reinforce the limitations of Jesus's human life, yet mark his transcendent status.

Alongside the prophecy from Jeremiah, Matthew relies on the review of Israel's history (Matt 2:16; Jer 31:15).[50] This serves as the fourth prophetic OT fulfillment. To demonstrate that the danger to Jesus is genuine and that the origin story merits additional evidence that Jesus is the Christ, Matthew continues the narrative of Herod's murderous plot. Both Matthew and Jeremiah refer to the mothers of Israel who lament the deaths of their sons. For Jeremiah, the mothers of Israel are those who wept over the loss of children due to the fall of the southern kingdom of Judah. For Matthew, the mothers are those whose sons, two years and under, are killed in Bethlehem and its vicinity (2:16).[51] Matthew's use of the humanity of Jesus implies that the Christ is killable. If killable, then human. If Jesus is not human, there is no need in the story for the dream or the flight to Egypt (2:13–15). For Matthew, the human story is crafted for the believability of OT fulfillment quotations in the opening narratives of the Gospel.

The fifth prophetic fulfillment pericope in the birth narratives is the identification of Jesus as a Nazarene. While the other fulfillment prophecies can be located in the OT, no explicit citation can be found regarding the Christ being a Nazarene.[52] Two differences stand out in Matthew's prophetic formula. First, instead of a singular prophet mentioned, as in the first four prophetic announcements, Matthew selects the plural τῶν προφητῶν ("prophets"). Second, he omits the participle λέγοντων ("saying") in three of the four other prophetic announcements.[53] These changes indicate that Matthew recognizes that this fulfillment is based on common instruction through the prophets.[54] Just as the prophets teach that the Messiah will be stricken, scorned, and rejected,[55] here, Matthew's selection of τῶν προφητῶν ("the prophets") suggests that he combines the thinking of OT authors such as David the Psalmist, Isaiah, and Daniel to predict a lowly human beginning to the Messiah's origin story.

Identifying Jesus as a Nazarene creates a negativity associated with his lowly position. Nazareth's status is not directly stated in Matthew but

50. Blomberg, *Matthew*, 68.

51. Brown, *Birth of the Messiah*, 36.

52. For the complexities of the fifth prophetic fulfillment, see Berger, "Jesus als Nasoräer/Nasiräer," 323–35; and Menken, "Sources of the Old Testament Quotation," 451–68.

53. Turner, *Matthew*, 98. See ch. 2, n42 above.

54. Turner, *Matthew*, 100.

55. Pss 22:6–8, 13; 69:8, 20–21; Isa 11:1; 49:7; 53:2–3, 8; Dan 9:26.

its negative reputation is mentioned in the Gospel of John (John 1:46–47; 7:41–42, 52).[56] With attention to the humble birth in Bethlehem and the obscurity of Nazareth as a village,[57] Matthew highlights the lowly, modest nature of Jesus's clearly human origin. Matthew's intentional use of Jesus's human identification is established through his hometown of Nazareth (Matt 2:23).[58] He grows up among his brothers and sisters (13:54–56), and he is understood by the townsfolk as a human carpenter's son who has Mary as his mother (13:55). As the final prophetic fulfillment in the origin story, the oral and source traditions Matthew maintains encourage belief in and understanding of the human Jesus as a Nazarene. As Matthew prioritizes the humanity of Jesus, the themes of humility and rejection will reappear in the Gospel narrative.[59]

As we can see, Matthew's portrayal of the humanity of Jesus within the origin story helps establish three features of Matthean Christology. First, as a descendant of David and Abraham, Matthew prioritizes the humanity of Jesus to establish his ethnic and legal Messianic position through the γενέσεως Ἰησοῦ Χριστοῦ ("genealogy of Jesus Christ," Matt 1:1–17). As he presents evidence that Jesus is the Messiah, the humanity of Jesus establishes how he meets the prophetic expectations of Jewish Christians.[60] Second, word choices show that Matthew purposely maintains the balance between the humanity and transcendence of Jesus.[61] Third, with identifying Jesus as Emmanuel, "God with us," we will see that Matthew crafts the main character's story so that Jesus's words and conduct connect.[62] This allows Matthew to establish Jesus as an exemplar so that his human life illustrates for the reader what God's presence can look like.[63] Each of these theological

---

56. For exegetical attempts to discern the provenance of this quotation, see Gundry, *The Use of the Old Testament*, 97–104; Davies and Allison, *Matthew 1–7*, 274–81; Hagner, *Matthew 1–13*, 39–42.

57. Gundry, *Use of the Old Testament*, 103. Reed, "Nazareth," 951.

58. Menken, "Sources of the Old Testament," 455.

59. Jesus's earthly humility (Matt 11:29; 12:19; 21:5) and rejection (8:20; 11:16–19; 15:7–8).

60. Matt 1:23; 2:6, 15, 18, 23.

61. Witherington, *Matthew*, 39, specifies that the opening narratives of Matthew provide the origin of Jesus, "both human and divine." Brown, *Birth of the Messiah*, 161, also describes the complementary nature of Jesus's existence as a Davidic and divine son. The description of the conception suggests the transcendent element of Jesus's existence (Matt 1:18–25). That, in conjunction with the omission of referring to Joseph as his father and repeated references to Mary as his mother, balances the transcendent and human portrait of Matthew's Jesus (1:1—2:23).

62. Allison, *Studies in Matthew*, 149.

63. Heil, *Death and Resurrection of Jesus*, 9.

points is possible through Matthew's biographical use of the humanity of Jesus in the origin story. Even though the origin story lacks any words of Jesus (1:1—2:23), Matthew's portrayal of Jesus demonstrates a fundamental concern for the human aspect of this character.

2.2 A BAPTISM TO FULFILL ALL RIGHTEOUSNESS (MATT 3:1–17)

Following Matthew's attention to the humanity of Jesus through the origin story, Matthew shifts the scene to Jesus's baptism.[64] The baptismal pericope begins with a call for the Jewish crowd to repent (Matt 3:2 // Mark 1:4 // Luke 3:3), but only Matthew adds that John baptizes with water εἰς μετάνοιαν ("associated with repentance," Matt 3:11).[65] The Greek meaning of the term "repentance" in the Gospels refers "both to an inner change and to a change in behavior—mainly, a turning away from an ungodly life to one reoriented toward God."[66] Matthew has yet to depict Jesus in a manner that would require a baptism associated with repentance. While Matthew maintains much of Mark's portrayal of Jesus's baptism (Matt 3:1–17 // Mark 1:2–11), Matthew redacts the pericope to explain why Jesus is baptized.

Matthew adds a pre-baptismal dialogue between Jesus and John the Baptist that reinforces the human and transcendent balance Matthew strives to uphold (Matt 3:14–15 // Mark 1:9–11 // Luke 3:21–22). As John attempts to prevent the baptism of Jesus, Matthew provides Jesus's first words in the Gospel, "Let it be so at this time, for thus it is fitting for us to fulfill all righteousness" (Matt 3:15).[67] As the first words from the mouth of his main character, Matthew's Jesus is concerned with righteousness. Only Matthew portrays that Jesus's baptismal purpose is πληρῶσαι πᾶσαν δικαιοσύνην ("to fulfill all righteousness," Matt 3:15 // Mark 1:9–10 // Luke 3:21). Kingsbury notes that as a "root character trait" for Matthew's Jesus,[68] δικαιοσύνη

---

64. For background on baptism, see McDonnell, *Baptism of Jesus*.

65. Bauer, "εἰς," BDAG, 291. Discussion of interpreting the εἰς ("associated with") as a causal preposition in Matt 3:11 and Acts 2:38 has been debated between J. R. Mantey and Ralph Marcus. Applying a causal understanding of εἰς ("associated with") leads to interpreting repentance as a result of baptism. In Matthew's thinking, baptism is a result of bearing fruit that reflects repentance (Matt 3:7–8). Therefore, according to Bauer, "εἰς," BDAG, 291, the εἰς ("associated with") in 3:11 is best understood as a "marker of a specific point of reference." For a fuller discussion on the causal use of εἰς, compare Mantey, "Causal Use of *Eis*," 45–58; and Ralph Marcus, "On Causal *Eis*," 129–30.

66. Mendez-Moratalla, "Repentance," 771.

67. Zerwick, *Grammatical Analysis*, 7.

68. Kingsbury, "Significance of the Earthly Jesus," 62.

("righteousness") and its meaning is a topic of interest for Matthew.[69] Bauer defines δικαιοσύνη to be "of specific action *righteousness* in the sense of fulfilling divine expectation not specifically expressed in ordinances."[70] Matthew portrays Jesus as the one who fulfills the divine expectations of a well-pleased Father after the baptism and transfiguration (Matt 3:16; 17:5), but Matthew's Jesus is not the only one who is to fulfill divine expectations.

The sense of fulfilling divine expectations is "a present ἕξις ["practice"] of man" according to the Greek understanding of δικαιοσύνη ("righteousness").[71] Matthew's Jesus is not the only human who is responsible to fulfill all righteousness as evidenced by the use of ἡμῖν ("us") to connect Jesus and John (Matt 3:15). Applying δικαιοσύνη ("righteousness") to Jesus identifies him and the Baptist as ones who are πληρῶσαι πᾶσαν δικαιοσύνην ("to fulfill all righteousness," 3:15). Based on Matthew's clear interest in the humanity of Jesus thus far and using the pronoun ἡμῖν ("us"), Luz correctly suggests that it "is almost unquestionable that the thought [of righteousness], as in 5:10, 20, and 6:1, is of a human act. This is the idea in the Qumran writings and especially in the Tannaitic literature, where, unlike the OT, it becomes increasingly clear that צְדָקָה ["righteousness"] becomes an ethical religious norm and refers to human conduct."[72] Part of Jesus's role as a human is to fulfill the divine expectations for human conduct,[73] and Matthew not only provides discourses that teach humanity how to live (Matt 5:1—7:28; 10:5–11; 18:1—19:1), but also portrays Jesus as the moral exemplar whom his followers should emulate.[74] Jesus and John the Baptist are connected to fulfill the divine expectation of righteousness as humans (3:15).

69. Matthew uses forms of δικαιοσύνη ("righteousness") and δίκαιος ("righteous") more than any other Gospel author. Matt 1:19; 3:15; 5:6, 10, 20, 45; 6:1, 33; 9:13; 10:41 (twice); 13:17, 43, 49; 20:4; 21:32; 23:28–29, 35 (twice); 25:37, 46; 27:19. Mark 2:17; 6:20. Luke 1:6, 17, 75; 2:25; 5:32; 12:57; 14:14; 15:7; 18:9; 20:20; 47, 50. John 5:30; 7:24; 16:8, 10; 17:25.

70. Bauer, "δικαιοσύνη," BDAG, 248, (emphasis original). *Cels.* 7, 18, 39.

71. Matt 5:10, 20; 6:1. Schrenk, "δικαιοσύνη," *TDNT* 2:193.

72. Luz, *Matthew 1–7*, 142. Przybylski, *Righteousness in Matthew*, 39, 75–76, specifies Tannaitic literature spanned 10–220 CE beginning with the disciples of Shammai and Hillel and ending with R. Judah ha-Nasi. Przbylski argues that צְדָקָה [("righteousness")] signifies "all aspects of religious teaching which are normative for man's conduct . . . Righteousness is the demand of God upon man." Matthew's perception of Jesus's human existence requires that he meets all of God's righteous requirements not only as a moral exemplar, but also in light of his human existence.

73. See ch. 3.1.4, n24 below.

74. Matt 3:15; 4:1–11, 23–25; 9:2–7, 35–38; 10:24–25; 12:46–50; 15:29–31; 16:24–28; 17:24–27; 19:13–15; 26:36–46; 28:18–20.

By connecting Jesus and John, Matthew portrays both as obedient to God.[75] Even though John the Baptist is a fellow human model for the readers (Matt 11:7–19), the Gospel follows the story of Jesus as the prototype and model.[76] According to Luke Timothy Johnson, "The most obvious element defining Jesus' human character is his obedient faith in God."[77] While obedience is important to the Jesus story, as has been seen and will be seen, it is not the most obvious element of Jesus's humanity in Matthew's portrayal.

The baptism pericope prepares the reader for the temptation narratives. In light of Matthew's baptism narrative, Luz correctly suggests that "Jesus is presented as the exemplary obedient and humble one. For Matthew, his first words in the Gospel refer to this. Jesus' conduct has fundamental significance."[78] Prioritizing the human story of Jesus in a manner that connects Jesus with other humans who should meet divine expectations, Matthew's perspective that Jesus is a model begins with baptism as an example to fulfill all righteousness (Matt 3:15). Purposely pointing to the humanity and transcendence of Jesus at the baptism, Matthew's Jesus will now be tempted.

2.3 A TEMPTED HUMAN (MATT 4:1–11)

Using Q, Matthew and Luke depict Jesus being led into the wilderness to be tempted (Matt 4:1–11 // Luke 4:1–13). Examination of the temptation narrative raises questions that assist in the study of Matthew's use of the humanity of Jesus. For example, how can Jesus actually be tempted if Matthew does not prioritize the humanity of Jesus? Is the best translation of πειράζω "tempt"? Do the temptations Jesus faces evoke a desire in the human Son of God to disobey the Father's will? These questions contribute to our understanding of the role the humanity of Jesus plays in Matthew's portrait.

When describing Jesus's time in the wilderness, πειράζω is traditionally translated "temptation." The existence of temptation narratives in Mark (Mark 1:12–13) and Q (Matt 4:1–11 // Luke 4:1–13), and in conjunction with another Jewish Christian writing, the Epistle to the Hebrews (Heb

---

75. While it will be seen throughout this project that Matthew's Jesus is obedient to God, John is also depicted in this manner (Matt 3:1–14; 11:7–19; 14:1–12).

76. Luz, *Matthew 1–7*, 142.

77. Johnson, "Learning the Human Jesus," 174.

78. Luz, *Matthew 1–7*, 142. Matt 3:15; 4:1–11, 23–25; 9:2–7, 35–38; 12:46–50; 15:29–31; 16:24–28; 17:24–27; 19:13–15; 26:36–46; 28:18–20.

2:18; 4:15),[79] suggests that an awareness of a tempted human Son of God exists in the first-century. In light of Matthew's interest in Jesus as the Son of God,[80] Birger Gerhardsson argues for a shift in the meaning of πειράζω from "tempt" to "test."[81] While both "tempt" and "test" are valid options for translating the term,[82] Gerhardsson contends that Matthew is more concerned with divine "testing" than Satanic "tempting,"[83] but in Matthew's temptation pericope there is a distinction between tempt and test.

Matthew uses πειρασθῆναι ("to tempt," Matt 4:1) and οὐκ ἐκπειράσεις ("you will not test," 4:7) in the same pericope. This distinction is reinforced by the setting of both the temptation scene in Matthew and a description of Israel before going into the Promised Land in Deuteronomy (Deut 8:2; Matt 4:1-2).[84] William Stegner considers "testing" to be one of four important words found in the LXX that connects the two narratives,[85] however, he does not point out that Matthew changes the LXX description from the term for ἐκπειράζω ("test," Deut 8:2; Matt 4:7) to πειράζω ("tempt," Matt 4:1). Matthew's change in language indicates he perceives a difference between ἐκπειράζω ("test") and πειράζω ("tempt"). This evidence suggests that Matthew uses πειράζω to describe a temptation rather than test.

Each of the temptations reflects real human experiences. The first temptation relates to a physical human need for food.[86] Just as Jesus's disciples experience hunger (Matt 12:1), Matthew assumes Jesus is human

---

79. Longenecker, *Christology*, 20, classifies Hebrews as a Jewish Christian writing. Recall that the author of Hebrews announces Jesus πεπειρασμένον . . . κατὰ πάντα καθ᾽ ὁμοιότητα χωρὶς ἁμαρτίας ("has been tempted . . . in every way as we are, [was] yet without sin," Heb 4:15).

80. Matt 3:17; 4:3, 6; 8:29; 14:33; 16:16; 26:63; 27:40. For an extended discussion regarding the importance of the "Son of God" title to Matthew, see Kingsbury, *Matthew*, 40–83.

81. Gerhardsson, *Testing of God's Son*, 2.1: 25–28. See France, *Gospel of Matthew*, 126–28, and Turner, *Matthew*, 124–31 for scholars who side with Gerhardsson to nuance Matthew's use of the term πειράζω ("tempt").

82. Bauer, "πειράζω," BDAG, 792–93.

83. Gerhardsson, *Testing of God's Son*, 25–35. France, *Gospel of Matthew*, 126, reinforces the idea by pointing out that the entire testing pericope occurs through the guidance of the Spirit and consequently God's purpose.

84. Stegner, "Temptation Narrative," 7–8, connects Israel in Deuteronomy and the Matthean temptation narrative by pointing to "has led," "forty," "wilderness," and "testing."

85. Stegner, "Temptation Narrative," 8.

86. France, *Gospel of Matthew*, 131, points out that a similar response can be found in Wis 16:26: "[T]hat thy sons, whom thou didst love, O Lord, might learn that it is not the production of crops that feeds man, but that thy word preserves those who trust in thee."

by describing him as hungry after forty days and nights (4:2).[87] While a transcendent being does not need food in Jewish thought,[88] the tempter entices the human Jesus, as the Son of God, to change stones into bread. Jesus faces the temptation to use power in a self-serving manner due to hunger (4:2). After fasting forty days and nights,[89] hunger is a point of human frailty, yet Jesus relies on God for nourishment (4:4).[90] Jesus subjects himself "as the human Son of God, to a commandment that specifically refers to a human being (ὁ ἄνθρωπος) living by God's word (Deut 8:3; Matt 4:4)," as Donald Hagner puts it.[91] While Jesus does not fall prey to the temptation as evidenced by the work of the ministering angels at the end of the pericope (Matt 4:11), Jesus's victory over the first temptation serves as an example for the reader. Just as the rest of humankind must trust in the provision of the Father, so does Jesus (4:4; 6:25–33; 7:9–11).

The second temptation involves the opportunity for Jesus to prioritize himself over the Father's will. After Jesus overcomes the first temptation using scripture, the devil challenges Jesus to throw himself off of the temple (Matt 4:5–6). The devil quotes a Psalm to tempt Jesus to disobey the Father and put God and his word to the test (4:6–7; Ps 91:11–12). The question is whether Jesus should take a leap of faith.[92] The human Jesus can experience physical harm as has been seen with the flight to Egypt (Matt 2:13–15). Therefore, the temptation involves not only protection from mortal danger,[93] but also, and more specifically, the temptation to act with a belief that God exists to serve the Son rather than the opposite.[94] This temptation provides the striking image that while God promises protection for his people, courting those risks does not benefit God's covenant community.[95]

87. Matthew references the hunger of Jesus at the scene involving the cursing of the fig tree (Matt 21:18).

88. One can cite the requirement of the placement of the "Bread of the Presence" (Exod 25:30), but Durham, *Exodus*, 362, suggests that "whatever primitive people may think about food for their gods, the people of Israel cannot by any stretch of the socio-theological imagination be put into such a category." While care for the gods in ancient Mesopotamia includes feeding the gods, the OT and NT are devoid of any evidence that the Judeo-Christian God needed food for sustenance. Also see Oppenheim, *Ancient Mesopotamia*, 183–98.

89. Scripture portrays Moses and Elijah fasting forty days and nights (Exod 34:28; 1 Kgs 19:8).

90. Morris, "Deuteronomy in the Matthean and Lucan Temptation," 293.

91. Hagner, *Matthew 1–13*, 66.

92. Turner, *Matthew*, 129.

93. Gerhardsson, *Testing of God's Son*, 61.

94. Keener, *Commentary*, 141.

95. France, *Gospel of Matthew*, 133.

A similar attitude is expressed by the Israelites at Massah and Meribah (Exod 17:1–7).[96] As the Israelites yearn for water, they demand miraculous intervention to save their lives.[97] Their demand not only reflects the idea that God is there to serve the covenant son, Israel, but also their attitude provokes Moses to ask, "Why do you test the Lord?" (Exod 17:2). Israel fails by putting God to the test. Jesus, on the other hand, overcomes the temptation and responds with a command. "Do not put the Lord your God to the test" (Matt 4:7; Deut 6:16a).[98] Jesus's response does not test God.[99] Just as God has established a new covenant with the Jewish Christians, they will be tempted to put God to the test by placing their desires before God's will. Only Matthew's readers are to seek first the kingdom of God and his righteousness (Matt 6:33). Just as Jesus chooses to put the will of God before his will, the Jewish Christian audience will need to follow the exemplar and do the same.

The third temptation involves riches and idolatry.[100] The devil leads Jesus to a mountain to see the kingdoms of the world so that he can offer them to Jesus if he worships the devil (Matt 4:8–9). By doing so, Jesus will follow his desires and cease to obey God.[101] This is not the only instance Matthew's Jesus faces a similar temptation. The temptation to follow his own desires returns as σκάωδαλον ("a stumbling block") later in the Matthean narrative (16:22–23). Bauer defines σκάωδαλον as "an action or circumstance that leads one to act contrary to a proper course of action or set of beliefs."[102] He translates Matthew's use of σκάωδαλον as "you are tempting me to sin."[103] Matthew applies the term elsewhere to refer to other humans in the world and the role it plays in temptation (18:7). After ordering the disciples not to tell anyone that he is the Messiah (Matt 16:20 // Mark 8:30), Matthew and Mark portray Peter telling Jesus that he will never be killed by the chief priests, elders, and scribes. Both depict Jesus's response as a rebuke, ὕπαγε ὀπίσω μου, σατανᾶ ("get behind me, Satan," Matt 16:23 // Mark 8:33). The rebuke is similar to the response to the third temptation as Jesus says, ὕπαγε, σατανᾶ ("be gone Satan," Matt 4:10). However, only Matthew adds Jesus's

---

96. France, *Gospel of Matthew*, 133.

97. France, *Gospel of Matthew*, 133.

98. Bauer, "ἐκπειράζω," BDAG, 306, defines the term ἐκπειράζω as "to subject to test or proof," yet translates the term as "tempt."

99. Keener, *Commentary*, 141.

100. Gerhardsson, *Testing of God's Son*, 62.

101. Seesemann, "πεῖρα," *TDNT* 6:23–36 (35).

102. Bauer, "σκάωδαλον," BDAG, 926.

103. Bauer, "σκάωδαλον," BDAG, 926.

rebuke of Peter, σκάωδαλον εἶ ἐμοῦ ("you are a cause of stumbling to me," Matt 16:23 // Mark 8:33).

In both the third temptation and the rebuke of Peter's earthly thoughts, Matthew's Jesus is tempted to follow his own desires, achieve worldly power, and forsake the Father by committing idolatry and worshiping the devil (Matt 4:8–10). The third temptation is to worship and to serve someone other than God (4:10). As God's covenant people, the readers can observe the exemplar as they remember to worship and serve God alone (4:10; Deut 6:4, 13).

Humankind can be seduced to disobey through temptation,[104] and out of the heart comes evil (Matt 15:18–19). Bauer defines καρδία ("heart") as the "seat of physical, spiritual and mental life,"[105] and he describes the term in several ways to suggest it can refer to the center of "moral decisions," "the emotions, wishes, desires," and "the will and decisions" of an individual.[106] Only Matthew describes Jesus as gentle and humble in heart (11:29), and Matthew depicts Jesus expressing each of the nuanced meanings for καρδία ("heart"). For example, Jesus makes moral decisions in the temptation pericope (4:1–11). Jesus ἠθέλησα ("desired") to gather the people of Jerusalem under God's protective wings (23:37).[107] In the Garden of Gethsemane, Jesus not only possesses a will, but also a will contrary to the Father (26:36–46).[108] These examples demonstrate Jesus possesses a heart that is the seat of life. Matthew portrays Jesus as one who faces real temptation to make his own moral decisions, to follow his own desires, and to disobey because he possesses his own will.

In light of Matthew's portrayal of the human Jesus and the pericope itself, a better understanding of πειράζω is "tempt." Matthew's narrative demonstrates a difference between tempting and testing and each of the temptations reflects real human experiences. The temptations of whether to trust God for provisions, to treat God as your servant, and to worship someone other than God are real human temptations. Early Christian thought considers Jesus is tempted as we are (Heb 2:15), and as has been seen, Jesus

104. Seesemann, "πεῖρα," *TDNT* 6:33.

105. Bauer, "καρδία," BDAG, 508.

106. Bauer, "καρδία," BDAG, 508–9.

107. Keener, *Commentary*, 558.

108. Crisp, *Divinity and Humanity*, 49, in light of the Council of Chalcedon, suggests that it is difficult to imagine that Jesus can be truly human without a will distinct from the will of the Father. For a "theologically orthodox" development of this argument from an abstract-nature incarnation perspective, see Crisp, *Divinity and Humanity*, 57–58.

faces similar temptations encountered by others including Israel.[109] The way Matthew makes that possible is through his portrayal of the humanity of Jesus in his writings not only with the use of πειράζω ("tempt," Matt 4:1) but also in light of the temptations themselves.[110]

Matthew and Mark, unlike Luke, end the temptation narrative to inform the reader that angels arrive and διηκόνουν αὐτῷ ("ministered to him," Matt 4:11 // Mark 1:13 // Luke 4:13).[111] Διακονέω ("minister") carries a nuance that means "to give to eat."[112] In light of forty days without food (Matt 4:2), it seems reasonable to conclude that providing nourishment is one result of the angelic ministry. If Matthew wants to portray Jesus primarily as a transcendent figure, why is a physical, human need met by the ministering angels? Why not omit this conclusion as Luke did? Matthew is in the process of building Jesus's transcendent status as the Son of God. Jesus, depicted as a human figure capable of hunger, death, and misuse of power through temptation, exists as dependent on the Spirit to lead him into the wilderness and, at the end, receiving the angels' ministry to him (4:1, 11).

If Matthew desires to prioritize the transcendent nature of Jesus and limit his humanity, then he could have provided a portrayal similar to the Gospel of John.[113] The author of John's Gospel explicitly writes to encourage people to believe that Jesus is the Christ, the Son of God (John 20:31). John's portrayal of Jesus does not include Matthean emphases such as the human genealogy, temptation, transfiguration, and agony in Gethsemane. Matthew's primary focus is not to identify the transcendent status of Jesus in the temptation pericope. Even though he is identified as the Son of God twice (Matt 4:3, 6),[114] Matthew indicates Jesus is led by the Spirit (4:1),

---

109. Schottroff and Stegemann, *Jesus and the Hope of the Poor*, 54.

110. According to Seesemann, "πεῖρα," *TDNT* 6:33, in light of Matthew's internal evidence, Mark, Q, and other Jewish Christian literature, "there is no doubt that the life of Jesus is [in Heb 2:18; 4:15] understood as a life in temptation."

111. Turner, *Matthew*, 589, reinforces that Jesus "needed ministry" from the angels after the temptation.

112. Davies and Allison, *Matthew 1–7*, 374, reference Matt 8:15; 25:44; Luke 22:27; John 12:2; Acts 6:2; Josephus, *Ant.* 11:163, 166 and compare the experience of Jesus and Elijah in the wilderness (1 Kgs 19:4–8). Bauer, "διακονέω," BDAG, 229, acknowledges one function of the term can be "attention at meals."

113. This assumes a post-Matthean authorship of the Gospel of John and a knowledge of the temptation story. For a discussion on the order of the Gospels, see Hengel, *Four Gospels*, 38–47. For a brief discussion suggesting a late first-century date of Johannine authorship of the Gospel, see Michaels, *Gospel of John*, 37–38. For a discussion on John's dependence on and interaction with the Synoptics, see Denaux, *John and the Synoptics*.

114. Gerhardsson, *Testing of God's Son*, 22–23, indicates that this "Son of God" theme can be applied to "Anointed One" and to "God's people" (Deut 1:31; 8:5; 14:1;

hungry (4:2), distinct from God (4:7, 10), ministered to by angels (4:11), and tempted rather than tested because God is not to be tested (4:1, 3, 7). Matthew's temptation narrative shows that he desires to emphasize the humanity of Jesus in conjunction with Jesus's transcendent status. By doing so, Matthew maintains a distinction between Jesus and God.

Matthew connects the horizontal, human, and vertical, transcendent, components of the life of Jesus.[115] While this foreshadows the interest of what became the two natures doctrine of the early church, Matthew's interest in establishing Jesus as the Son of God does not eliminate his interest in Jesus's humanity.[116] From Matthew's perspective, Jesus is tempted and exemplifies how to endure temptations. As the model who fulfills all righteousness (Matt 3:15), Matthew's portrayal of the human Jesus models for his audience ways to respond to temptation (4:1–11). Because Matthew prioritizes the human element, legitimate temptations overcome by Jesus justify belief in him as the moral exemplar.

2.4 AN EARTHLY MINISTRY INITIATED (MATT 4:12–16)

The final section of a portrait of the human beginning sets up Jesus's ministry. Comparing the Synoptics assists to identify that Matthew addresses the initiation of Jesus's ministry differently (Matt 4:12–16 // Mark 1:14–15 // Luke 4:14–15). Luke's depiction portrays Jesus returning to Galilee in the power of the Spirit teaching and being glorified (Luke 4:14–15). In Mark, after the arrest of John the Baptist, the audience reads Jesus's first words in the Gospel that initiate his ministry to proclaim the Gospel of God in Galilee (Mark 1:14–15). While Matthew maintains the arrest of John the Baptist as a signal to initiate the ministry (Matt 4:12), Matthew's portrayal includes its own unique qualities that reinforce his interest in using the humanity of Jesus to tell the story.

The first indicator of Matthew's interest in the humanity of Jesus is his addition of Isaiah's prophecy (Matt 4:15–16; Isa 9:1–2). As Matthew portrays Jesus withdrawing into Galilee and settling in Capernaum, only Matthew points out that this is within the region of Zebulun and Nephtali.

32:5, 6, 18–20).

115. Luz, *Studies in Matthew*, 96.

116. Kingsbury, *Matthew*, 41, considers Son of God to be the "central Christological title" for Matthew. As a result, Kingsbury highlights this theme and title throughout Matthew at the expense of exploring the humanity of Jesus.

As seen with the examples of prophetic fulfillment in the origin story,[117] Matthew's interest in this region lies within his christological purpose of identifying Jesus's humanity through prophetic fulfillment. In this pericope, Matthew geographically connects the prophetic utterance of Isaiah to the earthly location of Jesus's ministry beginnings (4:14–16).

In Isaiah, the house of Judah brought trouble and judgment on themselves, yet a prophecy led to hope that light would come to Jerusalem once again (Isa 1:1–31; 3:1–26; 9:1–7).[118] This hope is not limited to the Jews (Isa 9:1; Matt 4:15). Isaiah's phrase, "Galilee of the nations" describes an area between the Sea of Chinnereth and the Mediterranean where Hebrews, Canaanites, Arameans, Hittites, and Mesopotamians live.[119] Galilee is the location where Israel encounters the rest of the world, hence the phrase, "Galilee of the nations," in Isaiah (Isa 9:1).[120] The inclusion of this prophecy, unique to Matthew, denotes a missional interest.[121]

Even at the beginning of his ministry, Matthew portrays Jesus's mission to include being a light to the Jews and the gentiles as demonstrated by the inclusion of this prophecy. In spite of Jesus focusing on the Jews (Matt 10:5–7), his fame and ministry spreads to the gentiles (4:13–16; 15:21–39). In the end, just as Galilee is the launching point for Jesus's ministry and the location where Jews encounter people from other nations, the Jewish Christians following Jesus, the moral exemplar, are to make disciples of all nations (28:18). This unique section not only reinforces another prophetic fulfillment, it also urges the audience to see that their mission is a mission to Jews and gentiles through the example of Jesus's ministry.[122]

The second unique human feature in this pericope, though not as obvious, is Matthew's redaction to Jesus's response to the arrest of John the Baptist. Luke omits the relationship between Jesus's ministry initiation and the arrest of John, but Matthew and Mark, describing the situation differently, connect the events (Matt 4:12 // Mark 1:14 // Luke 4:13–15). Mark simply indicates that ἦλθεν ("he came," Mark 1:14) into Galilee after John's arrest, yet Matthew changes the language to ἀνεχώρησεν ("he withdrew," Matt 4:12).

117. See ch. 2.1 above.

118. Goldingay, *Isaiah*, 70; Watts, *Isaiah 1–33*, 24:134.

119. Oswalt, *Book of Isaiah 1–39*, 239.

120. Oswalt, *Book of Isaiah 1–39*, 239.

121. Keener, *Commentary*, 145.

122. Keener, *Commentary*, 146.

Mark's description that ἦλθεν ("he came") means to "proceed on a course" or be in "movement from one point to another,"[123] and Matthew's term, ἀναχωρέω ("withdraw"), means to "withdraw, retire, take refuge."[124] Matthew describes Jesus taking refuge by withdrawing into Galilee after the arrest of John the Baptist.[125] In the birth narratives unique to Matthew, it has been observed that Jesus is protected from the threat of Herod's genocidal command (Matt 2:13–16). There are other times Jesus withdraws in the context of hostility or danger.[126] For example, after he heals the man with the withered hand, Jesus withdraws because the Pharisees conspire about how to destroy him (12:14–15). However, Matthew is not always consistent with Jesus's movement due to danger. Matthew omits a scene where Mark describes Jesus telling the disciples to have a boat ready (Mark 3:7–8). The reason is due to the multitude of people pressing in on him. Mark's Jesus is concerned that θλίβωσιν αὐτόν ("they might crush him," 3:9). Here, Matthew's change in terminology connects the arrest of John the Baptist to Jesus's withdrawal, and reinforces that the withdrawal for Jesus is strategic in the case of potential physical danger.[127]

While danger is implied with the use of ἀναχωρέω ("withdraw," Matt 4:12), Matthew relies on the human story to explain Jesus's geographic movements to make narrative sense because Matthew depicts Jesus as a human who faces physical danger (2:13–16; 4:12). Matthew prioritizes the human story to connect the withdrawal and another fulfillment prophecy (Matt 4:15–16; Isa 9:1–2). That prophetic fulfillment is used to describe the initiation of Jesus's ministry to Jew and gentile (Matt 4:13–16). As an example of the Great Commission (28:18–20), Matthew describes the initiation of Jesus's ministry as a model of missional interest to all nations. Matthew intentionally uses the human characteristics of his primary character not only to establish the prophetic fulfillment for belief but also to demonstrate Jesus is an example of a minister to all nations.

CONCLUSION

As has been seen in this chapter, Matthew's portrayal of the origin story, baptism, temptation, and initiation of Jesus's earthly ministry displays an interest in the human Jesus. Through the use of the humanity of Jesus,

---

123. Bauer, "ἔρχομαι," BDAG, 393–94.

124. Bauer, "ἀναχωρέω," BDAG, 75.

125. Davies and Allison, *Matthew 1–7*, 376.

126. Matt 4:12; 12:15; 14:13; 15:21. France, *Gospel of Matthew*, 156.

127. Turner, *Matthew*, 132.

Matthew's Christology focuses on concern for his audience's belief in Jesus as a fulfiller of prophecy.[128] As a result, Matthew prioritizes the human story by weaving it into the narrative to meet those expectations as an apologetic to affirm belief. That portrait would resonate with what is known by the Jewish Christian audience. For those readers, Matthew's perspective on the human story of Jesus establishes him as the moral exemplar for the audience at the baptism, temptation, and ministry initiation. In the transition from Judaism to Jewish Christianity, presenting Jesus as a model of what it means for humans to be righteous before God provides direction for those who read Matthew's Gospel.

As the Gospel of Jesus's humanity,[129] Matthew purposely balances Jesus's identity as a human and transcendent figure more than the other Gospel authors, especially in the portrait of the human beginning (Matt 1:1—4:16). However, Matthew's interest in the humanity and transcendence of Jesus will begin to lead to an inconsistent portrayal of the main character. At times Matthew will develop the case for Jesus's transcendence and others he will prioritize the human element of his main character. As Matthew attempts to tell the human story as he builds an argument for Jesus's transcendent status, the portrayal will demonstrate Matthew's perspective on the importance of Jesus's humanity.

128. See ch. 2.1 above.

129. Irenaeus, *Haer.* 3.11.8.

3

Portrait of the Human Life with Transcendent Status

(Matthew 4:17—16:20)

WITH THE STRUCTURAL MARKER ἀπὸ τότε ἤρξατο ("from that time he began," Matt 4:17), Matthew shifts the focus of Jesus's human story from his beginnings to his ministry. Initiating the story of Jesus with reassuring his audience of Jesus's identity,[1] Matthew portrays Jesus as Emmanuel (1:23), the Son with whom the Father is pleased (3:17). Yet, even in the narrative shift to Jesus's ministry, Matthew continues to follow the human life of Jesus. Before coming to the narrative of the activities of Jesus's ministry, the reader has already been informed that Jesus is the Messiah (1:1, 16–18; 2:4), the Son of David (1:1, 20), fulfiller of multiple prophecies,[2] a bearer of the Spirit (3:16; 4:1), and the Son of God (3:17; 4:3, 6).[3] Shifting to Jesus's ministry, the reader will engage with activities from the time he began his public ministry to the affirmation that Jesus is the Christ, the Son of the living God (4:17—16:20). It will be seen that Matthew constructs an argument for belief in Jesus's transcendent status in the midst of his emphasis on the human portrayal.

From the initiation of Jesus's ministry to Peter's proclamation of his identity (Matt 4:17—16:20), the Matthean narrative can be divided into two segments. The first portrays Jesus's two discourses, multiple healings, and

---

1. Luz, *Studies in Matthew*, 34.
2. Matt 1:22; 2:15–17, 23; 4:14.
3. Davies and Allison, *Matthew 1–7*, 426.

growing questions about Jesus's identity (4:17—10:42). As the questions increase,[4] the second section focuses on responses to Jesus's teaching and activities (11:1—16:20). These responses feature an increasing polarization of attitudes toward Jesus,[5] which lead to Jesus teaching in parables (13:1–52), a temporary shift in mission (15:21–39), as well as Peter's climactic confession (16:13–20).

Prioritizing the human story, Matthew employs the narrative to interject explicitly Jesus's status as the Son of God three times between ministry initiation and confession. The first comes from demon-possessed men (Matt 8:29). The second from the mouths of the disciples after Jesus walks on water and calms the sea (14:33). The third reference is Matthew's culminating christological statement from Peter that Jesus is the Christ the Son of the living God (16:16).[6] While Matthew provides evidence for Jesus's transcendent status, he focuses on using the human portrayal to fulfill prophecy,[7] to portray him as a moral exemplar,[8] and to build the identity for belief in a human and transcendent character.[9] Combining these elements, Matthew employs the humanity of Jesus to portray the human life with transcendent status.

3.1 A LIFE WITH TRANSCENDENT RESULTS (MATT 4:17—10:42)

After Matthew's portrait of the human beginning (Matt 1:1—4:16), Jesus's ministry initiation differs from Luke's in two primary ways (Matt 4:17 // Luke 4:14–15). First, Luke's Jesus begins his ministry filled with the Spirit

4. Matt 7:28–29; 8:18–9:8; 9:10–17; 9:32–34.

5. Matt 11:2–6; 11:18–19; 12:1–14; 12:22–32; 12:38–42; 13:53–58; 15:1–9. Blomberg, *Matthew*, 89.

6. Kingsbury, *Matthew*, 8. Luz, *Studies in Matthew*, 92, connects the Son of God to "divine sonship," therefore suggesting that transcendence is connected to Matthew's descriptive title.

7. Matt 8:17 // Isa 53:4; Matt 12:17–21 // Isa 42:1–4; Matt 13:14–15 // Mark 4:12 // Isa 6:9–10, 35. Three of the four prophetic fulfillments are only located in Matthew's Gospel, and Mark's use of the fulfillment is only partial.

8. See chs. 2.2 and 2.3 above. As has been illustrated with Jesus's desire to fulfill all righteousness and his ability to overcome temptation (Matt 3:15; 4:1–11), preserving the human story of Jesus throughout the narrative strengthens Matthew's emphasis on the *imitatio Christi* (10:24–25; 28:18–20). Davies and Allison, *Matthew 8–18*, 5, reinforce the idea that in the miracle chapters Jesus models behavior worthy of imitation. Luz, *Studies in Matthew*, 93, describes Jesus's life as "the model character" for the disciple.

9. Matt 8:23–27; 9:2–8, 18–26; 12:15, 25, 46–50; 16:16; 26:57–68.

(Luke 4:14). Second, Luke describes Jesus as being glorified by all (4:15).[10] Matthew employs neither of these descriptors to initiate Jesus's ministry. Moreover, Matthew reserves δοξάζω ("glorify") as a descriptor for God the Father and Jesus's future return as the Son of Man.[11] Matthew does not initiate Jesus's ministry trying to convince the people of his identity as Son of God, Son of Man, God, or even the Messiah. Rather, he introduces Jesus's ministry with preaching repentance because the kingdom of heaven is at hand (Matt 4:17). While this is Jesus's message, these events involve a call to model Christ.[12] Just as Jesus preaches, Matthew parallels Jesus's activities with his instructions to his disciples in the second discourse (4:17 // 10:6).[13]

At the Sea of Galilee Jesus asks the disciples to follow him, setting up parallels between Jesus and the disciples (Matt 4:18–22). The story of calling the first disciples closely resembles Mark's description (Matt 4:18–22 // Mark 1:16–20). Luke, on the other hand, adds a miraculous catch of fish that acts as a catalyst for Peter, James, and John to accept the call to be fishers of men (Luke 5:1–11). Matthew's portrayal sets aside the need for a supernatural event to convince these disciples to follow him. The Gospel narrative itself neither refers to any prior interaction between the disciples at the scene by the Sea of Galilee nor requires a public demonstration of transcendence for the disciples to drop their nets and follow (Matt 4:18–22). The fame of Jesus does not spread until he teaches in synagogues, preaches the gospel, and heals afflictions, including epilepsy, demon-possession, and paralysis (4:23–25). The narrative progression suggests that Jesus's preaching sufficiently convinces Peter, Andrew, James, and John to hear, leave their boat, leave their father, and follow Jesus (4:17–22). Relying on neither fame nor transcendence, Jesus, the human disciple maker, models for his readers the ability to gather followers without transcendent activities.

After Jesus preaches and calls disciples, the narrative depicts Jesus performing miracles (Matt 4:23). How can Jesus accomplish transcendent, miraculous activities that extend beyond the norm of human experience? Besides conception ἐκ πνεύματος ἁγίου ("by the Holy Spirit," 1:18), the Spirit comes on Jesus in the form of a dove (3:16), and, later in the Matthean

10. Green, *Gospel of Luke*, 205, parallels praising God and thanking Jesus in Luke (Luke 17:15–16).

11. Matthew uses δοξάζω ("glorify") for God the Father on multiple occasions (Matt 5:16; 9:8; 15:31; 16:27). The other uses describe Jesus's glory by referring to the future state (19:28; 24:30; 25:31).

12. Davies and Allison, *Matthew 1–7*, 412.

13. Davies and Allison, *Matthew 1–7*, 411–12, reinforce Jesus as a model commenting that he wants his missionaries to "do exactly what he has done" in the second discourse (Matt 10:1–42).

narrative, Jesus indicates he casts out demons ἐν πνεύματι θεοῦ ("by the Spirit of God," 12:28). Prior to that disclosure to the Pharisees, Matthew refers to a prophecy from Isaiah that the Spirit of God rests on him as depicted at the baptism scene (3:16; 12:18; Isaiah 42:1). In contrast, Luke more directly connects the role of the Spirit to Jesus's power.[14] He portrays Jesus as full of the Spirit (Luke 4:1) and in the power of the Spirit (4:14). In the Synagogue, Luke's Jesus proclaims the Spirit rests on him at the beginning of his ministry (4:18). While Matthew and Luke claim Jesus is led by the Spirit (Matt 4:1 // Luke 4:1), only Matthew indicates that Jesus casts out demons ἐν πνεύματι θεοῦ ("by the Spirit of God," Matt 12:28 // Luke 11:20). As Matthew's Jesus depends on the Spirit of God, Gerald Hawthorne correctly observes that reliance on the Spirit serves as another "proof of the genuineness of his humanity . . . the Holy Spirit was the divine power by which Jesus overcame human limitations, rose above his human weakness, and won out over his human mortality."[15] Therefore, Matthew, as well as Luke, depicts transcendent power stemming from the presence and power of the Spirit not from his transcendent status as the Son of God. In other words, Jesus exists as a human with transcendent power from the Spirit. As Jesus is empowered by the Spirit, his followers can be also.[16]

As a result of healing and preaching, great crowds follow Jesus as he proceeds to sit on a mountain to teach (Matt 4:23—5:1).[17] The portrayal connects the stories of God speaking to Israel through Moses and Jesus.[18] Matthew does not depict God speaking to Israel directly. Rather, in both Exodus and Matthew's Gospel, the message comes through humans, Moses and Jesus. Here, only Matthew refers to Jesus opening his mouth (5:1-2) to teach them the first of five discourses (5:3—7:27).[19] Commonly called the Sermon on the Mount, Matthew's Jesus teaches as one with authority (7:29).

14. Stronstad, *Charismatic Theology of St. Luke*, 37–54, describes Jesus as the "Charismatic Christ" due to Luke's christological understanding of the Spirit's role in Jesus's power.

15. Hawthorne, *Presence and the Power*, 35.

16. Kirk, *Man Attested by God*, 41.

17. According to Turner, *Matthew*, 149, Jesus sits to teach (Matt 13:1-2; 24:3), but in some contexts teaching occurs to "pronounce eschatological judgment" (19:28; 20:21, 23; 22:44; 25:31; 26:64). According to Keener, *Commentary*, 164, a sitting Jesus follows the proper pattern of cultural instruction (Luke 4:20; Pesiq. Rab Kah. 18:5). Davies and Allison, *Matthew 1–7*, 423, comment that the mountain serves as the location for Jesus to proclaim "weighty words" (Matt 5:1; 17:9; 28:16).

18. Exod 19:3, 12; 24:15, 18; 34:1-4. Luz, *Matthew 1–7*, 182. For a detailed argument that Matthew intentionally connects the stories of Moses and Jesus, see Allison, *New Moses*.

19. Matthew 10:5-42; 13:1-52; 18:1-35; 23:1—25:46.

Jesus is covered in God's authority,[20] but, unlike the scribes, he teaches concerning the kingdom of God and righteous principles which serve as commands for others to follow as members of that kingdom.[21] Matthew balances Jesus's identity through connecting Jesus with Moses yet hints at transcendent status through his teaching with authority.

In light of our topic, four elements of the Sermon on the Mount discourse deserve attention.[22] First, the principles taught by Jesus in the Sermon are embodied by him as the model to be emulated.[23] To make this possible, Matthew customizes Jesus's human existence in light of Sermon principles.[24] For example, the Sermon depicts οἱ πραεῖς ("the humble one") shall inherit the earth (Matt 5:5), but only Matthew uses πραΰς ("humble") to describe Jesus elsewhere (11:29; 21:5).[25] According to the Sermon, those who hunger and thirst for righteousness are blessed (5:6), yet only Matthew's Jesus desires to fulfill all righteousness (3:15). The peace makers are blessed, and Matthew expands the depiction of Jesus's ability to make peace navigating a drawn sword at the Garden of Gethsemane.[26] As the exemplar,[27]

20. Garland, *Reading Matthew*, 91, connects the end of the first discourse with the end of the narrative prior to the second discourse to connect the crowd's astonishment at Jesus's authority.

21. Hagner, *Matthew 1–13*, 82.

22. Allison, "Structure of the Sermon," 423–45, for a discussion of this portion of Matthew's Gospel (Matt 5:3—7:27).

23. Davies and Allison, *Matthew 1–7*, 467.

24. Betz, "Portrait of Jesus," 174–75, (italics original), defends two conclusions regarding Jesus as an "ἄνθρωπος ["man"] *par excellence.*" 1). Jesus as a teacher exemplifies the wise one who builds his house on the rock (Matt 7:24). 2). Jesus presents himself as a human being including himself in the model prayer to the Father (6:9).

25. According to Davies and Allison, *Matthew 1–7*, 449, Jesus is the "model" of meekness and his life on earth provides "content to his words." Turner, *Matthew*, 152, indicates meekness is a characteristic of "authentic kingdom spirituality" (Matt 11:25–30; 18:1–5; 19:13–15), which Jesus exemplifies in his earthly existence.

26. Matt 5:9; 26:51–54 // Mark 14:47–50 // Luke 22:50–51. Keener, *Commentary*, 172. Luz, *Matthew 1–7*, 276, adds that Matthew's Jesus is the reader's "model" of non-retaliation during the Passion Week (Matt 26:47–68; 27:27–44).

27. Below are additional examples that demonstrate Matthew connects the principles of the Sermon on the Mount with Jesus's behavior. Hagner, *Matthew 1–13*, 96, summarizes the beatitudes, they can be "taken as a description of the behavior of Jesus himself." Matthew's Jesus mourns as he laments the spiritual status of cities and, in particular, Jerusalem (Matt 5:4; 11:20–24; 23:37–39). In the Matthean Gospel, Jesus demonstrates mercy. When asked for mercy, Jesus extends it to two blind men (9:27–29; 20:29–34), the Canaanite woman (15:21–28), and a demon-possessed son (17:14–18). Most visible is Jesus's suffering on account of righteousness, something Matthew clearly illustrates not only in the passion narratives (27:4, 19, 23), but also in the persecution of the prophets (21:34–36; 22:6). See France, *Gospel of Matthew*, 173. As the exemplar,

Matthew's Jesus teaches the principles of the kingdom in the Sermon on the Mount and lives these same principles during his time on earth.

Second, Matthew's reliance on Jesus's humanity not only fulfills OT prophecy,[28] but also OT Law. Within the Sermon, only the Jesus of Matthew indicates he did not come to abolish but to fulfill the law and the prophets (Matt 5:17).[29] Nowhere in the first Gospel does Matthew portray Jesus breaking the OT law, at least according to the author's description of Jesus's actions.[30] This portrayal of Jesus brings the law and prophets to their divinely intended goal.[31] Jesus not only fulfills OT prophecies as the Messiah, he intends to fulfill the requirements of all righteousness (3:15; 5:17). Third,

---

Jesus is not only righteous but through him all righteousness becomes fulfilled (3:15; 5:17; 27:4, 19). Also see Davies and Allison, *Matthew 1–7*, 467. Matthew's Jesus is never portrayed with a lustful thought, a marriage with which he could divorce, or a need to swear (5:27–37). According to Keener, *Commentary*, 195, Jesus avoids oaths. There is a prohibition of anger (5:22). While Matthew's Jesus clearly uses hyperbole in his rhetoric in the Sermon on the Mount (5:27–30, 38–42, 48; 6:1–4), Jesus's teaching in relation to his own anger merits attention. Twice, Matthew removes Mark's explicit mention of Jesus's anger or fury (Matt 19:14 // Mark 10:14; Matt 12:12–13 // Mark 3:5), however, Matthew retains Jesus's implicit anger at the cleansing of the temple and increases the woe proclamations (Matt 21:12–13; 23:13–36). It should be noted that Keener, *Commentary*, 183, clarifies that the anger Jesus describes in the Sermon on the Mount is the type that can "generate murder if unimpeded." That type of anger is considered equivalent to murder itself. Anger itself is not wrong but the type of anger becomes the issue (Eph 4:26; 1 John 3:15; T. Gad 4:1–7). In addition, Manson, *Sayings of Jesus*, 53, suggests a difference exists for Matthew's Jesus that the attacks are "not so much against persons as against abuses in the system." The condemnation is against the system of ideas, not the individuals. A life lived in light of the principles of the Sermon on the Mount continues as Jesus does not retaliate against his enemies, even those who torture him before and during the crucifixion (5:38–39; 26:47–68; 27:27–44). The death of Jesus serves as the ultimate example and expression of love for one's enemies (5:43–44). Jesus demonstrates that he serves God by overcoming temptations and following his Father's will (6:19–21, 24; 4:1–11; 16:22–23; 26:36–46). As far as fasting, Jesus fasts in the wilderness (4:2), but during his ministry, he only anticipates its later occurrence (9:15). Each of these examples reinforce Matthew's Jesus models his teaching in the Sermon on the Mount.

28. Matt 1:22–23; 2:5–6, 15, 17–18, 23; 4:14–16; 8:17; 12:17–20; 13:14–15, 35; 21:4–5; 27:9–10.

29. Luz, *Studies in Matthew*, 8, states: "I find it significant that Matthew does not adopt Mark's freedom from the ritual law. The Matthean community does observe the Sabbath (24:20) and emphasizes that justice, mercy, and faith are more important than tithing (23:23)."

30. France, *Gospel of Matthew*, 180, notes that Jesus takes issue with literal observance of the law and provides a nuanced understanding of its application in Matthew's Gospel (Matt 5:21–48; 9:13).

31. Davies and Allison, *Matthew 1–7*, 485–87.

the repeated phrase "your Father"[32] in the Sermon suggests Jesus perceives a distinction between himself and the Father. Fourth, establishing Jesus's authority above and beyond the skills and influence of the teachers of the law is, as France comments, a "bold claim" (7:28–29).[33] This bold claim reinforces, as Turner claims, a "transcendent authority" that other earthly teachers do not possess.[34]

Although Jesus possesses authority unlike others, Matthew establishes this authority while balancing the human story with the Sermon on the Mount in two ways. First, his earthly mission foreshadows a transcendent status as an eschatological judge (Matt 7:21–23). Second, even though Matthew's Jesus refers to God as "my Father,"[35] Matthew never instructs the readers to pray to Jesus, but rather to God the Father.[36] The Matthean Jesus neither specifies that he is the figure that the readers should glorify (5:16) nor from whom they receive good things (7:11). Maintaining his status as a future eschatological judge and preserving a distinction between Jesus and the Father, Matthew's Jesus does not consider himself solely transcendent. In spite of preserving a distinction that Jesus is not solely transcendent, the First Evangelist ends the Sermon elevating Jesus's authority at the expense of the scribe's (7:28–29). This prepares the readers for an initiation into the developing and deepening controversies over Jesus's identity and status.[37]

3.1.1 Jesus's Human Touch and Human Reactions (Matt 8:1–17)

After coming down from teaching on the mountain, Matthew's Jesus performs ten miracles. Even though there are ten miracles, there are nine stories that are grouped in three triads (Matt 8:1–17; 8:18—9:8; 9:18–35).[38] The grouping of these triads illustrates Matthew's intentionality with

---

32. Matt 5:16, 45, 48; 6:4, 8, 14, 18, 26; 7:11.

33. France, *Gospel of Matthew*, 298–99.

34. Matt 7:29; 9:8; 10:1; 21:23–27. Turner, *Matthew*, 225.

35. Matthew builds the argument that Jesus is in a unique relationship with the Father through repeated references of "my Father" throughout the narrative (Matt 7:21; 10:32–33; 11:27; 12:50; 15:13; 16:17; 18:10, 19, 35; 20:23; 26:29, 39, 42, 53). Comparing the Synoptics, there are fewer connections between Jesus and "my Father" in Luke (Luke 2:49; 10:22; 22:29; 24:49) and none in Mark.

36. By contrast, see John 14:14.

37. Matt 9:2–17; 12:1–14, 22–45; 13:53–58; 15:1–9; 16:1–4; 19:3–9; 21:14–17, 23–46; 22:15–46. See Repschinki, *Controversy Stories*, for Matthean redaction controversy stories from the healing of the paralytic to Jesus's interaction with the Sadducees.

38. Luz, *Studies in Matthew*, 221–22.

narrative organization.[39] Jack Dean Kingsbury argues that Matthew rearranges his source material to present Jesus "above all as the Messiah, the Son of God."[40] Even though "Son of God" appears only once in these triads (8:29), Jesus's activities and Matthew's various christological identifiers, such as Son of Man (8:20; 9:6), Lord,[41] Son of David (9:27), and servant from Isaiah (8:17),[42] are arranged to build toward Peter's confession that Jesus is the Christ, the Son of the living God (16:16). While presenting Jesus above all as Messiah and Son of God is a sufficient summary,[43] it is more accurate to say that in the midst of building the argument for Jesus's transcendent status through miracles and discourse, Matthew attempts to describe Jesus's identity in a multitude of ways. In Matthew's mind, Jesus's identity includes many aspects,[44] including human. As will be seen, in the midst of building a case for Jesus's transcendence, Matthew prioritizes the human elements of Jesus's story to picture a human life with transcendent status that designates Jesus is the Christ, the Son of the living God (16:16).

The first of the three miracle triads models Jesus's authority, power, and willingness to heal outsiders in Jewish society.[45] Jesus heals a ritually unclean leper (Matt 8:1–4), a gentile centurion's servant (8:5–13), and Peter's mother-in-law, a second-class citizen at the time (8:14–15).[46] Within each of these miracle accounts, Matthew adjusts elements of Jesus's story. While Ulrich Luz suggests that Matthew abbreviates many of the scenes to emphasize the dialogue,[47] it appears that in some instances Matthew achieves more than accentuating discourse in his descriptions of healing outsiders in Jewish society.

39. It is generally agreed that Matthew groups the ten miracles in a triadic fashion topically not chronologically. See Thompson, "Reflections on the Composition," 365–88; Kingsbury, "Observations on the 'Miracle Chapters,'" 559–73; Moiser, "Structure of Matthew," 117–18. France, *Gospel of Matthew*, 362.

40. Kingsbury, "Observations on the 'Miracle Chapters,'" 572.

41. Matt 8:2, 6, 21, 25; 9:28.

42. Davies and Allison, *Matthew 8–18*, 4.

43. Kingsbury, "Observations on the 'Miracle Chapters,'" 572.

44. Hill, "In Quest of Matthean Christology," 140, states: "Because [Matthew] portrays Jesus by means of a story no one category—teacher, healer, Wisdom, incarnate, triumphant Son of man, not even Kyrios or Son of God—is adequate to contain that Jesus reverenced by the church, the Jesus on whom Matthew reflects in his book."

45. Davies and Allison, *Matthew 8–18*, 8. Turner, *Matthew*, 230.

46. Compton, "Was Jesus a Feminist?," 4, argues Jesus challenged social taboos of the day including care for the "marginal" individuals such as non-Jews, the poor, children, and women.

47. Luz, *Matthew 8–20*, 3.

Matthew and Luke maintain Mark's portrayal of Jesus touching a leper to heal the unclean outsider (Matt 8:3 // Mark 1:41 // Luke 5:13).[48] It should be remembered that in most societies and religions power or energy can emanate from a holy man or healer.[49] Since that is the case, these initial healings neither require the disciples nor the readers to perceive Jesus as a solely transcendent figure. Rather, in light of Jesus's authority (Matt 7:29), Matthew builds the argument for Jesus's transcendence, not only in the narrative, but also through the organization of these triads.

As Matthew portrays Jesus's physical touch of the leper (Matt 8:3), the healing entails human contact. For the Jewish observers at the time, Jesus's gesture would be considered abnormal in at least three ways.[50] First, touching a leper would be perceived as contradicting the Law of Moses (Lev 5:3), but, by making him clean, Jesus fulfills the law.[51] The command to sacrifice afterwards remains as a requirement in the story so that the priest can restore the healed leper to community (Matt 8:4).[52] Second, there is no need for Matthew to maintain Jesus's physical healing touch. The next miracle narrative depicts Jesus healing a centurion's servant from a distance (8:5–13). Third, and most important, Matthew preserves the human touch of Jesus to show he extends compassion even to those considered unclean.[53] However, Matthew removes Mark's motivation to σπλαγχνίζομαι ("be moved with pity," Matt 8:3 // Mark 1:41). Through touching the leper, Jesus breaks the taboos of Jewish society for the purpose of compassion.[54] For Matthew's Jewish Christian audience, retaining that level of emotional detail is unnecessary because compassion is implied.[55] Although Matthew adds compassion elsewhere in the narrative (Matt 20:34 // Mark 10:52 // Luke 18:22), this is the first instance of Matthew removing an emotion of Jesus, yet it will not be his last.

After Jesus heals the leper, Mark's Jesus ἐμβριμησάμενος ("sternly charged") him to keep the miracle a secret (Mark 1:43). Both Luke and Matthew retain Mark's portrayal that the healing should be kept secret, but

---

48. For a brief synopsis on the significance of healing touch, see Theissen, *Miracle Stories*, 62–63.

49. Josipovici, *Touch*, 62. Davies and Allison, *Matthew 8–18*, 13.

50. Blomberg, *Matthew*, 139.

51. Lev 13:3, 8, 10, 13, 17. Gundry, *Matthew*, 140.

52. Viljoen, "Jesus Healing the Leper," 7.

53. Keener, *Commentary*, 261.

54. Viljoen, "Jesus Healing the Leper," 7.

55. France, *Gospel of Matthew*, 307.

they remove the ἐμβριμάομαι ("stern charge," Matt 8:3–4 // Luke 5:14).[56] However, only Matthew later adds another situation where Jesus ἐνεβριμήθη ("sternly charged") others not to report their healing (9:27–31). Even though Matthew removes the emotion to σπλαγχνίζομαι ("be moved with pity," Matt 8:3 // Mark 1:41) in the leper's healing, he is the only Synoptic author to add that Jesus σπλαγχνίσθεὶς ("was moved with pity") when healing two blind men outside Jericho (Matt 20:34 // Mark 10:52 // Luke 18:42). These two examples demonstrate Matthew's inconsistent use of the emotions of Jesus. This suggests that Matthew uses the humanity of Jesus for his own storytelling and theological purposes.

The theological purposes are particularly observable with the emotion included at the healing of the second outsider, a centurion's servant. Using a Q pericope, Matthew and Luke portray Jesus ἐθαύμασεν ("marveled") at the faith of the centurion (Matt 8:10 // Luke 7:9). While the point of Jesus's amazement at the centurion's answer contrasts the lack of faith in Israel with the gentile's faith,[57] Matthew's use of θαυμάζω ("marvel") communicates that Jesus is "extraordinarily impressed or disturbed by something."[58] Θαυμάζω ("marvel") repeatedly appears in Matthew's narrative as an emotion expressed by humans as a result of Jesus's activity.[59] Θαυμάζω ("marvel") is a human emotion shared by Jesus and the crowd.

Again, Matthew handles this emotion differently elsewhere in his narrative. Matthew maintains the ἐθαύμασεν ("marveled") response to the gentile's faith (Matt 8:10), yet, in comparison to Mark, Matthew removes that emotion from Jesus in Nazareth (Matt 13:58 // Mark 6:6). Jesus does not marvel at lack of faith in Nazareth. Although France suggests that Matthew "typically omits" matters that are considered "unessential" to the story,[60] it

56. Luke changes the description to παραγγέλλω ("command," Luke 5:14).

57. Keener, *Commentary*, 268. Hagner, *Matthew 1–13*, 205.

58. Bauer, "θαυμ," BDAG, 444.

59. At the stilling of the storm, Matthew and Luke use ἐθαύμασαν ("they marveled"), but Mark has ἐφοβήθησαν ("they feared," Matt 8:27 //Mark 4:41 // Luke 8:25). Both Matthew and Luke describe the response to casting out a demon with ἐθαύμασαν ("they marveled," Matt 9:33 // Luke 11:14). Only Matthew selects θαυμάζω ("marvel") to describe the gentile crowd's response to multiple healings (Matt 15:31). Only Matthew describes the disciple's emotional reaction to the withered fig tree as ἐθαύμασαν ("they marveled," Matt 21:20 // Mark 11:20). Matthew, Mark, and Luke use different forms of the root verb θαυμάζω ("marvel") to describe the response to Jesus's teaching on paying taxes to Caesar (Matt 22:22 // Mark 12:17 // Luke 20:26). Matthew and Mark describe the reaction of Pilate to Jesus's silence using θαυμάζειν ("to marvel," Matt 27:14 // Mark 15:5).

60. France, *Gospel of Matthew*, 309.

appears Matthew is relying on the emotions of Jesus to assist in telling the story.

Faith is a topic of interest for Matthew.[61] In the Nazareth narrative, the religious leaders treat Jesus with contempt and suspicion,[62] and the Nazarenes question his identity (Matt 13:54–55). To what extent would it make narrative sense to preserve Jesus being "extraordinarily impressed or disturbed by something"[63] as a response to the lack of faith in the Jewish town of Nazareth? As early as his second reported healing miracle, Matthew's Jesus has already pointed out the lack of faith in Israel in contrast to a gentile's faith (8:10). Therefore, the later omission of θαυμάζω ("marvel") in Nazareth is not because of the emotion being "unessential" to the story in the words of France.[64] Rather, Matthew intentionally adjusts the human emotions of Jesus for theological and storytelling purposes. He relies on Jesus's emotion to point out a lack of faith displayed by Israel in contrast to a gentile's faith (8:10). Pointing out Israel's lack of faith is not only due to Israel's history with prophets (5:11–12; 11:11–24; 13:57), but also their response with a human prophet standing before them (21:45–46; 23:29–39).

After the miracle with the Centurion's servant (Matt 8:5–13), Jesus heals Peter's mother-in-law as the final miracle of the first triad (8:14–15). While each of the Synoptics includes this miracle (Mark 1:29–31 // Luke 4:38–39), only Matthew's shortened version combines Jesus ἐλθών ("came"), εἶδεν ("saw"), and ἥψατο ("touched") Peter's mother-in-law. Each Synoptic author uses an active form of the root ἔρχομαι ("come") to describe Jesus's entrance into Peter's house (Matt 8:14 // Mark 1:29 // Luke 4:38). Unlike people informing Jesus of her sickness in Mark and Luke (Mark 1:30 // Luke 4:38), Matthew's Jesus heals without any intervention, interaction, or request from those in or outside Peter's house (Matt 8:14–15). Adding the human element that Jesus εἶδεν ("saw") her sickness demonstrates Jesus's initiative to heal without an expression of the mother-in-law's faith.[65] While it could be suggested that no one wanted Peter's mother-in-law healed, it is more

61. With minor characters, Jesus points out the faith of the gentile (Matt 8:5–13), the people carrying the paralyzed man (9:2–7), the hemorrhaging woman (9:20–22), and the Canaanite woman (15:21–28). Olivares, "Term ὀλιγόπιστος," 281, stresses that the term functions as a rebuke for failure to believe, pointing out the disciples' bad memory, and teaching discipleship. Of the times "little faith" receives attention in the Synoptics, Matthew refers to it five times, only once paralleling with Luke, and it does not appear in Mark (Matt 6:30 // Luke 12:28; Matt 8:26; 14:31; 16:8; 17:20). Kingsbury, *Matthew as Story*, 27, designates the minor character's faith as "foils for the disciples."

62. Matt 9:3, 10–11, 34; 12:1–2, 14, 24.

63. Bauer, "θαυμ," BDAG, 444.

64. France, *Gospel of Matthew*, 309.

65. Davies and Allison, *Matthew 8–18*, 33–34.

likely this healing reinforces that Jesus possesses the authority and power to heal without a request or an expression of faith.[66] The initiative, authority, and power deserves greater attention because Matthew adjusts the description of Jesus's humanity. Matthew makes use of the humanity of Jesus as he comes, sees, and touches Peter's mother-in-law to display the initiative and power.

Matthew ends the first triad with a focus on Jesus's human existence for prophetic fulfillment. Jesus displays his authority over demons by casting them out with a word and curing the sickness of all brought to him (Matt 8:16–17). Luke describes demons coming out of people and crying Jesus is "the Son of God" earlier in his narrative, but Matthew is the only Synoptic author to quote the prophet Isaiah (Matt 8:16–17 // Mark 1:34 // Luke 4:41). In spite of an opportunity to state explicitly Jesus's transcendent status similar to Luke's description, Matthew instead focuses on the humanity of Jesus through this prophetic fulfillment. Matthew quotes Isaiah to remind the readers that Jesus is the Suffering Servant of Isaiah[67] and will bear the people's weakness and sickness (Isa 53:4; Matt 8:17).[68] According to Maarten Menken, "The illnesses are considered to be a punishment for 'our' sins, and the servant vicariously bears the punishment for these sins (see Isa 53:4–6, 8, 10–12)."[69] He adds, "It is anyhow striking that Matthew only describes Jesus' sufferings and death as vicarious in terms which seem to have been derived from Isaiah 53 when he finds these terms in Mark (Matt 20:28 // Mark 10:45; Matt 26:28 // Mark 14:24)."[70] While both Matthew and Mark present Jesus as the one who will give his life as a ransom for many (Matt 20:28 // Mark 10:45), only Matthew's birth narrative connects Jesus with saving people from their sins (Matt 1:21). Only Matthew adds the role of Jesus's blood in the new covenant for the forgiveness of sins (26:28). As a result of prioritizing characteristics of Jesus's human existence, birth and death play a clearer role in the redemption of humankind for Matthew.

The miracles of Jesus healing a leper, a Centurion's servant, and a mother-in-law fulfill prophecy and demonstrate that miraculous work is available to Jews and those deemed outsiders.[71] These scenes foreshadow not only another prophecy of Isaiah that will include gentiles as beneficiaries

---

66. Turner, *Matthew*, 234.

67. Twelftree, *Jesus the Miracle Worker*, 111.

68. Watts, "Messianic Servant," 91–92, argues Matthew has this prophecy of Isaiah in mind when he frames the healing.

69. Menken, "Source of the Quotation," 323.

70. Menken, "Source of the Quotation," 324.

71. Twelftree, *Jesus the Miracle Worker*, 111.

of a Messiah (Matt 12:17–21) but also Jesus's future earthly ministry to the gentiles (15:21–39). In spite of Jesus's ministry to outsiders, Matthew's narrative focuses attention on further developing Jesus's identity through the authority of his human yet transcendent character.

3.1.2 What Kind of Man Is This? (Matt 8:18—9:8)

The second triad of miracles demonstrates Jesus's authority over nature, demons, and sin. This triad further balances the humanity and transcendence of Jesus. Matthew's Jesus exhibits authority over disease earlier in the narrative (Matt 4:24; 8:1–17), and in the second triad Jesus identifies himself as the Son of Man who forgives sins (8:20; 9:6). The disciples inquire what sort of man Jesus is (8:27), and the demons call him the Son of God (8:29). As Matthew builds toward Peter's confession that Jesus is the Christ the Son of the living God (16:16), the humanity of Jesus remains a central part of the story so that Matthew can adequately support belief in the human and transcendent identity he depicts.

For the first time, in response to a scribe and a disciple who display a desire to follow him, Matthew uses the enigmatic phrase υἱὸς τοῦ ἀνθρώπου ("Son of Man," Matt 8:19–22).[72] Matthew selects this title more than any other title to describe Jesus,[73] yet no consensus exists for what Matthew means by the phrase Son of Man and how the audience may perceive the meaning.

The book of Daniel and some non-canonical materials are central to understanding the meaning of Son of Man (Dan 7:13; 1 En. 37–71; 4 Ezra 13). A literal translation of son of man is "human being."[74] As the primary

---

72. Hagner, *Matthew 1–13*, 213–15, indicates the phrase Son of Man is "very problematic" and a *"crux interpretum"* in scholarship in the twentieth-century. In light of its limited use outside the Gospels (Acts 7:56; Rev 1:13; 14:14), it is not a phrase commonly used to describe Jesus's identity. Luz, *Studies in Matthew*, 97–112, devotes an entire chapter on "The Son of Man in Matthew: Heavenly Judge or Human Christ?" He acknowledges that questions regarding the "Son of Man" and its meaning remain unresolved. Davies and Allison, *Matthew 8–18*, 43, describe the scholarly debate over the Son of Man title as a "specialized field of its own wherein scholarly discord reigns supreme." For additional research on Son of Man, see Lindars, *Jesus Son of Man*; Muller, *Der Ausdruck "Menschensohn"*; and Hurtado and Owen, *'Who Is This Son of Man?'*

73. Matthew uses the title "Son of Man" thirty times (Matt 8:20; 9:6; 10:23; 11:19; 12:8; 12:32, 40; 13:37, 41; 16:13, 27–28; 17:9, 12, 22; 19:28; 20:18, 28; 24:27, 30, 37, 39, 44; 25:31; 26:2, 24, 45, 64); "Son of God" ten times (4:3, 5; 5:9; 8:29; 14:33; 16:16; 26:63; 27:40, 45, 54); and "Son of David" ten times (1:1, 20; 9:27; 12:23; 15:22; 20:30–31; 21:9, 15; 22:42).

74. Bock, "Son of Man," 894, reinforces this commenting that "'son of man' simply

title for Matthew's Jesus, "Son of Man" depicts: (1) A future heavenly glory;[75] (2) earthly suffering;[76] (3) present status and authority.[77] While debate continues regarding the meaning of Son of Man, each of these descriptors can be connected to Jesus's existence as a human being. In the immediate context, its first mention describes Jesus's existence as the Son of Man in human terms (Matt 8:18–22). Matthew describes Jesus's earthly living situation as one of personal poverty and homelessness.[78] In light of the son of man in the Psalms, any Jewish speaker could understand his own life in terms of this text (Ps 8:4).[79] In turn, Davies and Allison rightly conclude that it would be "methodologically unsound to approach the synoptic data with the assumption that most first-century Jews . . . would have immediately thought of a transcendent redeemer figure."[80] The primary title Jesus employs to describe himself and the context where Matthew first places the term attests to his interest in Jesus's humanity.[81]

Matthew's use of the phrase υἱὸς τοῦ ἀνθρώπου ("Son of Man") lends itself to preserving a distinction in his main character. It helps explain Jesus's desire not only to maintain a level of secrecy as to his identity,[82] but also to communicate Matthew's and his church's interest in the ministry of the "human Son of Man as one who was at the same time the Son of God,"[83] as Donald Hagner puts it. Matthew employs both Son of Man and Son of God, but never interchangeably in his use of Q and Mark.[84] In other words,

---

refers to a human being." France, *Gospel of Matthew*, 326.

75. Matt 10:23; 16:27–28; 19:28; 24:27, 30, 37, 39, 44; 25:31; 26:64.

76. Matt 8:20; 11:19; 12:40; 17:9, 12, 22; 20:18; 26:2; 26:24, 45.

77. Matt 9:6; 12:8, 32; 13:37, 41; 16:13. France, *Gospel of Matthew*, 327. Davies and Allison, *Matthew 8–18*, 43, observe that these three categories assist to understand the title. The present status, suffering, and future return in glory all occur as a result of Jesus's humanity. Davies and Allison, *Matthew 8–18*, 50–51, point out that of the thirty uses, thirteen refer to Jesus's future coming, ten to death and resurrection, and seven to earthly activity. This title shows up more than Son of God, and Matthew's Jesus never directly titled himself Son of God.

78. Luz, *Matthew 8–20*, 18. Pamment, "Son of Man," 119–20, makes a connection between Son of Man and every other individual who follows Jesus (Matt 8:20; 9:6–8).

79. Smith, "No Place," 100.

80. Davies and Allison, *Matthew 8–18*, 46.

81. See ch. 3, n73 above. Kingsbury, *Matthew*, 113.

82. Novakovic, "Jesus as the Davidic Messiah," 164–69, addresses Matthew's Messianic Secret and its purpose to avoid open conflict with the leaders of the land until Jesus enters Jerusalem.

83. Hagner, *Matthew 1–13*, 213–15.

84. Mark uses the phrase "Son of Man" thirteen times (Mark 2:10, 28; 8:31, 38; 9:9, 12, 31; 10:33; 13:26; 14:21, 41, 62). Matthew uses the title thirty times and only omits

Matthew preserves the distinction between a title describing a human being, Son of Man, and the developing transcendent status as Son of God. Throughout the narrative Matthew expands the transcendent description of Jesus alongside his human existence as the Son of Man. Matthew's treatment of the disciples, the demons, and the detractors further clarifies the identity of his main character in this second triad.

The first miracle involves a sea storm rescue. Before the rescue, Jesus is asleep on a boat.[85] Sleep is a very natural, human activity, but Jesus is awakened to save the disciples from the windstorm on the sea (Matt 8:23–25). After the seas and winds obey him, only Matthew's disciples ask ποταπός ἐστιν οὗτος ("what sort of man is this," Matt 8:27 // Mark 4:41 // Luke 8:25).[86] While there are non-canonical sources that include nature miracle narratives that demonstrate a human's ability to control wind, rains, and other forms of nature,[87] the narrative focus is not how but who calms the sea. The disciples wrestle with the tension between the human they follow and the transcendent power they witness because, in the OT tradition, the seas only obey the God who creates them.[88] The tension leads them to ask what sort of man Jesus is (Matt 8:27).

As Matthew's Jesus arrives in the country of the Gadarenes, he meets two demoniacs (Matt 8:28). Even though Jesus recently refers to himself as a human being using the phrase υἱὸς τοῦ ἀνθρώπου ("Son of Man," 8:20) and the disciples ask ποταπός ἐστιν οὗτος ("what sort of man is this," 8:27), the demons declare another aspect of Jesus's identity by calling him the υἱὲ τοῦ θεοῦ ("Son of God"). The disciples do not give Jesus the title "Son of God" until he walks on the water (14:33). Here, Matthew's Jesus displays his authority over nature with the calming of the sea (8:23–27) and then over demons by casting them out (8:28–34). In the midst of Jesus's human story, arranging this miracle section in this manner is part of slowly building the

---

Mark's use of Son of Man once (Matt 16:21 // Mark 8:31 // Luke 9:22). Luke uses the title twenty-five times and Matthew omits the phrase on four occasions (Matt 5:11 // Luke 6:22; Matt 10:32 // Luke 12:8; Matt 26:50 // Luke 22:48; Matt 28:6–7 // Luke 24:7).

85. Batto, "Sleeping God," 153–77, argues that this pericope points to divine rule. Allison and Davies, *Matthew 8–18*, 72, provide OT examples of people seeking to wake God from sleep (Ps 35:23; 44:23–24; 59:4; Isa 51:9). However, these examples are neither narrative nor reflect what occurs at the sea storm when the narrative depicts the disciples awakening Jesus.

86. Even though the term ἄνθρωπος ("man") is not used here, Matthew selects the singular, masculine form of οὗτος ("this").

87. Keener, *Commentary*, 279, provides a list of non-canonical sources (Diogenes Laertius, *Lives of Eminent Philosophers* 8.2.59; Porphyry, *Life of Pythagoras*, 29; Iamblichus, *De Vita Pythagorica*, 29). Also see Keener, *Miracles*, 1:579–99.

88. Job 38:8–11; Pss 29:3–4; 65:5–7; 89:8–10; 93:4; 106:9; 107:23–32.

case for his transcendent status as the characters in the story begin to see what the readers know.

After providing the narrative of Jesus's authority over demons, Matthew edits Mark's account of Jesus healing a paralytic to conclude the second miracle triad. Three particular modifications show the intentional portrayal of the humanity of Jesus in Matthew. First, only Matthew removes the question, "Who can forgive sins but God alone?" (Matt 9:3 // Mark 2:7 // Luke 5:21). Contrasting the Synoptics, Luz specifies that Mark's inclusion of the question places Jesus "on the same level with God."[89] Here is an opportunity for Matthew to reinforce the case he is slowly building for Jesus's transcendent status, yet he removes this question. While each Synoptic portrays the Son of Man possessing the authority to grant forgiveness (Matt 9:6 // Mark 2:10 // Luke 5:24),[90] only Matthew's crowd glorifies God for giving that authority to men (Matt 9:8). In Matthean theology, human beings also possess the capacity to forgive the sins of others (16:19; 18:18).[91] Even in the OT, human beings are credited with the capacity to obtain forgiveness from God for others through prayer (Exod 32:31–33; Num 14:19). Therefore, Matthew removes the question "Who can forgive sins but God alone" because God has granted the authority not only to the Son of Man but also other humans. In an instance where Matthew could further his case for Jesus's transcendence and preserve the question located in Mark and Luke, he chooses to connect the portrait of Jesus's human activity and authority with other human beings to forgive sins.

Second, Matthew adjusts the crowd's reaction to the scene. After preserving the crowd glorifying God (Matt 9:8 // Mark 2:12 // Luke 5:26), only Matthew's crowd glorifies God for granting authority for forgiveness to ἀνθρώποις ("humans"). Although Turner suggests Jesus's act of forgiving sins is the "most crucial aspect of Jesus's authority,"[92] God receives glory. Unlike Jesus in John's Gospel, Matthew does not directly equate Jesus and

---

89. Luz, *Matthew 8–20*, 28.

90. Martin, "It's My Prerogative," 71.

91. Hagner, *Matthew 14–28*, 472–74; 532–33, correctly connects binding and loosing, unique to Matthew (Matt 16:19; 18:18), with the authority of forgiveness within the members of the community. Basser, "Derrett's 'Binding' Reopened," 299–300, states in reference to binding and loosing in the *Didascalia Apostolorum*, "There is no hint here of 'permitting' or 'forbidding' activities. Even where 'binding' and 'loosing' are connected to the law in the *Didacalia*, the terms still refer to 'chaining (imprisoning)' and 'freeing.'" For Semitic arguments to understand binding and loosing, see Duling, "Binding and Loosing" 3–31.

92. Turner, *Matthew*, 247.

God (John 10:30).[93] The First Evangelist's alteration to the crowd's reaction emphasizes Jesus's identity as a human.

The modification to the crowd's reaction raises the question of Matthew's view of Jesus's identity. Matthew's crowd glorifies God because God grants the authority to forgive to ἀνθρώποις ("humans").[94] In prior scenes the disciples ask, "What sort of man is this?" (Matt 8:27) and the demons address Jesus as the "Son of God" (8:29). Matthew's adjustment to the crowd's response indicates their perception of Jesus's existence as a human. Matthew's emphasis on the Son of Man connects Jesus with other humans as authorized to forgive sins.[95] This is consistent with Matthew's view that Jesus dispenses the authority to forgive (16:19; 18:18). Jesus, as the exemplar, calls humans to offer God's forgiveness, clarifying that God's forgiveness occurs in conjunction with human forgiveness (6:12–14; 18:15–35).[96]

Third, healing a paralytic involves conveying Jesus's knowledge. Comparing the Synoptic accounts of healing the paralytic, each of the authors select ἰδών ("seeing") to describe Jesus's ability to discern the faith of those bringing the paralytic to Jesus (Matt 9:2 // Mark 2:5 // Luke 5:20). The faith of the friends is physically observable through their activity. However, later in this pericope Matthew modifies the description of Jesus's ability to discern the thoughts of the scribes (Matt 9:4 // Mark 2:8 // Luke 5:22). To describe Jesus's insight, Mark and Luke employ ἐπιγνοὺς ("perceiving"), yet Matthew chooses to use ἰδών ("seeing," Matt 9:4 // Mark 2:8 // Luke 5:22) again. Adela Yarbro Collins argues that the choice of ἐπιγινώσκω ("perceive") in Mark and Luke implies that Jesus possesses "special insight not available to ordinary human beings,"[97] in other words, a transcendent awareness. While an alternate translation of ἰδών ("seeing") could be "perceiving,"[98] Matthew's choice to maintain ἰδών ("seeing") does not require Jesus to possess transcendent knowledge.[99]

93. Hagner, *Matthew 1–13*, 234.

94. Hagner, *Matthew 1–13*, 234.

95. France, *Gospel of Matthew*, 348. As a basic order of the church, Luz, *Matthew 8–20*, 28–29, correctly assesses Matthew's thematic interest in forgiveness as a basic directive for the church (Matt 18:15–35). Garland, *Reading Matthew*, 192, points out that this section encourages the church to seek after the one who sins. Following this pericope Jesus commands "unlimited forgiveness" (18:21–35).

96. As Twelftree, *Jesus the Miracle Worker*, 117, states, "This story thus serves as a paradigm for Matthew's readers in their ministry of healing and forgiveness."

97. Collins, *Mark*, 185.

98. Bauer, "ὁράω," BDAG, 785, provides one definition that indicates "to be mentally or spiritually perceptive."

99. Matthew employs this term throughout his narrative in several ways. For example, Herod realizes the wise men trick him (Matt 2:16). Judas realizes his condemnation

Only Matthew applies ἰδὼν ("seeing") to Herod (Matt 2:16), to Judas his betrayer (27:3), and to Pilate (27:24), effectively Jesus's executioner.[100] Would Matthew's readers consider these villainous characters capable of transcendent knowledge? France correctly suggests that Jesus ἰδὼν ("seeing") the scribes' thoughts is possible through noting body language and whispering together (9:3–4).[101] Therefore, human observation serves as the only requirement for knowing what the scribes thought. Consequently, Matthew's redaction and choice of ἰδὼν ("seeing") implies no need for transcendent knowledge. It will become obvious that Matthew's Jesus is not all-knowing based on his admission that he was unaware of the day or hour of his return (24:36).[102] It is also clear that at a moment when Matthew can reinforce "special insight not available to ordinary human beings,"[103] he, instead, chooses to keep Jesus's knowledge on the human level.

Herein is another example of an apparent inconsistency of Matthew's use of the humanity of Jesus. This results in Matthew's attempt to portray Jesus as a human with transcendent status. According to France, Matthew would have no hesitation ascribing transcendent knowledge to Jesus (Matt 12:25; 22:18),[104] yet, in both examples France provides, Matthew selects two different terms to describe Jesus's knowledge, εἰδὼς ("knowing," 12:25) and γνούς ("having awareness," 22:18).[105] Below we will see evidence for Matthew's seemingly inconsistent approach to Jesus's knowledge.

In France's first example, Jesus knows the thoughts of the Pharisees after healing a blind and mute demoniac (Matt 12:22–25). Matthew retains the term εἰδὼς ("knowing") from Q (Matt 12:25 // Luke 11:17). While Matthew employs εἰδὼς ("knowing") in this confrontation with the Pharisees, derivatives of οἶδα ("know") describe the knowledge of other humans throughout Matthew's narrative.[106] Unlike Mark and Luke, Matthew previously establishes that the Pharisees suspect that Jesus casts out demons by the prince of demons (Matt 9:34). Later, Jesus casts out demons a second time (12:22–23)

(27:3), and Pilate realizes his attempts to thwart the death of an innocent man get him nowhere (27:24). Several uses include the literal ability to observe someone or something (3:7; 5:1; 8:18; 9:22–23, 36; 21:19).

100. Consider Pilate, a villain in Matthew's story. He ᾔδει ("knew") that out of envy the chief priests, elders, and scribes deliver Jesus to him (Matt 27:18).

101. France, *Gospel of Matthew*, 346.

102. Other passages suggest the Jesus's lack of knowledge (Matt 13:51–52; 14:12–13; 27:34, 46). For a fuller discussion, see Brown, "How Much Did Jesus Know," 315–45.

103. Collins, *Mark*, 185.

104. France, *Gospel of Matthew*, 346.

105. Matt 12:15; 16:8; 22:18; 26:10.

106. Matt 7:11; 20:22, 25; 24:42; 25:13; 26:2; 27:65.

and, in both instances, the Pharisees claim that Jesus's power comes through Beelzebul, the prince of demons (Matt 9:34; 12:24 // Mark 3:22 // Luke 11:15). Considering the development of the narrative and connecting the two scenes, there is no need for Jesus to possess transcendent knowledge to know the thoughts of the Pharisees, which may explain why Matthew selects the term εἰδὼς ("knowing") to describe Jesus's perceptivity. In light of these examples, the Jesus of Matthew possesses human knowledge akin to the rest of humanity.

France's second example shows that the Jesus of Matthew possesses transcendent awareness in the scene of paying taxes to Caesar (Matt 22:15–22 // Mark 12:13–17 // Luke 20:20–26).[107] Each of the Synoptic authors selects a different term to describe Jesus's knowledge of the Pharisee's malice, hypocrisy, and craftiness (Matt 22:18 // Mark 12:15 // Luke 20:23). Luke selects κατανοήσας ("noticed"),[108] a term that Luke and Matthew apply to human observation and consideration.[109] Mark chooses εἰδὼς ("knowing"), a term he later ties to Herod (Mark 6:20). Matthew opts for γνούς ("aware").[110] As a term Matthew repeatedly uses to describe Jesus's knowledge,[111] γνούς ("aware") describes "intelligent comprehension of an object or matter."[112] Examination of Matthew's choice to use the aorist tense of γνούς ("aware") when only applied to Jesus denotes the possibility that Jesus possesses the capacity to perceive things because of his "supernatural knowledge," as Luz describes it.[113] Although Matthew limits his use of the aorist tense of γινώσκω ("knowledge") to Jesus,[114] he applies other forms of γινώσκω (knowledge) to the disciples (Matt 13:11), a character in the parable of the talents (25:24), the Pharisees (12:7; 21:45), and those living in the days of Noah (24:39). France observes that both passages hint at Jesus's supernatural knowledge, yet, as we have seen, Matthew appears to portray the knowledge of Jesus inconsistently. In some cases, Jesus's knowledge is akin to the rest of humanity and, in other instances, Jesus possesses transcendent knowledge.

107. In light of each of the Synoptic narrative progressions of the relationship between Jesus and the religious leaders, perception will not require transcendent insight by Jesus to discern their malice (Matt 22:18), hypocrisy (Mark 12:15), or craftiness (Luke 20:23).

108. Bauer, "κατανοέω," BDAG, 522–23.

109. Matt 7:3; Luke 6:41; 12:24, 27.

110. Bauer, "γινώσκω," BDAG, 200, defines the term as "awareness of something."

111. Matt 12:15; 16:8; 22:18; 26:10.

112. Bultmann, "γινώσκω," *TDNT* 1:689.

113. Luz, *Matthew 21–28*, 337, references examples (Matt 12:15; 16:8; 22:18; 26:10).

114. Matt 12:15; 16:8; 22:18; 26:10.

Matthew's apparent inconsistent approach to Jesus's knowledge represents an attempt to balance Jesus's human existence and transcendent status. Even though the second triad of miracles validates Jesus's authority, the issues of Jesus's emotions, knowledge, and personal identification as the Son of Man suggest Matthew also tells the human story of Jesus. The First Evangelist develops an understanding of Jesus's identity that demonstrates a balanced combination of a transcendent status as Son of God and a human Son of Man.

3.1.3 Nothing Like This in Israel . . . Ever (Matt 9:9–38)

As with the first two triads, the third miracle triad adds to the case that Jesus's actions and activities are unique in Israel's history (Matt 9:33). We will see that Matthew continues to build the argument for Jesus's transcendence, but not at the expense of the human portrayal. Prior to the final triad, the narrative includes a brief description of the call of Matthew as well as an interaction between Jesus and the disciples of John regarding fasting (9:9–17).[115] In the midst of that conversation, a request comes to Jesus to bring a daughter back to life (9:18–19). This initiates the third miracle triad that Matthew ends distinctively, not only with the crowds realizing that nothing like this has ever occurred in Israel, but also with the Pharisees attributing Jesus's miraculous power to the prince of demons (9:33–34).

Two miracles in one scene display Jesus's miraculous power as Matthew portrays the healing of a woman with a hemorrhage and the raising of a dead daughter (Matt 9:18–26 // Mark 5:21–43 // Luke 8:40–56). Of the Synoptic accounts, Matthew provides the shortest account. We will see that, while omitting elements of the story that reinforce Jesus's transcendence, the First Evangelist retains aspects that hold the humanity and transcendent status of Jesus in balance.

After being asked to raise a daughter from the dead,[116] Jesus heads to the ruler's house (Matt 9:18–19). On the way, a woman suffering from a hemorrhage for twelve years believes that if she touches the clothing of Jesus,

---

115. According to Jeremias, *Eucharistic Words of Jesus*, 231–37, to sit and eat with sinners implies that fellowship with sinners and tax collectors is a form of approval. Jesus's earthly existence as the moral exemplar reminds the reader of the priorities for the Christ follower. Matthew portrays Jesus sitting at the table eating with tax collectors and sinners (Matt 9:10–11).

116. Even though Mark and Luke indicate she is dying when the request is made, she is described as dead before Jesus makes it to the house (Mark 5:23, 35 // Luke 8:42, 49).

she will experience healing (9:20–21).[117] In this pericope, Matthew has the opportunity to reinforce the transcendence of Jesus, yet he does not. First, Matthew preserves healing through the woman touching Jesus's clothes. Belief that healing occurs through clothing worn by a holy individual is neither a cultural anomaly nor does it require the individual to be transcendent (Matt 14:36, Mark 6:56; Acts 19:12).[118] Second, the word δύναμις ("power") in the LXX describes "the power of God himself."[119] Mark and Luke say that δύναμιν ("power") leaves Jesus (Mark 5:30 // Luke 8:46). Considering Matthew's consistent use of the LXX,[120] keeping the word δύναμις ("power") to describe the power of God himself serves as another opportunity to connect Jesus directly to transcendent status, yet Matthew removes that term (Matt 9:21–22). Third, unlike Mark and Luke who apply ἐπιγινώσκω ("perceive") to describe Jesus's awareness that power leaves him (Matt 9:21–22 // Mark 5:30 // Luke 8:46), Matthew removes ἐπιγινώσκω ("perceive") in reference to Jesus. Fourth, even though Matthew removes ἐπιγινώσκω ("perceive"), only Matthew's account describes Jesus turning and seeing the woman (9:22). Matthew's portrayal maintains Jesus's ability to discern the one who touches him through normal human observation. In both Mark and Luke, Jesus asks who touches him because he perceives power leaves him (Matt 9:21–22 // Mark 5:30–31 // Luke 8:45–46). In Matthew, Jesus turns not because power leaves him but presumably because of her touch (Matt 9:22). Unlike Mark and Luke who depict Jesus surrounded by the crowds (Mark 5:24 // Luke 8:42), Matthew's Jesus is not surrounded. Matthew's Jesus possesses the natural ability to see and to know who touches his garment (Matt 9:22). Fifth, Matthew modifies the timing of the healing. Mark and Luke portray immediate healing after she touches the garment which releases subsequent power (Mark 5:28–29 // Luke 8:44). For Matthew it is the faith of the woman

117. This later occurs at Gennesaret (Matt 14:36).

118. Hagner, *Matthew 1–13*, 249. Allison and Davies, *Matthew 8–18*, 2:129. Meier, *Mentor, Message, and Miracles*, 709, notes that those wanting to "classify Jesus as a magician find this story a star witness." In response, Bromley, "Healing of the Hemorrhaging Woman," 17–18, examines Matthew's alterations to reinforce Jesus's ability to heal as the Messiah and remove the stigma of a magician performing the healing.

119. Hooker, *Gospel According to St Mark*, 149, uses the term "primarily" to describe the use of δύναμις ("power") in the LXX. However, review of the LXX suggests that it is used not only to describe the power of God (Exod 12:41; Josh 4:24; 1 Chr 12:23; 29:11) but also tribal or military power (1 Kgs 21:19; 2 Kgs 6:15; 25:1; 25:5).

120. While Matthew alters the LXX, it is clear that he regularly relies on it to tell the story of Jesus. E.g.: Matt 1:23 // Isa 7:14; Matt 2:6 // Mic 5:2; Matt 2:15 // Hos 11:1; Matt 2:18 // Isa 40:3; Matt 4:10 // Deut 6:13; Matt 4:15–16 // Isa 9:1–2; Matt 12:18–21 // Isa 42:1–4; Matt 13:35 // Ps 77:2; Matt 21:13 // Jer 7:11; Matt 21:16 // Ps 8:2; Matt 27:9 // Zech 13:7. Marcos, *Septuagint in Context*, 265, specifies that "most of the Old Testament quotations in the New follow the text of the LXX in one of its known forms."

that makes her well at that moment (Matt 9:22).[121] While Matthew may simply be shortening the story, his revisions reinforce that the sole concern is not to identify Jesus as transcendent. Rather, the portrayal relies on a human Jesus, wearing a garment, looking and seeing a woman in need, responding to her faith, and healing her.

After healing the hemorrhaging woman, the Jesus of Matthew raises a girl from the dead. Before raising her, Jesus declares that she is not dead but sleeping (Matt 9:24 // Mark 5:39 // Luke 8:52). Causing a level of ambiguity in the passage,[122] the perception of the family is that she is dead, as evident by the rhetoric in the story (Matt 9:24 // Mark 5:40 // Luke 8:53).[123] One might think that raising a girl from the dead strengthens Jesus's transcendent identity, but OT and NT literature portray other humans performing this miracle.[124]

The second miracle narrative in the third triad involves blind men requesting the Son of David to have mercy on them (Matt 9:27–31). After healing the blind men, only the Jesus of Matthew adds Jesus ἐνεβριμήθη ("sternly warned") them to remain silent (9:30).[125] Previously, Matthew removes Mark's ἐμβριμησάμενος ("he sternly warned") from the story of cleansing a leper (Matt 8:3–4 // Mark 1:43). This raises two questions. First, why does Matthew remove the stern warning in Mark (Matt 8:3–4 // Mark 1:43)? Morna Hooker rightly suggests that the stern warning in Mark invokes an "urgency with which Jesus sends [the leper] to fulfil the regulations of the Law: he is not to stop on the way to tell people what has happened."[126] Matthew's modifications support Hooker's explanation as both Matthew and Mark require the cleansed leper to go to the priest (Matt 8:3–4 // Mark 1:43). Second, why does Matthew add a stern warning after healing the two blind men near the end of the last triad (Matt 9:27–31)? Luz and France comment on the difficulty of explaining the addition of the warning,[127] but at this point in the narrative, Jesus's fame is growing (9:35). To emphasize the growing fame, Matthew uses the human emotions of Jesus for storytelling

121. Hull, *Hellenistic Magic*, 136, states: "Matthew changes the order of the healing so that the woman is not healed by the touching of the cloak and there is no power, no miracle-working aura surrounding Jesus which the superstitious can tap."

122. Collins, *Mark*, 285.

123. Twelftree, *Jesus the Miracle Worker*, 119. Collins, *Mark*, 285.

124. E.g., 1 Kgs 17:17–22; 2 Kgs 4:32–35, 13:20–21; Acts 9:36–41; 20:9–12.

125. Healing the two men is considered a doublet. Oyen, "Doublets," 278, demonstrates its identification as a doublet as early as the nineteenth century and defines it as a "doubly attested saying or narratives in one and the same gospel."

126. Hooker, *Mark*, 81.

127. Luz, *Matthew 8–20*, 49. France, *Matthew*, 369.

purposes. Matthew places the stern warning after healing the blind to feature that, in spite of the stern warning, Jesus's fame spread throughout the region (9:31).[128]

The final miracle of the three triads depicts Jesus healing a demoniac. Matthew's combination of the ten miracles sets up two statements that describe the results of Jesus's activity. First, Matthew's crowd proclaims that nothing like the miracles portrayed have ever been seen in Israel (Matt 9:33). Rather than attributing glory to God or acknowledging the possibility of Jesus's transcendent status, the portrayal of Jesus's humanity remains intact. Second, to emphasize the response, instead of recognizing this human with transcendent status, the Pharisees discount the crowd's perception by proposing that Jesus cast out demons by the prince of demons (9:34). While this foreshadows a future interaction with the Pharisees after healing another demoniac (12:22–24), the stage is set for Jesus's second discourse because Matthew has established Jesus's authority within the miracle triad.

Before the discourse, Matthew reviews the ministry of Jesus's human activity and authority (Matt 9:35–38).[129] Jesus teaches and heals "every disease and every affliction" (9:35). Describing Jesus's human activity with transcendent authority, Jesus models compassion to the harassed and helpless.[130] To assist the harassed and helpless, Matthew's Jesus establishes the need to listen to the call to be laborers (9:37–38). The call not only encourages more laborers in the kingdom but challenges the disciples to pray for fellow laborers (9:38). Immediately after this, the disciples receive their orders in the second discourse to preach and to accomplish the supernatural feats just as their exemplar has in the miracle triads.

3.1.4 Like the Master Teacher (Matt 10:1–42)

The second discourse depicts Jesus's commissioning of the disciples. While Mark's mission discourse serves as the basic text for Matthew (Matt 10:1–42 // Mark 6:7–11 // Luke 9:2–5), Matthew's expansion reinforces the idea that Jesus exists as the master and teacher one should emulate (Matt 10:24–25). In the previous pericope, only Matthew describes Jesus as healing πᾶσαν νόσον καὶ πᾶσαν μαλακίαν ("every disease and every infirmity," Matt 9:35 // Mark 6:6 // Luke 9:1). While each author's Jesus gives the disciples authority (Matt 10:1 // Mark 6:7 // Luke 9:1), only Matthew repeats the mention of

128. Anderson, "Double and Triple Stories," 77.

129. Turner, *Matthew*, 262. Matthew parallels Jesus's ministry description (Matt 4:23 // 9:35).

130. Matt 9:36; 14:14; 15:32; 20:34. Hagner, *Matthew 1–13*, 260.

the disciples possessing the authority to replicate the power to heal "every disease and every infirmity" (Matt 10:1). Matthew's alterations to Mark's commission not only reflect the church's mission (10:16–33),[131] but also challenge the readers to imitate Jesus, the master teacher (10:24–25).

Throughout the second discourse, Matthew exhorts the readers to experience his sufferings (Matt 10:16–23), to imitate the master and teacher (10:24–25), and to accept Jesus's mission (10:34–39).[132] Structuring the human story of Jesus reinforces Matthew's *imitatio Christi* motif not only throughout the Gospel narrative,[133] but also in preparation for and within the second discourse. The Jesus of each Synoptic Gospel commissions the disciples to go and preach (Matt 10:7 // Mark 3:14 // Luke 9:2), but Matthew's Jesus asks them to do more. The disciples will accomplish the same feats. In the previous narratives, Jesus cleanses a leper (Matt 8:1–4), heals the sick (8:5–17; 9:2–8, 20–22), casts out demons (8:28–34; 9:32–34), and raises the dead (9:23–31).[134] Only Matthew portrays Jesus commanding them in detail to perform the same feats, including raising people from the dead (10:8).[135] Raising people from the dead is not a power limited to Jesus. Elijah raised the son of the Zarephath widow (1 Kgs 17:17–22), and Elisha raised the son of a Shunammite woman (2 Kgs 4:32–35). The precedent for modeling and training others is therefore not new in Jewish literature.[136] Elijah trains Elisha (2 Kgs 2:3–18). Samuel receives training and trains others in his prophetic ministry (1 Sam 3:1; 19:20–24). The only type of miracle

131. Hagner, *Matthew 1–13*, 263, suggests this was particularly clear with the inclusion of the gentile mission (Matt 10:18).

132. Luz, *Matthew 8–20*, 124.

133. Allison, *Studies in Matthew*, 147–53 (151), comments that the first Gospel "goes out of its way to make the twelve disciples emulate their Lord in numerous particulars" as is seen above.

134. Kalin, "Matthew 9:18–26," 46, connects Matthew's organization of the miracle pericopae to the response to John's disciples defending his status as Messiah (Matt 8:1—9:34; 11:4–5). Even though Kalin suggests every miracle matches the defense, Matthew does not portray the deaf hearing (8:1—9:34). Matthew uses the term κωφός which pertains to "lack of speech capability" or "lack of hearing capability" according to Bauer, "κωφός," BDAG, 580. The better understanding in the scene is that the demoniac is healed of κωφός ("lack of speech capability") because the demoniac speaks after being healed (9:33). While it is arguable that Matthew organizes the miracle section to set up the defense to John the Baptist's disciples, it is clear that Matthew organizes the miracle section to set up his commands in the discourse because every miracle commanded in the discourse Jesus accomplishes beforehand.

135. Blomberg, *Matthew*, 171, points out that the book of Acts shows that through various Christians, each of these miraculous commands is performed except for the cleansing of lepers (Acts 3:1–10; 8:7, 13; 9:32–43; 14:8–10; 19:13–16; 20:7–12).

136. Keener, *Commentary*, 310.

the disciples are not commanded to perform in the second discourse are those over nature. In light of this omission, these parallels show that Matthew designs the narrative to demonstrate that, while the disciples should imitate Christ, a distinction remains.

In spite of this distinction in Matthew's narrative, the correlation between the discourse mission of the disciples and the human life of Jesus does not end with the miraculous. Nearly midway through the second discourse, Matthew emphasizes the *imitatio Christi* motif above and beyond Luke (Matt 10:24–25 // Luke 6:40). While both point out that the disciple should be ὡς ("like") the teacher, to re-emphasize the *imitatio Christi* theme Matthew adds another comparison between a servant and a master (Matt 10:24–25).[137] Only Matthew reinforces this comparison because, as Luz puts it, "to live as a disciple is to live as Jesus does."[138] Since that is the case for Matthew, to establish Jesus's transcendence at the expense of his human identity negates a narrative priority because this discourse matches a way of life for the disciple and their master.[139]

These comparisons between the disciples and Jesus become clear through the First Evangelist's narrative structure. Matthew has already arranged the Sermon on the Mount and miracle triads in such a manner that the disciples can imitate their teacher in word and deed (Matt 5:1–9; 10:1, 7–9).[140] In this discourse, the author also links proclamation and persecution.[141] Matthew's Jesus predicts flogging, being dragged before political leaders, and division among family.[142] Just as Matthew's Jesus takes up his cross to lose his life for humankind, Jesus expects the same from his followers (10:37–39; 27:27–32, 50). Jesus will experience what he predicts will be the fate of disciples.[143] Matthew's use of the humanity of Jesus causes him to structure the narrative for the disciple and servant of Jesus to be ὡς ("like") their teacher and master (10:24–25). As David C. Sim points out, Matthew "depicts Jesus as the perfect Christian role model."[144] Following Jesus means

---

137. Davies and Allison, *Matthew 8–18*, 194.

138. Luz, *Matthew 8–20*, 82.

139. Luz, *Studies in Matthew*, 159.

140. See ch. 3, n27 above.

141. Keener, *Commentary*, 321.

142. There are parallels between Matthew and Luke, but none exist with Mark. While Matthew and Luke predict being dragged before leaders and division among family (Matt 10:34–36 // Luke 12:51–53), only Matthew includes flogging (Matt 10:17–25 // Luke 12:11–12, 21:12–19).

143. Matt 13:53–58; 26:57–59; 27:11–13, 21, 26.

144. Sim, "Pacifist Jesus," 2.

to live in a manner that leads to persecution and hostility,[145] something the human exemplar faces in Matthew's Gospel.

Although the focus of Matthew's second discourse encourages the reader to imitate the human master and teacher, sections of the discourse remind the reader of Jesus's transcendent status. The human Jesus exists distinct from the rest of humankind, and Jesus extends authority to his disciples to be representatives of Jesus (Matt 10:17–18, 21–22, 37–40). Matthew's Jesus predicts that disciples will be delivered up and hated by all for his name's sake (10:17–18, 21–22). Jesus will be placed in a position to acknowledge his followers before his Father (10:32–33).[146] Those who carry their cross, lose their lives, or receive others in Jesus's name will not only be disciples but also receive rewards (10:37–42).[147] Matthew not only structures his narrative and the second discourse purposefully to contribute to building the case for Jesus's transcendence but also makes it possible for the disciples to imitate the human Jesus.

3.2 RESPONSES TO THE HUMAN JESUS AND HIS TEACHING (MATT 11:1—16:20)

As we will see, Matthew continues to develop the identity of Jesus through various interactions with and responses to him. Before and after the second discourse the readers can observe responses toward Jesus's teaching and activities prior to Peter's confession that Jesus is the Christ, the Son of the living God.[148] Responses to Jesus are a focus of this section, but Matthew has already laid the groundwork for increasing opposition.[149] While the parables in the third discourse focus on responses to the message of the kingdom (Matt 13:3–13, 16–34, 44–52), this section provides nine responses to Jesus, both Jew and gentile. Five exhibit negative, unbelieving responses,[150] and four display positive, belief-oriented responses.[151] We will

---

145. Hagner, *Matthew 1–13*, 262.

146. While both Matthew and Luke acknowledge Jesus's role to judge those who follow Christ, only Matthew's Jesus does so before his Father (Matt 10:32–33 // Luke 12:8–9).

147. France, *Gospel of Matthew*, 387.

148. Matt 8:27, 29; 9:3–7, 27–34; 11:1—16:20. Davies and Allison, *Matthew 8–18*, 294. France, *Gospel of Matthew*, 417.

149. Matt 5:20; 7:29; 9:3, 11, 33–34. Hagner, *Matthew 1–13*, 298.

150. Matt 13:53–58; 14:1–12; 15:1–20; 16:1–4, 5–12. Turner, *Matthew*, 357, provides more responses due to the way he has structured Matthew's narrative.

151. Matt 14:22–33; 15:21–28, 29–39; 16:13–20. Turner, *Matthew*, 357.

see that these responses intensify as opposition to Jesus and understanding his identity evolve.

3.2.1 Jewish Responses (Matt 11:1—13:58)

After Jesus finishes his second discourse, Matthew develops Jesus's identity through the voices of John the Baptist (Matt 11:2–6), the Pharisees (12:1–32), and residents of his hometown (13:53–58). As will be seen, Matthew maintains the humanity of Jesus but continues to interject Jesus's transcendence, holding Jesus's identity in balance. He begins with John the Baptist's response. Imprisoned (11:2), John the Baptist, the baptizer of Jesus (3:15–16), listener to a voice from heaven (3:17), and forerunner of the Messiah (3:1–4), asks whether Jesus is the one whom Israel anticipates (11:3). Rather than exploring Jesus's transcendent identity, John's question points to Jesus's human messianic status. This causes us to ask why John the Baptist's response and other Jewish responses in this section reinforce Matthew's continued interest in Jesus's humanity.

Based on what John the Baptist hears while in prison regarding the Messiah's activities (Matt 11:2), Jesus has yet to meet the expectations of the figure John proclaimed (3:10–12).[152] Jesus's failure to carry a winnowing fork in his hand to clear the threshing floor of unrepentance causes John to send his disciples to question Jesus's messianic status (11:3). Matthew has the opportunity to identify Jesus in numerous ways: Son of David, Son of Man, Son of God, Messiah, or even Lord. However, Jesus responds with none of these answers. Rather, he informs John the Baptist's disciples to consider the evidence by examining Jesus's deeds to decide (11:4–5). As W. C. Davies and Dale C. Allison Jr. state: "The man through whom the poor have the good news preached to them and through whom miracles have come can only be the anointed one of Isa 61.1, the bearer of the Spirit."[153] The Spirit rests on Jesus (Matt 3:16; 12:17–21). Jesus is not having his identity as the Son of God questioned by John the Baptist, but rather as a human messianic figure (11:3).[154] Matthew's maintenance of the human portrayal addresses the questions and expectations of his audience to reinforce belief in his messianic identity.

In spite of that status, Matthew and Luke provide reactions that explain people rejecting John the Baptist and Jesus (Matt 11:18–24 // Luke 7:31–35). In that context, those observing Jesus and John consider John the Baptist

152. Davies and Allison, *Matthew 8–18*, 241.

153. Davies and Allison, *Matthew 8–18*, 245–46.

154. See ch. 2, n5 above.

demon-possessed and Jesus a glutton who drinks and befriends tax collectors and sinners (Matt 11:16–19). As the Son of Man, Jesus faces persecution and experiences social alienation from the religious.[155] This bolsters not only the Jewish antagonism toward Jesus and John (11:13–19)[156] but also humanizes Jesus, the Son of Man, who eats and drinks with sinners.

Then Matthew lists specific cities, Chorazin, Bethsaida, Tyre, Sidon, and Capernaum, whose people fail to repent in spite of the mighty deeds performed in their midst (Matt 11:20–24). Even though Matthew preserves the perception of Jesus's activity as a human being who eats and drinks with tax collectors and sinners (11:19), he transitions to the case for the transcendence. In spite of the generation's rejection, only Matthew adds a section that interjects a reminder that Jesus's identity includes transcendence (11:25–30). Calling God his Father (11:27), Matthew reminds the reader not only of the unique relational status between the Father and the Son but also the distinction between them (11:25–27).[157] In spite of the response of cities such as Chorazin, Bethsaida, and Capernaum, Matthew's description of Jesus upholds the human story and builds the case for transcendence.

Continuing to develop the identity of Matthew's main character, the focus shifts to the response of Pharisees who exhibit a deepening antagonism toward Jesus.[158] The conflict between Jesus and the Pharisees intensifies as they question his understanding of lawful Sabbath activities (Matt 12:1–14). Jesus hints that something greater than the temple is present and declares that the Son of Man is lord of the Sabbath (12:6, 8). In the OT, the Sabbath belongs to God and exists for him.[159] For Matthew, the claim elevates Jesus's status to "authority on a par with God himself" according to France.[160] By doing so, Jesus undermines the authority of the religious leaders and deepens the hostility between the Pharisees and Jesus so intensely that the Pharisees seek to destroy Jesus for the first time (12:14).

Similar to the danger Herod presents to Jesus's life (Matt 2:13),[161] Matthew uses this scene to explain Jesus's withdrawal from a hostile situation (12:15).[162] Jesus's exit from danger leads to healing the crowds, setting up

155. Kee, "Jesus," 386.

156. Blomberg, *Matthew*, 183.

157. Blomberg, *Matthew*, 192.

158. Hagner, *Matthew 1–13*, 312.

159. Exod 16:23; 20:10; 31:13; 35:2; Lev 19:30; Isa 56:4.

160. France, *Gospel of Matthew*, 463.

161. In both instances Matthew selects the verb ἀπόλλυμι ("destroy, kill," Matt 2:13; 12:14). Luke removes the specific plot to kill Jesus in his pericope (Matt 12:14 // Mark 3:6 // Luke 6:11).

162. A strategic withdrawal is portrayed in several instances (Matt 2:12–15, 22;

another instance of prophetic fulfillment (12:15–21).[163] The inclusion of Isaiah's prophecy describes Jesus as the one who is God's servant on whom the Spirit dwells (Isa 42:1–4; Matt 12:18–21). This identifies Jesus's source of power.[164] Matthew's clarification of the source of power being the Spirit sets up the account of the Beelzebul controversy.[165]

In the Beelzebul controversy (Matt 12:22–32), Matthew has another opportunity to identify Jesus's transcendent status. Yet, in two instances, Matthew clarifies Jesus as a human figure. First, after Jesus heals a blind and mute demoniac brought to him (12:22), only the crowd in Matthew reacts with the question of Jesus's identity. "Can this be the Son of David?" (Matt 12:23 // Mark 3:22–23 // Luke 11:14–15). The identity in question is neither Son of God nor Son of Man. The identity in question connects Jesus with the human lineage as the Son of David. That, in combination with the additional prophetic fulfillment (Matt 12:18–21), draws out Matthew's interest in connecting Jesus's human story through the crowd to reinforce his audience's belief in his messianic status,[166] just as Matthew's Gospel begins (1:1–17).

Second, Matthew's Jesus identifies the source of his power to heal the blind and mute demoniac (Matt 12:27). For the second time, the Pharisees associate the source of his power with Beelzebul (9:34; 12:24). Demonstrating a flaw in their logic, Jesus rationally works the Pharisees through the absurdity of such an accusation (12:25–27). While Matthew could portray Jesus casting demons out due to his transcendent status as the Son of God, Jesus identifies the source of his power as something other than himself (12:28).[167]

The power source becomes clearer through comparing Matthew and Luke's description. Luke's language for the source of Jesus's power differs from Matthew's (Matt 12:28 // Luke 11:20). Luke portrays that the power to cast out demons is due to the "finger of God" (Luke 11:20). In Jewish

---

4:12; 14:13; 15:21).

163. Fulfillment of this prophecy also sets up additional hope for the gentiles, a group increasingly receptive in spite of the negative Jewish responses (Matt 15:21–39).

164. Twelftree, *Jesus the Exorcist*, 161, argues Jesus confesses the source of his power is the Holy Spirit even though his technique to cast out demons requires invoking a name or source.

165. Hawthorne, *Presence and the Power*, 35, emphasizes the importance of the Spirit in relationship to Jesus's mortality.

166. Kingsbury, *Matthew*, 99–100.

167. Twelftree, *Jesus the Miracle Worker*, 128, adds the "eschatological Spirit" empowers Jesus. Turner, *Matthew*, 321, indicates that the same Spirit involved in conception has been "empowering" him since the baptism as a fulfillment of Isaiah (Matt 3:16—4:1; 12:18).

literature, the finger of God indicates the "active power of God," as Joel Green puts it.[168] For Matthew, who builds his case for Jesus's transcendence, it appears that attributing the ability to perform miracles with the "active power of God" would have been more effective. However, Jesus implies that other humans successfully cast out demons.[169] While the use of δέ ("but") contrasts Jesus to other exorcists, he divulges the actual source of his power to cast out demons is not himself but the Spirit (Matt 12:28).[170] Only Matthew adds Isaiah's prophecy immediately before this pericope to claim the Spirit rests on Jesus (12:18). Here, Matthew describes Jesus's work as the work of the human Son of Man rather than the transcendent Son of God (12:8, 32, 40). In the Beelzebul controversy, the Pharisees belittle the work of the Spirit of God through a human,[171] and Matthew emphasizes Jesus's humanity using the titles Son of Man and Son of David (Matt 12:23, 32, 40).[172] The power Jesus displays comes from the Spirit of God as prophesied in Isaiah (Isa 42:1–4). Instead of using this as an opportunity to increase the case for the transcendence of Jesus, Matthew maintains the human element of Jesus's identity and attributes his power to the Spirit.

This human Jesus, empowered by the Spirit, also has a human family. Twice during Jesus's ministry, Matthew draws attention to the earthly family of Jesus (Matt 12:46–50; 13:54–58). His family includes sisters, brothers, and a mother (12:46–47; 13:55–56). In the first family interaction, Matthew alters Mark to point to something greater about Jesus (Matt 12:46–50 // Mark 3:31–35). Mark writes that whoever does the will of God is my brother, sister, and mother (Mark 3:35). While Matthew concludes with a similar challenge to do God's will, he elevates Jesus's status to connect family with

---

168. Exod 8:19; 31:18; Deut 9:10; Ps 8:3. Green, *Gospel of Luke*, 457. Twelftree, *Jesus the Exorcist*, 108, correctly emphasizes that finger of God equals the activity of God citing the Qumran *War Scroll* (1QM 18:1–15) and the Spirit of the Lord falling on Ezekiel (Ezek 8:1; 11:5).

169. Matt 7:22; 10:1, 8; 12:27. Twelftree, *Jesus the Exorcist*, 107.

170. Twelftree, *Jesus the Exorcist*, 109n50 contrasts his finding with Hengel, *Charismatic Leader*, 64n102. Hengel states: "It is quite likely that, by contrast with Jesus, contemporary apocalyptic-messianic prophets appealed freely to the 'Spirit'. According to the Easter texts and apocalyptic literature there was in Judaism nothing unusual in appealing to actual possession of the Spirit." Twelftree, on the other hand, has been unable to locate confirmation of an appeal to the "Spirit" as means for exorcism.

171. France, *Gospel of Matthew*, 480, describes Jesus as a "human being" to explain this scene.

172. See ch. 2, n5 above. Kingsbury, *Matthew*, 99, considers the title Son of David a title of "great importance" because of the number of times it is repeated (Matt 1:1–17, 20–21; 9:27; 12:23; 15:22–24; 20:30–31; 21:9, 15; 22:41–46).

doing the will of "my Father" (Matt 12:50).[173] Unlike Mark's description, Matthew personalizes Jesus's transcendent relationship with the Father, elevating Jesus's status. In spite of Jesus living amidst his human family,[174] Matthew alters his sources in a manner that maintains Jesus's humanity yet develops his transcendence. Matthew's Jesus commands obedience to the will of his Father rather than simply obeying the will of God (Matt 12:50 // Mark 3:35).[175]

After commanding obedience to Jesus's Father, Matthew brackets a third discourse with familial relationships (Matt 12:46–50; 13:54–58)[176] and interjects parables of the kingdom (13:1–53). Twice within this third discourse Matthew relies on the human activity of Jesus to fulfill prophecy (13:14–15, 35).[177] Even in the midst of the parables and, in some cases, explanations of those parables, Matthew's interest connects the human story of Jesus to OT prophetic fulfillment.

Ending the third discourse, Jesus returns to his hometown. In Nazareth, the residents question his identity (Matt 13:53–58), a subject that continues to develop throughout Matthew.[178] The Nazareth pericope contains three elements that reinforce Matthew's christological interests (Matt 13:53–58 // Mark 6:1–6a). First, Matthew brings Jesus's family into the story a second time, reinforcing the point that Jesus has brothers and sisters (Matt 12:46–50; 13:53–58). Second, Matthew redacts the crowd's description of his human family. Unlike Mark, who describes Jesus as a carpenter, Matthew's crowd refers to Jesus as a carpenter's son (Matt 13:55 // Mark 6:3).[179]

173. No parallels between Matthew and Mark exist that employ this phrase to establish a filial relationship between Jesus and the Father (Matt 7:21; 10:32–33; 11:27; 15:13; 16:17; 18:10, 19, 35; 20:23; 25:34; 26:29, 39, 42, 53).

174. According to Tertullian, as late as the third century, Marcion argues Jesus does not have a human family, yet Tertullian suggests Matthew's Jesus prefers faith to physical, blood relatives (*Marc.* 4:19).

175. Keener, *Commentary*, 370, points out the submission to God's will (Matt 7:21; 21:31; 26:42) which marks one as Jesus's true family member (12:50; 25:40; 28:10).

176. Davies and Allison, *Matthew 8–18*, 461.

177. The quotations for prophetic fulfillment are taken from Isaiah and Psalms (Isa 6:9–10; Ps 78:2). Matthew provides seven parables with intermixed narrative elements (Matt 13:3–52). The parable of the sower and its explanation describes the proclamation of the kingdom and various responses (13:3–23). The parables of the tares (13:24–30), mustard seed (13:31–32), leaven (13:33), hidden treasure (13:44), pearl (13:45–46), and the net (13:47–52) further illustrate those responses.

178. Matt 1:1–25; 4:1–11; 7:28–29; 8:26–27, 29; 9:3–7, 32–35; 11:1–6; 12:1–29, 38–42, 46–50.

179. Meier, *Roots of the Problem*, 317, points out that Matthew reworks Mark's description of Jesus as a carpenter to designate Joseph as a carpenter (Matt 13:55 // Mark 6:3).

Matthew's readers know that Jesus is the Son of God (Matt 1:18–25), yet Matthew upholds the crowd's perception that Jesus is the son of Joseph with a mother, brothers, and sisters (Matt 13:55 // Mark 6:3).[180] Third, Matthew changes the reason why Jesus fails to accomplish many mighty deeds in Nazareth. In Mark's portrayal, Jesus οὐκ ἐδύνατο ("could not do") a mighty work in Nazareth, but Matthew indicates that Jesus οὐκ ἐποίησεν ("did not do") many mighty works there (Matt 13:58 // Mark 6:5). On one hand, Mark's Jesus is more human because he lacks the power or ability to accomplish mighty works.[181] On the other hand, Matthew, in keeping with his interest in the balance between the humanity and transcendence of Jesus, purposely describes Jesus with the ability to choose to refrain from many mighty works due to the Nazarenes' lack of faith. Matthew's portrayal emphasizes Jesus's authority to perform miracles in light of or in spite of an expression of faith.[182] Matthew's choice to reinforce the existence of Jesus's human family is in contrast to Jesus's authority to perform miracles as one in control of a situation.[183] Once again, Matthew not only continues to build the argument for Jesus's transcendent status but also prioritizes the human story.[184]

Through this section on Jewish responses, the question of Jesus's identity arises by means of Jewish interactions with and reactions toward Jesus.[185] The Pharisees are upset that Jesus eats and drinks with sinners and casts out demons by Beelzebul (Matt 11:19; 12:24). Jesus's hometown and human family question the source of his wisdom and power (13:54). Relying on the human story of Jesus, Matthew slowly increases the frequency of identifying Jesus's transcendence within the framework of his human existence. Matthew continues to build into his portrayal a Jesus who claims God is his Father (11:25–27). He is the lord of the Sabbath (12:8) and possesses the authority to heal in the midst of unbelief (13:58). Using this slow

---

180. Luz, *Matthew 8–20*, 302, indicates that use of brothers and sisters should be understood with the simplest understanding that Jesus has physical siblings.

181. Hagner, *Matthew 1–13*, 406.

182. Matthew demonstrates the importance of faith in healing but performs miracles in light of or in spite of faith (Matt 8:10, 13, 26; 9:2, 22, 28–29; 14:31; 15:28; 17:20; 21:21–22).

183. Davies and Allison, *Matthew 8–18*, 460–61.

184. Luke's Gospel contains a similar account of the rejection of Jesus at Nazareth but locates this much sooner in his narrative (Luke 4:16–30). The ending of Luke's Gospel contains a description that is nowhere else in the Synoptics. Jesus, in the midst of a hostile situation, somehow passes through the midst of the angry crowd (4:29–30).

185. Hagner, *Matthew 1–13*, 298.

progression, Matthew continues to describe different responses toward Jesus that lead to Peter's central confession.[186]

3.2.2 Herod, the Disciples, and the Pharisees Respond (Matt 14:1—15:20)

After examining the different responses to Jesus through the eyes of John the Baptist, the Pharisees, and Jesus's hometown, Matthew continues to rely on interactions with characters in the story to flesh out Jesus's identity for the reader. In spite of the rejection by the religious leaders and his hometown (Matt 12:22–32; 13:54–58), Jesus's fame reaches the local ruler, Herod (14:1–2). In light of Jesus's growing notoriety, Herod perceives Jesus as John the Baptist raised from the dead in spite of his role in beheading John (14:2–12). Unique to Matthew and another signal of Jesus's human ignorance, Jesus becomes aware of the Baptist's death by hearing about his demise rather than through transcendent knowledge (14:13).[187] In response to the news, Jesus withdraws (14:13). The withdrawal sets up the scene for three nature miracles that lead to the disciples' response that signals their acknowledgment of the transcendence of Jesus.

The first nature miracle in this section is Jesus feeding at least five thousand individuals.[188] Jesus withdraws in a boat, but the crowds follow him (Matt 14:13). Out of compassion, Jesus heals them and later feeds them (Matt 14:14–21 // Mark 6:34–44).[189] This is not the only time Jesus performs a miracle out of σπλαγχνίζομαι ("compassion," Matt 9:36; 15:32; 20:34).[190] It signals not only performing the works of God but also the beginning of the messianic age.[191] Matthew's use of compassion combines the transcendent and human identity of Jesus.

---

186. Davies and Allison, *Matthew 8–18*, 294. France, *Gospel of Matthew*, 417.

187. Matthew applies the verb ἀκούω (hear) to Jesus (Matt 8:10; 14:13), Herod (2:3), Joseph (2:22), John the Baptist (11:2), and the young ruler (19:22). Jesus's ability to hear is akin to other human figures in Matthew's Gospel.

188. Matt 14:13–21 // Mark 6:32–44 // Luke 9:10–17 // John 6:1–15. While there are no other food miracles of this magnitude performed by anyone other than Jesus in the NT, numerically smaller OT examples exist in the portrayal of Elijah (1 Kgs 17:8–16; 2 Kgs 4:1–7, 42–44).

189. Only Matthew's Jesus heals them (Matt 14:14 // Mark 6:34 // Luke 9:11).

190. Voorwinde, *Jesus' Emotions*, 24, 42. Even though Voorwinde, *Jesus' Emotions*, 43, states: "Whenever Matthew specifically mentions Jesus' compassion, the recipients are therefore always Jews," it will be seen that Matthew's Jesus expresses compassion to gentiles later in the narrative (Matt 15:32).

191. Exod 16:1–16; Ps 146:7; Isa 29:18; 35:5; 42:6–7. Voorwinde, *Jesus' Emotions*,

The second and third nature miracles immediately follow as Jesus walks on the water and calms the sea (Matt 14:22–33). Calming the seas for a second time (8:26; 14:32), this combination of miracles culminates with the disciples responding to Jesus as a transcendent figure (Matt 14:22–33 // John 6:16–21). Matthew's narrative contains unique elements that not only bring clarity to the disciples' perception of Jesus's transcendent identity, but also portray their clearest christological confession to this point in the narrative.[192] The disciples' confession of Jesus's transcendent status occurs in six ways.

First, Jesus walks on water (Matt 14:25–26), a power initially reserved for God in the OT.[193] Second, Jesus rescues them from the sea (14:24, 32), and in Jewish tradition, only God can rescue from the sea.[194] Third, Jesus self-identifies as ἐγώ εἰμι ("I am"). For Matthew and his readers, the phrase will have a particular meaning due to the LXX's use of ἐγώ εἰμι ("I am"). It is the name of Yahweh (Exod 3:14; Isa 43:10; 51:12).[195] Fourth, only Matthew's disciples worship Jesus (Matt 14:33 // Mark 6:51–52 // John 6:21). Matthew's use of προσεκύνησαν ("they worshipped") is understood as a respectful bow or religious worship of a deity.[196] Fifth, the winds and sea become still after Jesus and Peter enter the boat (Matt 14:32). This is another transcendent power attributed only to God (Pss 65:7; 89:9–10).[197] Sixth, only Matthew's disciples declare Jesus is the Son of God (Matt 14:33). As Matthew builds upon the image of Jesus's transcendence in connection with multiple allusions to his status,[198] it becomes clear that the disciples finally perceive that his identity includes Son of God. However, for Matthew, Son of God, as a sole descriptor, inadequately describes Jesus's identity. This becomes evident through Peter's confession and the structural marker that immediately follows to transition the story (16:16–20). Matthew maintains and develops the human and transcendent element of Jesus's identity from the beginning. Consequently, this pericope and its redactions work to lead the reader to Peter's unique confession.

42–43.

192. Blomberg, *Matthew*, 231.

193. Job 9:8; Ps 77:19; Isa 43:16; Hab 3:15. Keener, *Commentary*, 406. France, *Gospel of Matthew*, 566, reinforces the symbolic language in these OT passages which suggests God's control over "unruly forces of his world."

194. Exod 14:10—15:21; Ps 107:23–32; Jonah 1:1–16; Wis 14:2–4; T. Naph. 6:1–10. Davies and Allison, *Matthew 8–18*, 503.

195. Hagner, *Matthew 14–28*, 423.

196. Matt 2:2, 8, 11; 8:2; 9:18; 15:25; 18:26; 20:20; 28:9, 17.

197. Davies and Allison, *Matthew 8–20*, 509.

198. Matt 1:18–25; 4:1–11; 8:29; 14:33.

Comparing the response of the disciples to the first calming of the sea, the disciples had asked ποταπός ἐστιν οὗτος ("what sort of man is this," Matt 8:27). Up to this point in the narrative, applying the title Son of God to Jesus has been used only by God (3:17), demons (4:3, 6; 8:29), and as an editorial aside (2:15).[199] Here, as Davies and Allison point out, "The disciples are beginning to catch up with the readers of the gospel."[200] It seems doubtful that Matthew intends the disciples in the narrative to perceive that Jesus is God incarnate,[201] yet Matthew's alterations to his sources demonstrate that the narrative could lead the readers to such a conclusion. In spite of using this pericope to portray Matthew's "highest Christology," as Graham Twelftree describes it,[202] Matthew's changes do not remove any of the human elements of the story. This is evident in two ways.

First, Jesus prays (Matt 14:23). While the contents of the prayer are not provided, if Jesus is solely transcendent, why would he pray prior to walking on the water? John Paul Heil suggests that Jesus's prayer before a "uniquely divine action" occurs as a result of the relationship with the Father.[203] Matthew preserves the humanity of Jesus with prayer because a distinction exists between Jesus and the Father.[204] Second, only Matthew's Peter, clearly a human in the narrative,[205] walks on water (Matt 14:29). Unlike the OT, walking on water no longer displays a power reserved for the transcendent. Here, Jesus extends that power to Peter and encourages him to join him on the water (14:28–29).

Peter leaves the boat, walks on water, begins to sink, and then Jesus admonishes him for possessing ὀλιγόπιστε ("little faith," Matt 14:31). Jesus's authority has been and will be transferred to the disciples so they can model the authority and power Jesus will grant them (10:1–15; 28:18–20), and the operating factor of such power involves faith.[206] With faith, the same authority granted to Jesus (11:27) will be granted to the disciples (28:18–20) and

199. France, *Gospel of Matthew*, 571.

200. Davies and Allison, *Matthew 8–20*, 2:510.

201. Hagner, *Matthew 14–28*, 424. Davies and Allison, *Matthew 8–20*, 504, 510, build the argument that Matthew's portrayal of Jesus's activities demonstrates that the "powers of the deity have become incarnate in God's Son."

202. Twelftree, *Jesus the Miracle Worker*, 132.

203. Heil, *Jesus Walking on the Sea*, 33.

204. The repeated phrase "your Father" in the Sermon suggests Jesus perceives a distinction between himself and the Father (Matt 5:16, 45, 48; 6:4, 8, 14, 18, 26; 7:11).

205. Peter has a mother-in-law, brother, expresses a lack of knowledge, gets hungry, indicates he can die, and sleeps (Matt 4:18, 8:14; 10:2; 12:1; 18:21; 19:27; 26:35; 26:40).

206. Matt 6:30; 8:26; 14:31; 16:8; 17:19–20; 21:20–22.

nothing will be impossible for them through faith (17:19–20; 21:20–22).[207] Matthew maintains the humanity of Jesus to demonstrate the need for and power of faith.[208] Faith can move mountains into the sea (21:21). Faith sustains Peter's walk on the water until he becomes frightened (14:30–31). Without maintaining the humanity, Matthew's Jesus as the exemplar will hold little weight for his readers if they are to imitate their teacher and master (10:24–25).[209]

Imitating Jesus the exemplar comes in different forms through the next interaction between Jesus and the Pharisees who journey from Jerusalem to Gennesaret (Matt 15:1–20). The Pharisees shift the focus of their challenges from the behavior of Jesus to his teaching.[210] Questioning the disciples' break from the tradition of the elders, Jesus responds, but not with his words. When quoting the command to honor father and mother, Mark's Jesus quotes Moses, but Matthew's Jesus quotes God (Matt 15:4 // Mark 7:10). These quotes remind the Jewish Christian reader that the commandments of God trump the tradition of humans (15:3–6). Jesus calls them hypocrites (Matt 15:7 // Mark 7:6), applies a prophecy of Isaiah to them (Isa 29:13; Matt 15:8–9), and, only according to Matthew's disciples in the narrative, offends the Pharisees (Matt 15:7–9, 12 // Mark 7:6–7). Maintaining the distinction between Jesus and God through the human story, Matthew's exemplar reminds the readers that failure to correct the blind guides can cause those blind to the truth to suffer the same fate (15:13–14).

As we have seen through the responses to Jesus from Herod, the disciples, and the Pharisees, the identity of Jesus continues to develop in preparation for Peter's confession (Matt 16:16). As Matthew builds toward the confession, he continues to demonstrate Jesus as an exemplar, and the exemplar's challenge in the interaction with Pharisees demonstrates that Jewish tradition needs to be evaluated critically.[211] Even though Matthew's Jesus believes that the law and prophets are still in force (Matt 5:17–20; 8:4), the tradition of humans will in some measure require rejection.[212] That rejection is more clearly demonstrated through Jesus's modeled efforts of reaching the gentiles.

207. Keener, *Commentary*, 407.

208. On multiple occasions, Jesus emphasizes the importance of faith (Matt 6:30; 8:10, 13, 26; 9:2, 22, 29; 14:31; 15:28; 17:20; 21:21–22).

209. Keener, *Commentary*, 407.

210. The Pharisees question the behavior as Jesus sits with tax-collectors and sinners (Matt 9:11; 11:19), casts a demon out of the mute man (9:32–34), and heals the man with the withered hand (12:22–24).

211. Davies and Allison, *Matthew 8–18*, 537.

212. Davies and Allison, *Matthew 8–18*, 537.

3.2.3 Gentiles Respond to Jesus (Matt 15:21–15:39)

As the moral exemplar, Matthew's portrayal of Jesus's earthly activity in this section grants the reader insight into his actions in their social milieu. The Jewish Christian social milieu consists of gentiles who need compassion and healing just like the Jews. Even though Matthew follows Mark's timeline here,[213] Matthew's depiction of each interaction continues to demonstrate varying reactions to Jesus's activity, humanity, and identity.

Jesus withdraws to the district of Tyre and Sidon and encounters a gentile woman (Matt 15:21–22 // Mark 7:24).[214] In the exchange, the exemplar tests, observes, and acts in response to the faith of a Canaanite. Two of Matthew's editorial changes deserve attention. First, even though Jesus places obstacles of faith for the gentile to overcome,[215] only Matthew's Jesus points out the greatness of her faith (Matt 15:28 // Mark 7:29). This is the second time in the Matthean narrative that Jesus explicitly responds to the faith of a gentile in the text (Matt 8:5–13; 15:28). This reinforces Matthew's belief that God's salvation is available to gentiles who express faith.[216] Even though Jesus communicates to the gentile that his mission centers on the Jews (15:24), he uses this to test the persistence of the Canaanite's faith.[217] As her faith stands the test of Jesus's seemingly derogatory remarks,[218] Jesus demonstrates that the faith of a gentile will not be ignored.

A second aspect of the interaction unique to Matthew involves what the Canaanite woman chooses to call Jesus (Matt 15:22 // Mark 7:25).

213. Hagner, *Matthew 14–28*, 410.

214. Mark describes the woman as a Syrophoenician (7:26).

215. Davies and Allison, *Matthew 8–18*, 541. First, Jesus does not answer her. Second, he indicates his mission is to the house of Israel. Third, Jesus questions the wisdom of misusing the gift offered to the children of God.

216. Matt 4:15–16; 12:18–21; 15:21–39; 28:18–20. Twelftree, *Jesus the Miracle Worker*, 133.

217. Keener, *Commentary*, 417.

218. Scott, "Matthew 15.21–28," 41, effectively argues from a narrative-critical perspective that a "sense of despair and frustration in Jesus" comes out in his encounter with the woman. We see Jesus at the temple, in the woe proclamations, and in the lament over Jerusalem expressing frustration and despair (Matt 21:12–13; 23:1–39). However, Scott, "Matthew 15.21–28," 43, indicates Jesus is "simply rude" in his interactions with the Canaanite woman no matter the historical, sociological, or intellectual situation. As we will see in the woe proclamations, to impose twentieth-century communication expectations on a first-century interaction would be presumptuous. As France, *Matthew*, 591, points out, "A good teacher may sometimes aim to draw out a pupil's best insight by a deliberate challenge which does not necessarily represent the teacher's own view — even if the phrase 'devil's advocate' may not be quite appropriate to this context!"

Requesting mercy, she addresses Jesus not as the Son of God but as κύριε υἱὸς Δαυίδ ("O Lord, Son of David").[219] Connecting κύριος ("Lord") to Jesus's transcendence may be part of the informed Christian confession, but it seems unlikely that this is what the Canaanite meant.[220] It seems more likely that the combination of κύριε υἱὸς Δαυίδ ("O Lord, Son of David") from the lips of the Canaanite acknowledges Jesus as a king who conquered her ancestors (Josh 12:7–24).[221] The Canaanite woman's address reinforces Matthew's depiction of Jesus as a human descendent of the Son of David. Using Son of David reinforces that ministry to the gentiles is a component of Jesus's Messianic ministry (4:14–16; 12:17–21).

After healing the Canaanite woman, Matthew continues to describe Jesus's ministry to gentiles in a manner that can be perceived in three ways.[222] First, Jesus heals multiple afflictions, and the God of Israel receives glory (Matt 15:31 // Mark 7:37). None of the other miracle accounts in the Gospels ends with the crowds specifically glorifying τὸν θεὸν Ἰσραήλ ("the God of Israel").[223] Why does Matthew specify glorifying the God of Israel if these miracles happen to the Jews? In light of our study and this pericope, Matthew wants to reinforce that God's work occurs among Jew and gentile alike, and Matthew wants to maintain the human element of Jesus's identity by glorifying God alone. Second, Jesus returns by boat to a Jewish territory in Magadan where he encounters Pharisees and Sadducees (Matt 15:39—16:1). A boat ride suggests that Jesus's ministry to the gentiles extends beyond the interaction with the Canaanite woman.[224] Third, Jesus performs miracles in gentile territory similar to ones performed among the Jews. For example, not only does Matthew provide similar summary lists of diseases healed among Jews (4:24; 9:35; 14:35–36) and gentiles (15:30–31), but also Matthew's Jesus feeds large crowds out of compassion.[225] Just as Jesus extends compassion to the Jews (9:36; 14:14; 20:34), he also compassionately

219. Frequently in Matthew, he refers to Jesus as "Lord" (Matt 7:21–22; 8:2, 6, 8, 21, 25; 9:28; 10:24–25; 12:8; 14:28, 30; 15:23, 27; 16:22; 17:4, 17; 18:21; 20:33; 25:37, 44; 26:22) and "Son of David" (1:1, 20; 9:27; 12:23; 20:30–31; 21:9, 15; 22:42). Davies and Allison, *Matthew 8–18*, 548, suggest that calling Jesus κύριος ("Lord") "lay somewhere between 'sir' and the informed Christian confession."

220. Hagner, *Matthew 1–13*, 198.

221. Keener, *Commentary*, 418.

222. France, *Gospel of Matthew*, 598–600.

223. Matt 9:8; Mark 2:12; Luke 5:25–26; 7:16; 13:13; 18:43.

224. Twelftree, *Jesus the Miracle Worker*, 133–35.

225. In Matthew, Jesus feeds two hungry crowds, one consisting of five-thousand in a Jewish territory and the other consisting of four-thousand in a gentile region (Matt 14:19–21 // 15:35–38). The second food miracle parallels the first, in particular the wording (14:19–21 // 15:35–38). See France, *Gospel of Matthew*, 600.

feeds the gentiles (15:32). Why repeat the miracles if for Jews only? The connections serve to assist the readers in realizing the need to include gentiles in Christian community.[226] As Matthew prioritizes the humanity of Jesus to portray his perspective on Jesus as the exemplar, this section serves to remind readers that imitating the ministry of Christ includes Jew and gentile alike.

Even though this section extends Jesus's ministry to gentiles, the gentile perception identifies Jesus as a human by drawing a distinction between Jesus and the God of Israel (Matt 15:31). This, in conjunction with the recognition of the Canaanite woman's plea to "Lord, Son of David,"[227] reminds the reader of the exemplar's human identity in Matthew's story. In spite of the disciples coming to grips with Jesus being the Son of God (14:33), the gentile interactions remind the reader of Jesus's human identity as Son of David and as someone distinct from the God of Israel. Even though Matthew's depiction of the Messiah ministers first to the Jews in accordance to the scriptures,[228] Jesus also acts as Israel's Messiah on behalf of Israel's God for the gentiles (12:17–21; 15:21–39).[229] This progression within the narrative sets up the question, "Who is Jesus?"[230] Matthew's audience is now prepared for Peter's proclamation that Jesus is the Christ, the Son of the Living God (16:16).

3.2.4 Pharisees, Sadducees, and Peter Respond (Matt 16:1–20)

Before the climactic proclamation of Peter (Matt 16:16) and the following shift of focus to Jesus's journey toward Jerusalem (18:1—20:34) where he will encounter crucifixion, death, and resurrection (27:27—28:10), Matthew provides one more interaction with the religious leaders. As Jesus returns to Jewish territory (15:39), the first interaction with the Sadducees in Matthew's Gospel occurs (16:1). Testing Jesus, the Sadducees and Pharisees ask for a sign from heaven (16:1). In spite of Jesus's activities up to this point, the religious leaders ask for something to authenticate his identity.[231] The audience has already read about the numerous acts that validate Jesus's unique

---

226. Luz, *Studies in Matthew*, 213.

227. See ch. 4, n220 below.

228. Davies and Allison, *Matthew 8–18*, 557.

229. Luz, *Matthew 8–20*, 344–45.

230. France, *Matthew*, 612.

231. 4 Ezra 5:4; Matt 24:27; Mark 13:24–25; Luke 21:11. Gibson, "Jesus' Refusal," 37. Twelftree, *Jesus: The Miracle Worker*, 135.

status at this point in the narrative.[232] Consequently, the request appears preposterous.[233] The only sign Jesus willingly alludes to for a second time is the sign of Jonah, and that sign foreshadows the resurrection (12:38–41; 16:4).

In the following pericope Peter proclaims the central christological confession and Jesus announces his death, burial, and resurrection for the first time (Matt 16:16–21). Peter's proclamation occurs as a result of Jesus's inquiries into the perception of his identity from people and his disciples (Matt 16:13–15 // Mark 8:27–29 // Luke 9:18–20). In Mark and Luke, Jesus initiates the dialogue by asking "whom do people say that I am" (Mark 8:27 // Luke 9:18). Matthew preserves the conversation partners but modifies the question. Matthew's Jesus asks the disciples who the people think the Son of Man is (Matt 16:13). In response to Jesus's inquiry, Peter confesses, "You are the Christ, the Son of the living God" (16:16). The confession, in connection with the modification of the question, intentionally connects three primary titles to help the readers comprehend Jesus's identity:[234] Son of Man,[235] Christ,[236] and Son of the living God.[237]

Further evidence of Matthew answering the identity question is the confession itself. Peter's confession varies in the Synoptics. In Mark it is "You are the Christ" (Mark 8:29). In Luke, Peter responds, "The Christ of God" (Luke 9:20). Matthew's Peter states: "You are the Christ, the Son of the living God" (Matt 16:16).[238] The first use of ὁ χριστὸς ("the Christ") in direct

232. At this point in the narrative, Jesus is the Son of David (Matt 1:1–17; 9:27; 12:23; 15:22), Son of God (4:3, 6; 8:29; 14:33), and Son of Man (8:20; 9:6; 11:19; 12:8, 32, 40). In addition, Jesus possesses unique authority (7:28–29), performs miracles (4:24; 8:1—9:35; 14:35–36; 15:30–31), forgives sin (9:1–8), and stands in unique relationship to God (11:25–27).

233. Davies and Allison, *Matthew 8–20*, 579.

234. Luz, *Studies in Matthew*, 85–96, validates the importance of each of these titles. Davies and Allison, *Matthew 8–18*, 617, suggest that the "Son of Man" and "Son of the living God" redactions bring together the three "major" christological titles for Matthew. Meier, *Vision of Matthew*, 109–10, integrates the three titles to explain one another. In other words, in Peter's confession Son of God and Messiah explain Son of Man and Son of Man explains how Jesus can be both Messiah and Son of God.

235. Matthew consistently links Jesus to being the Son of Man: 8:20; 9:6; 10:23; 11:19; 12:8, 32, 40; 13:37, 41; 16:13, 27–28; 17:9, 12, 22; 19:28; 20:18, 28; 24:27, 29–30, 37, 39, 44.

236. Matthew consistently connects Jesus to his messianic identity: 1:1, 16–18; 2:4; 11:2; 16:16, 20; 22:42; 23:10; 24:5, 23; 26:63, 68; 27:17, 22.

237. Matthew consistently links Jesus to an existence as a transcendent Son: 2:15; 3:17; 4:3, 6; 8:29; 11:27; 14:33; 16:16; 26:63; 27:40, 43, 54; 28:19.

238. Turner, *Matthew*, 404, indicates the phrase "living God" simply distinguishes false gods and the true Israelite God (Deut 5:26; 1 Sam 17:26; 2 Kgs 19:4; Pss 42:2;

speech in Matthew appears in Peter's confession, but for Matthew a solely Messianic descriptor fails to express the identity of Jesus adequately.[239] In light of the narrative progression leading to Peter's confession, Allison and Davies point out, "As Jewish messianism had anticipated, the Messiah in Matthew is certainly a human figure. But he also stands in a special relation to God, as God's Son."[240] In Matthean Christology and as seen throughout this project, ignoring either the human or the transcendent identity of Jesus leads to an inadequate description.[241] Even though Matthew elevates and expands Jesus's transcendence through Peter's confession, Matthew has intentionally preserved the human story of Jesus to portray Jesus as the messianic figure worthy of belief. Matthew's portrayal of the identity of Jesus requires both a human and transcendent description as Matthew purposely balances those aspects.

In an attempt to explain Matthew's changes, Davies and Allison suggest that the best way to resolve the differences may be due to an "imperfect assimilation of his sources."[242] However, observation of the narrative to this point demonstrates this is unlikely. Matthew's story, structure, progression, addition of human elements, and preservation of Jesus's human existence from source material demonstrates a human messianic figure. Prioritizing the human story, in conjunction with the development of the argument for Jesus as a transcendent figure, confirms Matthew intentionally edits the confession to reflect a character with a human and transcendent identity. Due to the nature of this confession and the use of the structural marker, ἀπὸ τότε ἤρξατο ("from that time he began") soon after the confession (Matt 16:16–21), Matthew builds his narrative to a point that provides a believability of Jesus's human as well as transcendent identity. To assimilate the sources imperfectly would not be consistent with the clear intentionality of what has led up to and follows this central confession. Even though Jesus exists as a human,[243] to identify him only as "the Christ" or only "Son of

---

84:2; Acts 14:15; Rom 9:26; 2 Cor 3:3; 6:16; 1 Thess 1:9; 1 Tim 3:15; 4:10; Heb 3:12; 9:14; 10:31; 12:22; 1 Pet 1:23; Rev 7:2). Meier, *Vision of Matthew*, 109, applies "living" to describe God, which stresses how God possesses life in and of himself. Whichever is the case, Peter's proclamation connects three central Matthean christological titles.

239. Keener, *Commentary*, 495.

240. Davies and Allison, *Matthew 8–18*, 642.

241. Davies and Allison, *Matthew 8–18*, 642, rightly raise the question regarding the functionality of Jesus's transcendence in light of the inability to describe Jesus's existence in solely human categories. However, Davies and Allison guide the conversation toward transcendence rather than attempting to present the humanity. As has been, and will be, seen through multiple redactions, Matthean Christology incorporates both.

242. Davies and Allison, *Matthew 8–18*, 621.

243. Hagner, *Matthew 14–28*, 468.

the living God" is incomplete and inadequate for Matthew. Instead, Matthew provides a christological identification through Peter's confession that adequately identifies the human and transcendent figure he depicts.

Matthew's narrative work in this section continues to tell the human story of Jesus. As he builds an argument for Jesus's transcendence, Matthew brings his understanding of the identity of Jesus together in Peter's confession (Matt 16:16 // Mark 8:29 // Luke 9:20). The confession proclaims what the implied author would have desired the reader to understand and believe in the narrative progression thus far. By maintaining the humanity of Jesus, it is possible for Matthew to argue for Jesus's Messianic status. In the midst of building the argument for Jesus's transcendence, Matthew uses the humanity of Jesus to keep Jesus and God as separate characters.[244] Jesus is a human with transcendent status. As Luz says, the First Evangelist "anticipates remarkably closely the doctrine of two natures in the later church."[245] A sufficient description of the identity of Jesus includes both a human and transcendent description. Peter's confession declares that the human Messiah in Matthew possesses transcendent status as God's Son.[246]

CONCLUSION

Spanning the beginning of Jesus's ministry (Matt 4:17) until Peter's confession (16:16) with the structural marker ἀπὸ τότε ἤρξατο ("from that time he began," 4:17; 16:21), we have seen that the readers of Matthew's Gospel can walk away with an understanding that Jesus lives a human life with transcendent status because he exists as both the human Messiah and transcendent Son of God (16:16). Although each Gospel depicts Jesus as a human, Matthew prioritizes the portrait in a different manner in three particular ways (4:17—16:20).

First, he continues to tell the human story to strengthen the belief in Jesus as a fulfiller of prophecy.[247] Casting out demons and curing the sick fulfills Isaiah's prophecy that Jesus bears the infirmities and sickness of others (Isa 53:4; Matt 8:16–17).[248] The others cured include gentiles because the Spirit rests on Jesus as Isaiah had prophesied (Isa 42:1–3; Matt 12:17–21).

---

244. Davies and Allison, *Matthew 8–18*, 642, point out that the term "God" never describes Jesus in the First Gospel.

245. Luz, *Studies in Matthew*, 96.

246. Davies and Allison, *Matthew 8–18*, 642.

247. Matt 8:17; 12:17–21; 13:14–15, 35.

248. Keener, *Commentary*, 273. See ch. 3.1.1 above.

Jesus teaching through parables also fulfills prophetic expectations.[249] As a result of Jesus's life as a human, the portrayal of fulfilled prophecies becomes reason to believe Peter's confession.

Second, even though Matthew constructs a case for Jesus's transcendent status through the narrative,[250] we observe that Matthew purposely balances the human existence and transcendent status of Jesus. For the credibility of Peter's confession, Matthew integrates the human and transcendent identity. In one situation Jesus possesses knowledge, or lack thereof, akin to the rest of humanity (Matt 9:3–4; 14:12–13), yet later, Matthew portrays Jesus possessing unique, transcendent knowledge (16:21; 22:18). Immediately after referring to himself as a homeless Son of Man, a title associated with humanity (8:19–20), Jesus calms the winds and the waves, causing the disciples to ask what sort of man is Jesus (8:23–27). In one scene Jesus walks on the water and is declared the Son of God (14:22–33), soon after, the gentiles glorify the God of Israel and Jesus crosses a sea by boat (15:31; 39). Matthew's story holds the human and transcendent identity of Jesus in balance to encourage readers to believe in and to emulate the main character.

Third, Matthew portrays Jesus as an exemplar.[251] For Matthew to develop his perspective on the *imitatio Christi* motif, he chooses to emphasize the human story. For example, Matthew's portrayal of the life of Jesus exemplifies the teaching of the Sermon on the Mount.[252] The miracle section establishes Jesus as the exemplar as he models and commands the disciples to accomplish the same miracles.[253] In the same discourse, Matthew's Jesus challenges them to emulate their master and teacher (Matt 10:24–25). The imitation includes responding not only to the faith of the Jews but also the gentiles (8:5–13; 15:21–39). For the audience to comprehend the implications of the call to be like their master and teacher, Matthew's Jesus necessarily exists as other humans because the humanity of Jesus functions as

---

249. Isa 6:9–10; Ps 78:2; Matt 13:14–15, 35.

250. Matt 8:23–27; 9:2–8, 18–26; 12:15, 25, 46–50; 16:16.

251. See ch. 3, n8 above.

252. See ch. 3, n24 above.

253. Matt 8:1–16; 8:28—9:8; 9:18–31; 10:1, 7–8. Davies and Allison, *Matthew 8–17*, 5, reinforce the idea that in the miracle chapters Jesus models behavior worthy of emulation.

the archetype for discipleship.[254] Even though Jesus possesses transcendent status,[255] the exemplar is depicted as a human.

Matthew will increasingly focus on Jesus's existence as a human with Jesus heading toward Jerusalem. We will see that the final act in Matthew's narrative portrait maintains a balance between the human existence and transcendent status of Matthew's primary character. The transcendent element of Jesus's status continues to develop, but, as will become clear, the focus of the end of Jesus's journey for Matthew is his humanity.

254. Johnson, "Learning the Human Jesus," 153, argues that even though many groups gather in the name of Christianity, they agree that the "humanity of Jesus somehow functions as the model and measure of Christian discipleship." As we observe in Matthew's narrative, that was the case then as is now.

255. Matt 8:23–34; 11:25–27; 12:8; 14:22–33; 16:16–19.

4

Portrait of the Human End
(Matthew 16:21—28:20)

TO THIS POINT MATTHEW has done a number of things to emphasize the humanity of Jesus. Matthew has taken the readers through Jesus's human beginning with an origin story, baptism to fulfill all righteousness, temptation, and ministry initiation (Matt 1:1—4:16). Establishing a transition in the story with ἀπὸ τότε ἤρξατο ("from that time he began," 4:17), Matthew shifts the focus to the ministry phase of Jesus's life (4:17—16:20). That section portrays a human life with transcendent status as Matthew preserves and elaborates on the human story while building a case for Jesus's transcendence. This final section is set apart by Matthew's last use of ἀπὸ τότε ἤρξατο ("from that time he began," 16:21). After Peter recognizes and proclaims Jesus's identity as the Christ, the Son of the living God (16:16), Jesus informs the disciples of his impending suffering, death, and resurrection (16:21).[1] The remainder of Matthew's Gospel fulfills that predictive summary statement.[2] With Peter's confession, the structural marker, and the first prediction of future demise, the final turning point in the Matthean narrative sets up a portrait of the end of a human life.[3] Drawing closer to the suffering and death of Jesus, it will be seen that Matthew's interest in the human story of Jesus is clear.

In this section, the First Evangelist shifts the focus to the human Son of God's journey toward Jerusalem and the Passion Week (Matt 16:21—28:20).

1. Davies and Allison *Matthew 8–18*, 659.

2. Turner, *Matthew*, 410.

3. Hagner, *Matthew 14–28*, 476–77.

In particular, Matthew uses conflict between Jesus and others while in Jerusalem in a manner that the reader can observe that Jesus's status as the human Son of David and transcendent Son of God contributes to the conflict that leads to his death. As Matthew leads the audience to the end of the life of his main character, we will see that the emphasis on the humanity of Jesus increases.

As demonstrated, Matthew's Jesus exists as "differentiated from animals on the one hand and God on the other; accordingly, certain elements—birth, family, life activities, death—constitute the outline of what we expect to be told about any human being."[4] This section portrays Jesus's temptation (Matt 16:23), hunger (21:18), anger (21:12–13), and lack of knowledge (24:36).[5] Facing sorrow and trouble (26:37–38), he confesses a will contrary to his Father's (26:39). Jesus suffers (26:67; 27:27–54), exhibits dependence,[6] dies (27:45–50), and rises bodily from the dead (28:9). As will be seen, the story of Jesus displays the portrait of a human end as an exemplar that reassures hope for a new beginning for the Jewish Christian community. This becomes possible through Jesus's obedience, suffering, death, burial, and bodily resurrection. In this Gospel, the storyline only serves as an apologetic for belief if Matthew maintains Jesus's humanity. The portrait of the human end provides not only a picture of what can happen to a disciple of Christ but also depicts hope of a future bodily resurrection.[7]

4.1 A PREDICTED DEATH AND RESURRECTION (MATT 16:21–28)

Matthew's application of the transitional phrase ἀπὸ τότε ἤρξατο ("from that time he began," Matt 16:21) provides a structural marker to indicate the final narrative shift as Jesus predicts the end of his life. Jesus announces he will go to Jerusalem, suffer, die, and resurrect from the dead (16:21). Unsatisfied with this prediction, Peter rebukes Jesus (16:22). The rebuke leads Jesus to specify that Peter's line of thinking hinders him (16:23). The prediction and response to the rebuke drive two questions: How does Peter's rebuke hinder the Son of God (16:23), and how can the Son of God die (16:16, 21)?

4. Thompson, *Humanity of Jesus*, 7.

5. Brown, "How Much Did Jesus Know," 315–45.

6. Matthew's Christology clarifies and repeats a dependence on God to raise Jesus from the dead as Matthew intentionally changes Mark's ἀναστήσεται ("will rise") to ἐγερθήσεται ("will be raised"), even though Luke retains Mark's descriptor (Matt 20:19 // Mark 10:34 // Luke 18:33). See ch. 4, n21 below for further explanation.

7. Matt 10:22–23; 24:9; 27:52–53; 28:8–10.

In order to understand Matthew's interest in Jesus's humanity, we begin with an examination of the prediction of his own death. Only Matthew's Jesus predicts his death four times.[8] Only Matthew includes the specificity of death by crucifixion in his predictions.[9] Death distinguishes Jesus from the solely transcendent God. The OT and NT assert that God will never die (Ps 90:2; Mal 3:6; Rev 1:8). A death prediction and physical death confirms for Matthew's readers that the identity of Jesus includes humanity (Matt 27:50). Based on the definition of human in this study and a portrayal of Jesus's self-perception, if Jesus proclaims he will die, then he knows that his identity includes humanity.[10]

Matthew's Jesus will go to Jerusalem not only to die but also to παθεῖν ("to suffer") many things (Matt 16:21). While the basic meaning of παθεῖν is "to experience something,"[11] the NT writers employ the term to describe an unfavorable experience.[12] The idea of πάσχω ("suffer") also involves "enduring something at someone's hands."[13] To emphasize suffering, the First Evangelist will provide the most graphic details of the physical suffering of Jesus.[14] Jesus's suffering will lead to his death at the hands of another as evidenced by ἀποκτανθῆναι ("to be killed," 16:21). For the narrative to resonate with the Jewish Christian audience regarding Jesus's demise, Matthew chooses to maintain the human story of Jesus in spite of his interest in establishing the perception of his transcendence immediately before the prediction (16:16).

As Matthew modifies the resurrection prediction, he emphasizes Jesus's dependence on something other than himself to be raised from the dead. Matthew, Mark, and Luke all employ similar, yet distinct language to describe the resurrection.[15] In Mark's resurrection predictions, he selects the

---

8. Matt 16:21; 17:22–23; 20:17–19; 26:1–2.

9. Matt 20:19 // Mark 10:34 // Luke 18:33 and Matt 26:2 // Mark 14:1 // Luke 22:1–2. Hagner, *Matthew 14–28*, 477.

10. Dunn, *Jesus Remembered*, 1:615–764, asks what Jesus thought of himself as God's Son, an eschatological agent, a priestly messiah, and/or a teacher. Dunn does not ask whether Jesus considers himself a human, which remains a question for discussion.

11. Michaelis, "πάσχω," *TDNT* 5:904–39 (904).

12. Matt 16:21; 17:12; Phil 1:29; 2 Thess 1:5; Heb 13:12; 1 Pet 2:21; 3:17. Bauer, "πάσχω," BDAG, 785.

13. Bauer, "πάσχω," BDAG, 785.

14. Matt 26:67–68 // Mark 14:65 // Luke 22:63–65; Matt 27:28–31 // Mark 15:17–20 // Luke 19:1–3.

15. Ennulat, *Die Minor Agreements*, 188–95, observes Matthean and Lukan disagreement with Mark in the passion predictions. As will be seen, the difficulty with this assumption is the interchangeable nature of the terms ἀνίστημι ("rise up") and ἐγείρω ("rise"). Bauer, "ἀνίστημι," BDAG, 83:7; Bauer "ἐγείρω," BDAG, 272:7.

verb ἀνίστημι ("rise up, come back from the dead")[16] employing the middle voice twice (Mark 9:31; 10:34) and an active infinitive once (Mark 8:31). In the words of A. T. Robertson: "In the active voice the subject is merely acting; in the middle the subject is acting in relation to himself somehow."[17] It is not until the Lord's supper that Mark uses the passive form of ἐγείρω ("rise") in reference to Jesus (14:28).[18]

Luke applies both ἀνίστημι ("rise up") and ἐγείρω ("rise") in the passion predictions. In the first prediction, Luke uses a form of ἐγείρω ("rise," Luke 9:22), but in the last forecast, he follows Mark's use of ἀνίστημι ("rise up," Mark 10:34 // Luke 18:33). Even though Luke removes the resurrection element in the second prediction (Matt 17:23 // Mark 9:31 // Luke 9:44), he relies on the active voice of ἀνίστημι ("rise up") to recall the prediction of the resurrection (Luke 24:7). The interchange of these terms leads R. T. France to indicate that "any attempt to draw a theological distinction between them is implausible."[19] While that may be the case, the question is whether Matthew perceives a theological distinction and thus a christological distinction.

Matthew consistently applies passive forms of ἐγείρω ("rise") throughout the narrative not only to describe raising others from the dead, but also in each reference to Jesus's resurrection in the narrative.[20] There are textual variants between the uses of ἀνίστημι ("rise up") and ἐγείρω ("rise") in Matthew's passion predictions (Matt 16:21; 17:23; 20:19).[21] However, none of

16. Bauer, "ἀνίστημι," BDAG, 83.

17. Robertson, *Grammar*, 804.

18. According to Albright and Mann, *Matthew*, 200, the NT writers "always" provide theological language that Jesus is raised by God or by the Spirit's power but "never" phrase the resurrection in a way that indicates Jesus is resurrected through his own power. If Jesus is solely transcendent, why do NT authors "always" indicate that Jesus is raised by some transcendent power other than himself?

19. France, *Gospel of Matthew*, 633. Also see Bayer, *Jesus' Predictions*, 208–11.

20. Matt 16:21; 17:23; 20:19; 26:32. Matthew uses ἐγείρω ("rise") to refer to Jesus rising from the dead in another part of the narrative (17:9). Matthew consistently selects passive forms of ἐγείρω ("rise") in terms of the resurrection of others (9:25; 11:5; 14:2; 27:52). The only active use of ἐγείρω ("rise") is in the command for the disciples to raise people from the dead in the second discourse (10:8). Clearly, Matthew's term of choice identifying Jesus and humans being raised from the dead is ἐγείρω ("rise").

21. France, *Matthew*, 633n12, considers these "significant textual variants" to maintain his position that ἀνίστημι ("rise up") and ἐγείρω ("rise") are interchangeable. However, examination of Matthew's entire narrative suggests that Matthew may not agree. The interchange resulting in the textual variants may be due to the editor's theological purposes. Examination of texts describing people being raised from the dead are as follows: Comparing the description of Jesus raising the leader of the synagogue's daughter, Mark and Luke use ἀνέστη ("rose") and only Matthew selects ἠγέρθη ("was raised")

the instances describing the resurrection of other individuals have a textual variant of ἀνίστημι ("rise up") attached to them.[22] Only within the prediction of the resurrection of Jesus does a textual variant exist for ἀνίστημι ("rise up") and ἐγείρω ("rise") among Matthew's passion predictions (16:21; 17:23; 20:19). Surveying passages that describe rising from the dead demonstrates that Matthew's term of choice is ἐγείρω ("rise") in various passive forms.[23] The passive suggests the subject receives the action.[24]

In the first resurrection prediction, both Matthew and Luke modify Mark's less theologically clear ἀναστῆναι ("to arise," Matt 16:21 // Mark 8:31 // Luke 9:22).[25] The passive form of ἐγείρω ("rise") more accurately reflects the church's language of the first century (Acts 10:40; 1 Cor 15:4).[26] This evidence, in conjunction with Matthew's consistent selection of ἐγείρω

---

without evidence of significant textual variance (Matt 9:25 // Mark 5:42 // Luke 8:55). Only Matthew mentions raising the dead as a role of the disciples in their commission during Jesus's ministry. He uses a form of ἐγείρω ("rise") and a textual variant is not currently listed (Matt 10:8 // Mark 3:7–8 // Luke 6:2–3). When Matthew describes Jesus's work to John the Baptist's messengers, both Matthew and Luke use ἐγείρονται ("raised") without any resulting textual variants (Matt 11:5 // Luke 7:22). All three of the Synoptic authors use ἠγέρθη ("was raised") to describe that Herod fears Jesus is John the Baptist raised from the dead (Matt 14:2 // Mark 6:14 // Luke 9:7). One other passage unique to Matthew describes those who fell asleep being raised (Matt 27:52). Matthew employs ἠγέρθη ("was raised"), and there is yet to be any noted evidence of a textual variant that changes the term from ἐγείρω ("rise") to ἀνίστημι ("rise up," 27:52). While "significant textual variants" exist in the passion predictions, there are none elsewhere as Matthew describes the resurrection of other human beings. Metzger, *Textual Commentary on the Greek New Testament*, 42–52, does not address these three textual variants in Matthew's predictions. Swanson, *New Testament Greek Manuscripts*, viii, suggests that the Codex Vaticanus is considered the "exemplar" and "superior to all other witnesses." The first prediction clearly supports the passive use of the term ἐγείρω ("rise," Matt 16:21). However, the other predictions are not as clear as to whether ἀνίστημι ("rise up") or ἐγείρω ("rise") is original. While the evidence suggests that ἀνίστημι ("rise up") is the original term in the previous two predictions (Matt 17:23; 20:19), Hagner, *Matthew 14–28*, 574, rightly assesses that the ἀναστήσεται ("he will rise") textual variants are due to assimilation to the synoptic parallels. As a result and in light of Matthew's consistent selection of ἐγείρω ("rise") to describe others being raised from the dead, there is room to agree with Aland, *Synopsis of the Four Gospels*, 157, 225, that the original reading in each of Matthew's passion predictions is ἐγερθῆναί ("to be raised"). Consequently, Matthew not only cares about the theology of Jesus's resurrection but also more clearly emphasizes the human dependence of Jesus to be raised from the dead.

22. The description of the bodies of the saints being raised does have a textual variant, but the variant is the difference between ἠγέρθησαν ("were raised") and ἠγέρθη ("has been raised"), both of which are forms of ἐγείρω ("rise," Matt 27:52).

23. Matt 9:25; 11:5; 14:2; 27:52.

24. Robertson, *Grammar*, 815.

25. Hagner, *Matthew 14–28*, 477.

26. Hagner, *Matthew 14–28*, 574.

("rise"), suggests that Matthew prefers the passive form. In addition, as Jesus forecasts his resurrection prediction for the last time, Matthew and Mark both select ἐγερθῆναί ("to be raised," Matt 26:32 // Mark 14:28). While both Mark and Matthew assume that God is the author of the resurrection,[27] Matthew consistently and more clearly establishes Jesus's dependence on something other than himself to rise from the dead. Even with Peter's proclamation of Jesus as the Christ, the Son of the living God, Matthew's human Son of God suffers, dies, and depends on the power of God to raise him from the dead (Matt 16:21). Therefore, if God authors the resurrection, then Jesus, as well as other humans, depends on God.

Another alteration in Matthew's narrative depicts Jesus as human after the first passion prediction. As Peter hears the death prophecy, he responds by rebuking Jesus (Matt 16:22 // Mark 8:32). Parts of the rebuke in Matthew and Mark are consistent with phrases such as "Get behind me, Satan" and "You are not on the side of God, but of men" (Matt 16:23 // Mark 8:33). However, Matthew adds a phrase, σκάνδαλον εἶ ἐμοῦ ("you are tempting me to sin").[28] The selection of the term σκάνδαλον depicts Jesus facing the temptation to act contrary to the prediction.[29] Ulrich Luz explains, "'Offense' (σκάνδαλον) is a strong word and means in substance the occasion for sin."[30] Matthew's addition to the rebuke, σκάνδαλον εἶ ἐμοῦ ("you are tempting me to sin"), reinforces the idea that Jesus endures temptation as he has explicitly in the temptation narrative (Matt 4:1–11) and will implicitly in the Garden (26:36–44). This serves as another example of the extent of Jesus's humanity and his temptation to decide whether to follow the plans of a human or God.[31]

After the rebuke of Peter, each Synoptic author connects the previous pericope to an expectation for a disciple to be willing to lose one's life, take up a cross, and follow Christ (Matt 16:24–28 // Mark 8:34—9:1 // Luke 9:23–27). Repeating an earlier explanation of the call of the disciples (Matt 10:38–39), Matthew has already explained that the life of a disciple should reflect the master teacher (10:24–25).[32] This, in conjunction with Matthew's

27. Allison and Davies, *Matthew 8–18*, 657. For further discussion, see Schnackenburg, "Jesus," 1–17, who points out that this is Paul's language in the first letter to the Corinthians (1 Cor 15:4), and God is thought of as the *Erweckende* ("Awakener").

28. Bauer, "σκάνδαλον," BDAG, 291; Davies and Allison, *Matthew 8–18*, 664. Wis 14:11; 1 Macc 5:4; Pss. Sol 4:23; Matt 18:7; Rom 16:7; Rev 2:14; Barn. 4:9.

29. Bauer, "σκάνδαλον," BDAG, 291, defines this as "an action or circumstance that leads one to act contrary to a proper course of action or set of beliefs."

30. Luz, *Matthew 8–20*, 382.

31. Matt 4:1–11; 16:22–23; 26:36–46.

32. Hagner, *Matthew 14–28*, 483; Turner, *Matthew*, 409.

addition of σκάνδαλον εἶ ἐμοῦ ("you are tempting me to sin"), connects the example of Jesus's temptation to follow the desires of humankind rather than God (16:23). Elements of the story demonstrate to readers Jesus's willingness to deny himself and die in spite of the temptation to follow his own will (16:23; 26:36–42). Here, the role of Jesus's humanity is exemplar.

4.2 FROM TRANSFIGURATION TO TAXATION (MATT 17:1–27)

As Jesus makes progress on his journey to Jerusalem, the development of the human and transcendent identity of Jesus continues in Matthew's narrative. Setting up the fourth discourse (Matt 18:1–35), Matthew's Jesus heals, teaches, pays taxes, and predicts his own suffering, death, and resurrection a second time (17:10–27). This section begins with Jesus's transfiguration (17:1–9). As Stephen C. Barton points out, the focal point of Matthew's transfiguration narrative is to portray Jesus as the Son of God.[33] For the second time in the Gospel, the Father identifies Jesus as the Son of God with whom he is well pleased (17:5; 3:17).[34] However, as will be seen, the human role of Jesus in Matthew's narrative during and after the transfiguration shines as Matthew maintains his interest in portraying Jesus as a teacher and exemplar.[35]

Matthew's transfiguration account renders both the transcendence and humanity of Jesus as christologically, anthropologically, and eschatologically important, particularly in comparison to Mark and Luke's (Matt 17:1–9 // Mark 9:2–10 // Luke 9:28–36). Jesus leads his inner-circle of disciples to a high mountain where μετεμορφώθη ("he was transfigured," Matt 17:2 // Mark 9:2).[36] With the passive, W. C. Davies and Dale C. Allison Jr. indicate that the transfiguration of Jesus is apparently divine because the passive verb establishes God as the cause.[37] Jesus is transformed by someone other than himself. If Jesus exists as a solely transcendent figure, he would not be depicted as relying on someone else for transformation. Once again, Matthew portrays his main character's human dependence.[38]

33. Barton, "Transfiguration of Christ," 240.

34. Luz, *Theology of the Gospel of Matthew*, 98–99. Also see, Kingsbury, *Matthew*, 67–69.

35. Luz, *Theology of the Gospel of Matthew*, 99.

36. Bauer, "μεταμορφόω," BDAG, 639. Luke removes μεταμορφόω ("transfigure"), Matthew and Mark use the passive form (Matt 17:2 // Mark 9:2 // Luke 9:29).

37. Davies and Allison, *Matthew 8–18*, 695.

38. Matt 17:2; 16:21; 17:23; 20:19; 26:32.

As a human being transfigured in the scene, Matthew preserves the description of Jesus's white garments (Matt 17:2 // Mark 9:3 // Luke 9:29) and adds ἔλαμψεν τὸ πρόσωπον αὐτοῦ ὡς ὁ ἥλιος ("[Jesus's] face shined like the sun," Matt 17:2). For Matthew's Jewish Christian audience, what happens to Jesus on the mountain resembles Moses's encounter with God on Mount Sinai (Exod 34:29).[39] Matthean Christology uses the human portrayal of Jesus not only to communicate a Mosaic comparison,[40] but also to connect to the disciples and the audience anthropologically.[41]

Luz points out that the transfiguration recalls Jewish and Christian anthropological and eschatological hope of a future resurrected human body that will be transformed wearing a white garment and having a radiant face.[42] For a disciple of Jesus, as in the Matthean parable of the tares (Matt 13:36–43), the righteous have hope that they also ἐκλάμψουσιν ὁ ἥλιος ("will shine like the sun") in the Father's kingdom (13:43).[43] As the exemplar, just as Jesus is baptized earlier to fulfill all righteousness and now shines like the sun at the transfiguration, the righteous disciples can possess hope that they too will be righteous and shine like the sun.[44] Matthew chooses to maintain an anthropology in his Christology because the disciples can also be sons of God in whom the Father is pleased (5:9).[45] Not only that, but Davies and Allison note that Matthew's Jesus provides a picture of what believers will become as God transforms "human beings into their divine destiny."[46] This is possible because of Matthew's intentional connections between the humanity of Jesus and the rest of humankind.

Prior to the end of the transfiguration, Mark's disciples experience fear, but Matthew moves and modifies the description of the disciple's reaction to

39. Barton, "Transfiguration of Christ," 240.

40. See Allison, *New Moses*.

41. Barton, "Transfiguration of Christ," 245. Also see Allison, *New Moses*, 243–48.

42. 1 Cor 15:51–52; 2 Bar. 51:3, 5, 9–12; Dan 12:3; 4 Ezra 7:97. Luz, *Matthew 8–20*, 397, proposes that the points of contact are not specific, but Matthew will demonstrate a continued interest in resurrection theology. As will be seen, not only is he the sole Gospel author to include a post-crucifixion resurrection of those who have fallen asleep and been raised from the dead (Matt 27:51–53), but he also redacts Mark's resurrection scene to maintain a physically resurrected body as the women at the empty tomb later take hold of his feet to worship him (Matt 28:9–10 // Mark 16:9–11).

43. Barton, "Transfiguration of Christ," 244.

44. Barton, "Transfiguration of Christ," 244.

45. Barton, "Transfiguration of Christ," 244, points out that the Sermon on the Mount connects the followers of Christ with the title of sons of God (Matt 5:9). This connection establishes a link between Jesus as the eschatological Son of God and followers of Jesus as sons of God.

46. Davies and Allison, *Matthew 8–18*, 697, 705.

the end of the story (Matt 17:6 // Mark 9:6). In order to maintain the balance between Jesus's human and transcendent identities, after the vision, the human Jesus returns to an ordinary existence without the visible glory of God (Matt 17:7–9).[47] To stress this, only Matthew's Jesus touches the disciples, commands them to rise, and challenges them to have no fear (17:7).[48] Even though Matthew emphasizes a sense of normalcy after the transfiguration,[49] each Synoptic author ends the transfiguration account with the disciples observing Jesus alone without a shining face or glowing garments (Matt 17:8 // Mark 9:8 // Luke 9:36). Jesus's illumination is temporary (Matt 17:6–9),[50] and the transfiguration glory is removed. While both Matthew and Mark remind the disciples of the Son of Man's resurrection (Matt 17:9 // Mark 9:9), only Matthew adds the reminder that the Son of Man will suffer at the hands of the scribes to keep the human element before the reader (Matt 17:12).

Each Synoptic author ends the transfiguration scene with Jesus alone after hearing God proclaim that Jesus is his Son and the disciples need to listen to him (Matt 17:5–8 // Mark 9:7–8 // Luke 9:35–36). Matthew's redactions—the touch and commands of Jesus—clarify that his actions occur through human form (Matt 17:7).[51] Even though Jesus's transfiguration glory fades and he is established as the Messianic Son of God prior to the fourth discourse (18:1–35),[52] Matthew's consistent emphasis on the humanity of Jesus demonstrates that he will accomplish God's will through death on a cross as the narrative reminds the reader two additional times after the transfiguration (17:9–12; 22–23).

Following the transfiguration, Jesus and the disciples come to a crowd where a man asks for mercy for his demon-possessed son (Matt 17:14–18 // Mark 9:14–27). After the demons leave the boy, the disciples privately ask Jesus why they lack the ability to cast out the demon (Matt 17:19 // Mark 9:28). Related to our topic is the way Matthew uses the interaction between Jesus and the disciples to shift the focus from the faith of the boy's father to the lack of faith by the disciples (Matt 17:19–21 // Mark 9:28–29).[53] Matthew places Jesus's humanity and position as the archetype before the readers. Notably, neither Mark nor Matthew's Jesus indicates that the healing

---

47. Hagner, *Matthew 14–28*, 490–91.

48. Matthew adds this phrase using two imperatives ἐγέρθητε ("you all rise") and μὴ φοβεῖσθε ("you all do not fear," Matt 17:7).

49. France, *Matthew*, 651.

50. Allison, *New Moses*, 248.

51. Luz, *Matthew 8–20*, 399.

52. Hagner, *Matthew 14–28*, 495.

53. Harrington, *Gospel of Matthew*, 258.

has anything to do with the transcendence of Jesus. While that could be implied from the context of the transfiguration, both Matthew and Mark provide different explanations for the power to cast out demons. In Mark, Jesus portrays that prayer drives out the unclean spirit, but Matthew's Jesus suggests that the disciples cannot cast out the demon because they possess little faith (Matt 17:20 // Mark 9:29). The ὀλιγοπιστίαν ("little faith") of the disciples remains a theme for Matthew.[54]

Used as a rebuke,[55] Jesus informs them they are unable to cast out demons due to a lack of faith in God's power to assist.[56] As the exemplar who has already cast out demons by the power of the Spirit (Matt 12:17–28), Matthew's Jesus shows what the presence of God's Spirit in one's life can produce. With faith the size of a mustard seed, Jesus declares that mountains move (17:21). For Matthew, just as nothing is impossible for Jesus as the exemplar, faith for the disciples makes nothing impossible for them (17:21). In spite of nothing being impossible for the disciples with faith the size of a mustard seed, the narrative immediately reminds the reader again that Jesus will die and be resurrected from the dead (Matt 17:22–23 // Mark 9:30–32 // Luke 9:43–45).

Only Matthew adds that the disciples experience great distress after this reminder of Jesus's demise (Matt 17:22–23 // Mark 9:30–32 // Luke 9:43–45). This raises the question, why are the disciples distressed at this prediction? Although the identity of Jesus as Son of God receives attention through the transfiguration (17:5), a shocking or, as Donald Hagner puts it, distressing "contradictory revelation" is reiterated.[57] For Matthew's disciples, it is distressing that the human Messiah and Son of the living God will suffer and die, as evidenced also in Peter's initial response to Jesus's first prediction (16:16, 22–23). Matthew uses their reaction to hold the story of the main character's human and transcendent identity before the reader as both appear in the following Matthean pericope (17:24–27).

---

54. Of the times "little faith" is mentioned in the Synoptics, Matthew refers to it five times, and only once does it parallel with Luke (Matt 6:30 // Luke 12:28; Matt 8:26; 14:31; 16:8; 17:20). Oliveras, "Term ὀλιγόπιστος," 274–91, observes that the First Evangelist's use of the term ὀλιγοπιστία ("little faith") operates in three ways. First is a "rebuke" for disbelief and lack of trust in God's providence. Second, it is a way to expose inadequate memory, and third, it serves as a method to teach disciples. Even though Jesus rebukes the disciples, he remains an example of faith and its power for disciples.

55. Oliveras, "Term ὀλιγόπιστος," 277.

56. Luz, *Matthew 8–20*, 409.

57. Hagner, *Matthew 14–28*, 489.

In the following scene, only Matthew portrays Jesus paying taxes (Matt 17:24–27).[58] When asked by the tax collectors whether Jesus pays taxes, Peter answers affirmatively (17:24–25). Then Jesus asks Peter to pay the tax for both of them with funds Peter will find in a fish (17:27). In this Matthean pericope,[59] the First Evangelist holds human activity and transcendent power in balance as Jesus pays the temple tax through supernatural means.[60]

While questions remain regarding why Matthew adds this story, it is clear that this pericope presents Jesus as an exemplar with the readers in mind.[61] The addition of the tax-paying teacher suggests paying taxes is a topic of interest to Matthew and his readers.[62] Through Matthew's use of humanity, Jesus the tax-payer accomplishes several things for his audience. First, as a moral exemplar,[63] Jesus's actions remind the disciples of their obligation to society as he does with the reminder to give to Caesar what is his (Matt 22:21).[64] According to David E. Garland, "Matthew included this account to provide precise moral guidance on the question of the payment of this tax."[65] Second, as the exemplar for the Jewish Christian community, Jesus interacts with Peter to teach the readers why one pays taxes. In this case, avoiding unnecessary offense motivates Jesus to pay taxes for himself and Peter (17:27).[66] Third, Jesus makes clear that just as sons of

58. Keener, *Commentary*, 443, referencing Exodus, indicates Jewish men in the Roman Empire pay the two-drachma tax annually for maintaining the Jewish temple. According to Horbury, "Temple Tax," 272, the early Christians used this text to confirm the need to pay Roman taxes, an issue Jesus addresses later in Matthew (22:15–22).

59. For a survey on the background of this section, see Horbury, "Temple Tax," 265–86.

60. Garland, "Temple Tax," 73, classifies the coin in the fish's mouth as a miracle.

61. Hagner, *Matthew 14–28*, 510; Keener, *Commentary*, 444n132; Luz, *Matthew 8–20*, 415.

62. This passage raises the question whether this story concerns a Roman or temple tax. Luz, *Matthew 8–20*, 415–19, suggests that the passage deals with the difficulties the church encounters during the rule of Domitian with the *fiscus Iudaicus* ("Jewish funds"). While he rightly contends there is no way to discern the provenance of the story, the story points out the need for the church to pay taxes through the example of Jesus. Also see Carter, "Paying the Tax to Rome," 3–31. For arguments for temple tax, see Horbury, "Temple Tax," 265–86.

63. Horbury, "Temple Tax," 286, considers Jesus's act of paying the tax as a prime example of other apostolic teachings for early Christians. Carter, "Paying the Tax," 3, 27–29, argues the passage is a theological object lesson for his audience. He also suggests that the story emphasizes God's sovereignty over creation and the tax.

64. Keener, *Commentary*, 444.

65. Garland, "Temple Tax," 76.

66. Bauer, "σκανδαλίζω," BDAG, 926, classifies the term as "to shock through word or action."

earthly kings do not pay taxes, the sons of God are exempt from paying taxes imposed in God's name (Matt 17:25–26).[67] According to Garland, the "miracle confirms that Jesus is, as he implied in the analogy, God's Son, because God provides the money for him to pay God's tax."[68] Fourth, the human Jesus pays the tax through supernatural means.[69] Matthew portrays Jesus with the foreknowledge not only of the question Peter will ask but also of the first fish Peter catches having a shekel to pay the tax for both himself and Peter (17:25, 27).[70] Although he uses the human story of Jesus to demonstrate him as a moral exemplar, Matthew continues to tell a human story with a transcendent status.

In this section, as Matthew strengthens the transcendent status of Jesus, he retains the human story for his audience. Jesus is transfigured and the Father proclaims that Jesus is the Son of God with whom he is well pleased (Matt 17:1–6).[71] Jesus then returns to his human appearance (17:7–9). Maintaining the balance, Matthew's Jesus heals, teaches, pays taxes through miraculous means, and predicts his own suffering, death, and resurrection for a second time (17:10–27). As the story leads the reader toward Jesus's death, Matthew clearly holds the humanity intact as he continues to build Jesus's transcendence. The human role of Jesus in Matthew's narrative carries the story toward the human Son of God's death. In spite of the impending death, Luz points out that throughout the journey toward Jerusalem, Matthew's Jesus is the "teacher and exemplar."[72]

4.3 JOURNEY TO JERUSALEM (MATT 18:1—20:34)

After the third discourse (Matt 18:1–35), Matthew returns to the narrative with his customary phrase καὶ ἐγένετο ὅτε ἐτέλεσεν ὁ Ἰησοῦς τοὺς λόγους

67. Allison and Davies, *Matthew 8–18*, 745.

68. Garland, "Temple Tax," 94, refers to the analogy because Jesus presumes he is exempt from the tax (Matt 17:25–26).

69. Garland, *Reading Matthew*, 190. Luz, *Matthew 8–20*, 418n49 provides a list of popular tales that contain jewelry or coins being found in fish (Heroditus, *Hist.* 3.42; Strabo, *Geogr.* 14.1.16), yet the difference here is that Jesus predicts the coin being located in the fish's mouth.

70. Both Luz, *Matthew 8–20*, 419, and Hagner, *Matthew 14–28*, 512, refer to the shekel in the fish as a "miracle."

71. Luz, *Theology of the Gospel of Matthew*, 98–99. Also see, Kingsbury, *Matthew*, 67–69.

72. Luz, *Theology of the Gospel of Matthew*, 99. As Matthew sets up Jesus's journey to Jerusalem, he provides a fourth discourse (Matt 18:1–35), a discourse that reminds the readers of the priorities of being a Christ-follower.

τούτους ("and it happened when Jesus finished these sayings," 19:1).[73] This section depicts Jesus nearing Jerusalem. Largely replicating the Markan depiction of the story,[74] topics and events on the journey include divorce and celibacy (19:3–12), welcoming children (19:13–15), riches and rewards (19:16—20:16), a third passion prediction (20:17–19), Christian service (20:20–28), and healing two blind men outside of Jericho (20:29–34). In the midst of teaching, Jesus's journey to Jerusalem reflects Matthew's human christological interests.

While this section contains more teaching and dialogue, the portrayal of the human Jesus advances him as an archetype of humility, gentleness, and compassion.[75] After discussing celibacy and divorce (Matt 19:3–12), Matthew and Luke maintain yet condense Mark's depiction of Jesus blessing children (Matt 19:13–15 // Mark 10:13–16 // Luke 18:15–17). Children in the first-century experience love but possess no social power.[76] However, the reader can observe them as objects of Jesus's mercy.[77] In Matthew's story, children experience healing (Matt 9:18–25; 15:21–28), and with the depiction of feeding both the four and five thousand, only Matthew adds children as recipients of food.[78] In spite of their low social status and Jesus's transcendent status, Matthew uses the humanity of Jesus to demonstrate humility and gentleness by taking the time to lay his hands on the children as a blessing (19:15).[79] With his ministry to children, Jesus continues to model the act of extending fellowship to Jewish society's marginalized.[80]

After Jesus blesses children, he interacts with a young man (Matt 19:16–22 // Mark 10:17–22 // Luke 18:18–25). Although Matthew maintains the storyline, his portrayal of the interaction between Jesus and the young man deviates from his source.[81] Mark depicts Jesus asking and responding

73. Matt 7:28; 11:1; 13:53; 19:1; 26:1.

74. Davies and Allison, *Matthew 19–28*, 1.

75. Davies and Allison, *Matthew 19–28*, 36.

76. This is not only evidenced by the disciples' intervention in the children coming to Jesus but also the portrayal of the disciples speaking sternly not to the children but to those who brought them (Matt 19:13–14). For a study of children in early Christianity, see Bakke, *When Children Became People*; Barton, *Family in Theological Perspective*. For a study of the significant difference Christianity makes in the lives of children historically, socially, and culturally, see Horn and Martens, *"Let the Little Children Come."*

77. Davies and Allison, *Matthew 19–28*, 35. See Matt 9:18–26; 14:13–21; 15:21–39; 18:3; 19:13–15.

78. Matt 14:21 // Mark 6:44 // Luke 9:16 // John 6:10. Matt 15:38 // Mark 8:9.

79. Gen 48:14–18; Deut 34:9; Acts 8:17.

80. Matt 8:1–17; 12:18–21; 15:21–39; 19:13–14. Davies and Allison, *Matthew 8–18*, 36.

81. For the problems that Mark's text creates for interpreters, see Taylor, *Gospel*

to a question, "Why do you call me good? No one is good but God alone" (Mark 10:18 // Luke 18:19). Matthew's Jesus responds, "Why do you ask me about what is good? There is only one who is good" (Matt 19:17). Even though Mark's portrayal of the interaction presents a humble Jesus who will not claim qualities for himself that belong to God,[82] Matthew changes the interaction in a significant manner that once again uses the humanity of Jesus when transcendence can receive greater attention.[83]

Two alterations allow Matthew to keep the humanity of Jesus before the readers and restructure Jesus's interaction with the young ruler. First, Matthew omits Mark's description of how the young man approaches Jesus. Normally, Mark describes people falling before Jesus,[84] and in Matthew's narrative, it is normal for people to kneel before Jesus.[85] Mark portrays the young man γονθπετήσας ("knelt") before Jesus (Mark 10:17), and Matthew typically selects a different expression, προσκυνέω+αὐτῷ ("kneel before him"). A favorite expression Matthew omits here,[86] προσκυνέω ("kneel") communicates a gesture of paying homage or worship.[87] Heinrich Greeven defines προσκυνέω ("kneel") as a "visible majesty before which the worshiper bows."[88] Avoiding the preferred expression, Matthew alters the approach to a generic form of προσέρχομαι ("come," Matt 19:16 // Mark 10:17). Matthew understands a distinction between γονυπετέω ("kneel") and προσκυνέω ("kneel") as evidenced by his intentional application of προσκυνέω+αὐτῷ ("kneel before him") elsewhere.[89] Maintaining Jesus's human identity, Matthew ignores an opportunity to reinforce the majesty of Jesus's transcendent status so that he might depict more accurately the attitude of the young man.

According to St. Mark, 426–27.

82. Collins, Mark, 476.

83. Boer, "Rich Young Ruler," 15–18.

84. Mark 3:11; 5:22, 33; 7:25.

85. For example, Matthew changes the language in the scenes with the man with leprosy (Matt 8:2 // Mark 1:40 // Luke 5:12), the synagogue ruler (Matt 9:18 // Mark 5:22), and the Canaanite woman (Matt 15:25 // Mark 7:25) to forms of προσκυνέω+αὐτῷ ("kneel before him"). Regarding the example of the man with leprosy, Metzger, Textual Commentary, 76, rightly argues Matthew's changes to προσεκύνει ("knelt before") and Luke's πεσὼν ἐπὶ πρόσωπον ("fell on his face") suggest the originality of γονυπετῶν ("kneeling") in Mark's account.

86. Matt 2:11; 8:2; 9:18; 14:33; 15:25; 18:26; 28:9, 17. Mark 5:6; 15:19. Luke does not use this combination. Davies and Allison, Matthew 8–18, 10.

87. Heinrich Greeven, "προσκυνέω," TDNT 6:763.

88. Greeven, "προσκυνέω," TDNT 6:765.

89. Matt 2:11; 8:2; 9:18; 14:33; 15:25; 18:26; 28:9, 17. Luz, Matthew 1–7, 114.

Second, using the humanity of Jesus for his own purposes, Matthew drops the ἀγαθέ ("good") from Mark's description of Jesus as a διδάσκαλε ("teacher," Matt 19:16 // Mark 10:17 // Luke 18:18). Matthew's removal of the adjective makes it possible for him to shift the question and response in Mark's portrayal. Mark depicts Jesus asking the man, "Why do you call me good?" Matthew, because he removes the ἀγαθέ ("good"), can modify the question to "Why do you ask me about what is good?" (Matt 19:17 // Mark 10:18 // Luke 18:19). This enables a different response. Mark and Luke's Jesus respond, "No one is good but God alone," but Matthew's Jesus states: "There is only one who is good" (Matt 19:17 // Mark 10:18 // Luke 18:19). Because Jesus is plainly signifying God the Father as good in this context,[90] these observations raise the question, why does Matthew redact Mark and Luke's portrayal of Jesus's interaction with the young man?[91]

One of Matthew's christological interests is to portray Jesus as the Son of God, yet Matthew's version of the interaction between Jesus and the young man attempts to avoid the possible inference that God is good and Jesus is not.[92] Mark and Luke's response to the man's question, "No one is good but God alone" leaves the reader in a quandary regarding Jesus's status as the Son of God (Mark 10:18 // Luke 18:19). Matthew's redaction removes the possibility that Jesus admits sinfulness by not being good or hinting at his own deity.[93] Even though Harry R. Boer argues that the Christian community tended to protect the transcendent at the expense of the humanity of Jesus,[94] Matthew's preservation of the human story clarifies the distinction between Jesus as a human with transcendent status and God.

As Matthew edits Mark's portrayal, the First Evangelist takes a different approach with the pericope. Is it possible that Jesus rejects the young man's question by asking, "Why do you ask me about what is good?"[95] (Matt 19:17). Jesus's response recalls commandments from the Torah (19:18–20; Exod 20:12–16). It appears that the young man knows the commands because he claims to observe them (Matt 19:20). The young man not only knows that the commandments are good, but also that the one who proclaimed them is good, God himself.[96] This approach better explains Jesus's reply, "There is only one who is good" (19:17). By managing the narrative in

90. Viviano, "God in the Gospel," 347.

91. Boer, "Rich Young Ruler," 15–18, discusses the significance of this change.

92. Davies and Allison, *Matthew 19–28*, 42.

93. Blomberg, *Matthew*, 297.

94. Boer, "Rich Young Ruler," 16.

95. Luz, *Matthew 8–20*, 511.

96. Luz, *Matthew 8–20*, 511.

this manner, Matthew sustains a distinction between God and the humanity of Jesus. In a pericope where Matthew could have chosen to redact the narrative to strengthen the case for the transcendence of Jesus, he instead contrasts Jesus's identity with God.

Using the story of the young man to teach on the difficulties of entering the kingdom of heaven and future rewards for the disciples (Matt 19:23–30 // Mark 10:23–31), Matthew adds the parable of the laborers in the vineyard (20:1–16). As Matthew ends the parable, he places the humanity of Jesus before the reader to predict his death a third time (20:17–19). The third passion prediction contains changes that not only point to Jesus's human story but more specifically reflect the narrative to come in two ways.[97] First, Matthew adds the prediction to specify the way in which Jesus will be killed, by crucifixion (Matt 20:19 // Mark 10:34). Crucifixion is also considered a potential death scenario for Jesus's followers (Matt 23:34), and the disciples are to take up one's cross to follow him (10:38; 16:24). In the words of Luz, "With Jesus as their model, his disciples then and now have the courage to bear their own cross and hope for their own resurrection."[98] The moral exemplar will face exactly what he asks of his followers and readers. Second, in keeping with the kerygma of the early church (Acts 10:40; 1 Cor 15:4),[99] Matthew clarifies the language of the resurrection of Jesus shifting it from Mark's ἀναστήσεται ("he will rise," Mark 10:34) to ἐγερθήσεται ("he will be raised," Matt 20:19) to specify Jesus's dependence on God for the resurrection (28:1–10).

Matthew's addition of the crucifixion within the prediction effectively increases the understanding of the role Jesus's suffering and death plays in the narrative for the disciples. In light of Jesus's impending death in Jerusalem, curiosity concerning position and prominence in the kingdom becomes a focus for the disciples. The desire for prominence and position juxtaposes Jesus's predictions of humility and suffering.[100] Although Matthew changes the originator of the question of position in the kingdom from James and John to their mother (Matt 20:20–21 // Mark 10:35–36), in both Matthew and Mark, the exemplar challenges them with the question, "Are

---

97. Davies and Allison, *Matthew 19–28*, 81, suggest that Matthew's portrayal brought the "prophecy and the events" described closer together using the shift from Mark's "after three days he will rise" to Matthew's "he will be raised on the third day" as the primary example (Matt 20:19 // Mark 10:34). France, *Gospel of Matthew*, 753, notes that the reader, familiar with the story, will recognize the accuracy of the prediction.

98. Luz, *Studies in Matthew*, 375.

99. Hagner, *Matthew 14–28*, 574, 576. See argument above in ch. 4, n27.

100. Turner, *Matthew*, 485.

you able to drink the cup I am to drink?" (Matt 20:22 // Mark 10:38). A question in and of itself that emphasizes Jesus as the exemplar.

As a common OT metaphor, the cup represents suffering.[101] Jesus predicts he will endure being mocked, scourged, and crucified (Matt 20:19). A call of the disciples is to endure what Christ endured (16:24; 20:23). Later, the reader will observe Jesus in the Garden of Gethsemane requesting that this cup of suffering be passed from him (26:39–44). Even as the human Jesus does not want to partake in the suffering, he epitomizes what it means to obey the Father's will. Again, Matthew uses the humanity of Jesus to identify with the disciples and their suffering. Just as Jesus will drink the cup of suffering, he indicates that the disciples will suffer (20:19, 23). This christological section demonstrates that his human life, suffering, and death matter.[102]

Immediately after the third prediction, Jesus is asked who will sit at his right and left in the kingdom. In response, he informs the reader of his intent to give his life as a ransom for many (Matt 20:28). While Jesus specifies the decision of who sits where is not his to make, Matthew alters Mark's depiction of the response to clarify the choice belongs specifically to μου πατρός ("my father," Matt 20:23 // Mark 10:40). The Jesus of Matthew specifies it is his Father who grants the decision for who will sit beside him. Again, Matthew clarifies that Jesus is not solely transcendent and confirms a distinction between Jesus and the Father because Jesus is the one who gives his life as a ransom for many (Matt 20:28 // Mark 10:45).[103]

While the idea that one individual's death can universally serve to atone for others may seem far-fetched,[104] Joachim Jeremias effectively argues that the idea has its roots in the Suffering Servant passage of Isaiah (Isa 52:13—53:12).[105] Matthew's Jesus recognizes that his role includes being a servant and a human sacrifice (Matt 20:28; 26:28). Providing a pattern to follow, the Matthean narrative inspires the readers to imitate Christ's giving of himself for others,[106] an attitude to which the followers should orient themselves.[107]

---

101. See Matt 26:37–39; John 18:11; Ps 11:6; Jer 25:15–17; 51:7; Ezek 23:31–34; Hab 2:16; Zech 12:2.

102. Davies and Allison, *Matthew 19–28*, 101.

103. For a discussion on the authenticity of the ransom logion, see Page, "Authenticity," 1:137–62.

104. See Barrett, "Background of Mark 10:45," 1–18; Hooker, *Jesus and the Servant*, 92–97.

105. Jeremias, "Das Lösegeld für Viele," 216–29.

106. France, *Gospel of Matthew*, 761.

107. Luz, *Matthew 8–20*, 546.

After portraying Jesus as the one who will give his life as a ransom (Matt 20:28), Jesus leaves Jericho to continue his journey toward Jerusalem. Two blind men sit by the roadside crying out to him twice (20:29–30).[108] With the first cry, the blind men ask for mercy from the Son of David (20:30). Once again, Son of David serves as a title for the human Jesus.[109] In the second cry to Jesus from the blind men, Matthew adds the vocative κύριε ("Lord," Matt 20:33 // Mark 10:51). The use of κύριος ("Lord") acknowledges that Jesus heals with divine authority.[110] Combining Lord and Son of David in the cries of the blind men holds these two titles of the identity of Jesus in balance. Luz rightly concludes, "Our text thus becomes, as it were, in the form of language the husk of the meeting with the one who is true God and at the same time is human."[111] As we continue to see, Matthew's Jesus is human and transcendent.[112]

The emphasis of a human and transcendent identity is even more pronounced in light of Matthew's alterations at the conclusion of the pericope. In this pericope, the crowds rebuke the blind men and tell them to be silent (Matt 20:31 // Mark 10:48 // Luke 18:39). Again, using the humanity of Jesus for his own theological interests, only Matthew adds σπλαγχνισθεὶς δὲ ὁ Ἰησοῦς ἥψατο τῶν ὀμμάτων αὐτῶν ("and Jesus, moved with pity, touched their eyes," Matt 20:34 // Mark 10:52 // Luke 18:42).[113] Contrasting the crowd's lack of compassion, Matthew's addition of σπλαγχνίζομαι ("pity") uses the crowd as a foil to sharpen the recognition that Jesus models benevolence to the begging blind men,[114] especially in light of the previous declaration that the Son of Man is here to serve (20:28). Matthew's addition stresses Jesus as the archetype not only responding to the faith of the blind beggars but also acting in compassion and healing them (20:34).

Throughout this section, Matthew continues to use the human journey of Jesus to accomplish his christological purposes. Matthew uses the

108. The difficulties with this pericope are numerous. Arguing this scene as a doublet serves as a forensic approach to bear witness that Jesus is the Son of David. See Loader, "Son of David," 570–85.

109. See Strecker, Der Weg der Gerechtigkeit, 118–20; Hummel, Die Auseinandersetzung, 116–22.

110. Kingsbury, Matthew, 113.

111. Luz, Matthew 8–20, 550.

112. Kingsbury, Matthew, 110.

113. Voorwinde, Jesus' Emotions, 42, argues that compassion is the "major emotion" Matthew attributes to Jesus. Even though the σπλαγχνίζομαι ("pity" or "compassion") of Christ is an emotion Jesus expresses in Matthew's portrayal (Matt 9:36; 14:14; 15:32), each of these examples parallels Mark's narrative. The example here reinforces that Matthew uses the emotions of Jesus for his own theological and storytelling purposes.

114. Voorwinde, Jesus' Emotions, 40.

human story of Jesus to demonstrate Jesus as the exemplar. Matthew's Jesus blesses children (Matt 19:13–15), exemplifies service (19:16—20:28), and demonstrates compassion to those the crowds try to silence (20:29–34). In addition, we see Matthew maintaining the humanity of Jesus even when given the opportunity to enhance Jesus's transcendent status through the interaction with the young ruler (19:16–22). As Jesus prepares to enter Jerusalem, he confesses his purpose is to give his life for others (20:28), a purpose that Matthew makes possible through the physical death of his human main character.

4.4 JESUS IN CONFLICT IN JERUSALEM (MATT 21:1— 25:46)

Jesus's journey toward Jerusalem is ending and his death in Jerusalem looms as Matthew provides details of the last week of Jesus's human existence. It will become clear that he allows the secret of Jesus's identity to become known in Jerusalem.[115] Even though Matthew follows much of Mark's storyline, his alterations to it not only reinforce and refine the expressions of Jesus's humanity but also heighten the religious leaders' awareness of his transcendent status.

As Matthew's Jesus draws near to Jerusalem with his disciples, the role the humanity of Jesus plays in the triumphal entry could be overlooked. Only Matthew's crowd connects Jesus as a descendant of David with shouts of "Son of David" as Jesus enters Jerusalem.[116] There are preparations (Matt 21:1–5), the triumphal entry (21:6–9), and the response of the crowds (21:10–11)[117] before entering the temple in Jerusalem (21:12). Through foreknowledge, Jesus sends two disciples to retrieve an ass and a colt (21:2–6),[118] but only Matthew uses the human activity of Jesus to clarify for the reader that the ride into Jerusalem on a donkey fulfills a prophecy (21:4–5; Zech 9:9). In their messianic expectations, a promised descendant of David will establish the promised kingdom,[119] yet as the narrative moves

115. Kingsbury, *Matthew as Story*, 80–93.

116. Matt 21:9 // Mark 11:9–10 // Luke 19:38 // John 12:14. Son of David connects to Jesus's human genealogy. See ch. 2, n5 above.

117. Turner, *Matthew*, 493.

118. Luz, *Matthew 21–28*, 7. Matthew redacts the number of animals Jesus asks the disciples to retrieve (Matt 21:2 // Mark 11:2 // Luke 19:30). For a summary of the views explaining the alteration, see Davies and Allison, *Matthew 19–28*, 120–21. For a more complete discussion of Matthew's number of animals, see Instone-Brewer, "Two Asses," 87–98.

119. Matt 23:39; Ps 118:25; b. Pesah. 119a; Midr. Ps. 118:24. Hagner, *Matthew*

toward the cross, the accurate but incomplete perception for the crowd and religious leaders of the identity of Jesus develops clarity within the narrative.

The readers of the Gospel can also observe that the Son of David heals people,[120] yet there is something more for the reader to consider. Previously in the narrative, Jesus charges two blind men and the disciples to keep his messianic identity a secret (Matt 9:30; 16:20). With Jesus's triumphal entry, the messianic secret is no more.[121] In Jerusalem, Jesus affirms, not only his identity as the Son of David who is a prophet from Nazareth, but also the narrative will portray Jesus's affirmation that he is the Son of God to those other than his disciples (21:33–44; 26:63–64; 27:54).[122] The identity comes into focus so the author can uphold the balance between the humanity and transcendence of Jesus. As his identity becomes more public, the readers further comprehend the growing conflict between Jesus and the religious leaders.[123]

As the crowd's prophet, who is the Son of David, enters the temple of God, Matthew's portrayal of the temple tantrum holds the human and transcendent identity of Jesus in balance. First, we see the human emotions of Jesus (Matt 21:12). Allison correctly suggests that even though there is no explicit comment on Jesus's anger,[124] it is difficult to imagine a situation where tables are overturned and people are driven out of the temple without Jesus expressing some level of anger. At this scene of Jesus's expression of this emotion, only Matthew adds Jesus's transcendent power as he heals the blind and lame who approach him in the temple (Matt 21:14 // Mark 11:17 // Luke 19:46). While this is the last healing account in Matthew, it serves the purpose of presenting the picture of Jesus's identity especially in light of the children's response that follows.

Adding the children's response, only Matthew portrays Jesus being praised by children and his acknowledgement and reception of worship (Matt 21:16–17). The placement of the partial quote of an LXX Psalm directs the reader to a praise applied to God that children now apply to Jesus (Ps 8:3).[125] Jesus's time in the temple allows the readers to observe an emo-

---

14–28, 596.

120. Matt 9:27–30; 12:22–24; 15:22–28; 20:30–34.

121. France, *Gospel of Matthew*, 774.

122. Dunn, *Jesus Remembered*, 1:660–64, develops the argument that Jesus considers himself a prophet (Matt 13:57). In addition, through the Jesus tradition, it is remembered that Jesus practices both prophetic insight and foresight (20:23; 24:2; 26:12, 29, 34).

123. Matt 21:14–17, 23–46; 22:15—23:36; 26:1–5.

124. Allison, *Studies in Matthew*, 246.

125. Luz, *Matthew 21–28*, 14.

tional Jesus respond to misuse of the temple one moment and then receive praise from children the next. While each Synoptic portrays the emotions and reactions of Jesus in the temple due to its misuse (Matt 21:12 // Mark 11:15 // Luke 19:45), only Matthew adds healing and receiving the praise of children. Instead of removing the human element of Jesus's temple tantrum in favor of his transcendence, Matthew maintains the humanity of Jesus.

The morning following the temple tantrum, Jesus states he is hungry (Matt 21:18 // Mark 11:12). Earlier in the narrative, Jesus eats with tax collectors, sinners, and the disciples.[126] The human Jesus needs food, yet Matthew turns Jesus's hunger into an opportunity to remind the reader of the power available by faith through the example of Jesus's cursing of the fig tree (21:18–19).

Although the disciples marvel at the immediate withering of the fig tree (Matt 21:20), Jesus indicates that with a doubtless faith, the disciples can not only do what has been done to the fig tree but also their faith can move mountains (21:21–22). Matthew's Jesus possesses power through the work of the Spirit (12:17–21, 28), but his example leads to discussions on faith.[127] Matthew's preservation of the human portrayal includes establishing what a human can do through faith. This pericope sets up the lack of faith expressed by the religious leaders in Jerusalem which prompts three parables exploring Jesus's source of authority (21:28—22:14).[128]

After instructing the disciples on the concept of faith again,[129] Jesus returns to the temple to teach (Matt 21:23). The chief priests and elders approach Jesus in order to trap him by attempting to trick him into revealing the source of his authority (21:24–27).[130] Matthew's Jesus uses three parables to respond to the religious leaders' question regarding Jesus's authority.[131] While each parable severely critiques Jewish leadership of the day,[132] the parable of the wicked tenants most clearly links the parable and Israel's historical rejection of the prophets and the Son of God (21:33–44).[133] While

---

126. Matt 9:11; 11:19; 26:20–21, 26–29.

127. Matt 8:26; 14:31; 16:8; 17:20; 21:21–22.

128. Hagner, *Matthew 14–28*, 608.

129. Matt 8:26; 14:31; 16:8; 17:20; 21:21–22.

130. According to Keener, *Commentary,* 506, it is clear throughout the narrative that the source is God. Matthew depicts this at the birth (Matt 1:23), the baptism (3:17), the temptation (4:1–11), Peter's confession (16:16), and transfiguration (17:5) narratives.

131. The parable of the two sons (Matt 21:28–32), the wicked husbandmen (21:33–46), and the great supper (22:1–14) draw this out for the reader.

132. Keener, *Commentary,* 507.

133. Hagner, *Matthew 14–28*, 624.

the message is implied,[134] the priests and the Pharisees who understand the parable can grasp the implication that Jesus calls himself the Son of God through the parable (21:37–38, 45–46).[135] However, only Matthew holds the crowd's perception that Jesus is a prophet.[136] Matthew's reinforcement of the perception of Jesus's status as a prophet and Son of God maintains the balance between the human and transcendent identity.

After the parables, the religious leaders and Jesus ask questions that challenge one another (Matt 22:15–46). Jesus effectively answers three questions designed to defeat him (22:15–40), and then he poses questions of his own that lead to stumping the religious leaders (22:41–46). Matthew's Jesus asks, "What do you think of the Christ?" and "Whose son is he?" (22:42). Only Matthew provides the Pharisee's answer that the Christ is the Son of David and points out that the Pharisees consider the Christ a son, implying a human descendant of David (22:42).

Jesus asks the Pharisees a follow-up question, "If David thus calls him Lord, how is he his son?" (Matt 22:45 // Mark 12:37). The readers of Matthew's Gospel know Jesus is a human descendant of David (Matt 1:1–17), yet a transcendent descendant of God (1:18–25).[137] In other words, Jesus is David's son because of human lineage, but more mysteriously, Jesus is David's Lord because he is God's Son. The Pharisees have little to no chance of answering the question, but the readers know how this is possible through Matthew's portrayal of the life of Jesus.[138]

While the question is difficult for the Pharisees to answer, the readers of the entire story can observe Matthew's developing argument that Jesus is more than the human Son of David. He is also the transcendent Lord of David because his identity includes Son of God.[139] Describing this pericope Luz says that "[w]hile he is human, he is not only and not primarily human."[140] Even though Peter and the disciples understand that Jesus is the Christ, the Son of the Living God (Matt 16:16), the public identity question begins to build again. The question builds and develops in the public arena

---

134. France, *Gospel of Matthew*, 811.

135. Kingsbury, *Matthew as Story*, 93; Luz, *Matthew 21–28*, 43.

136. Matt 21:11 // Mark 11:11 // Luke 19:45. Matt 21:46 // Mark 12:12 // Luke 20:19.

137. Luz, *Matthew 21–28*, 89.

138. Turner, *Matthew*, 541.

139. Acts portrays Peter assuring Israel that God made Jesus "Lord and Messiah" (Acts 2:36). Keener, *Commentary*, 532–33, points out that the use of the term "Lord" is ambiguous enough to avoid betraying monotheism, yet makes the point that this "Lord" is someone greater than David. Luz, *Matthew 21–28*, 90.

140. Luz, *Matthew 21–28*, 91.

until it culminates a second time when the high priest asks Jesus if he is the Christ, the Son of God (26:63–64).[141]

Only Matthew points out that the Pharisees are unable to answer the question (Matt 22:46 // Mark 12:37 // Luke 20:44). This sets up the story of Jesus's interaction with the chief priest and the council later in the narrative (Matt 26:57–68). This council seeks to question whether Jesus considers himself the Christ, the Son of God. The Pharisees have not confronted the mysterious possibility that a human being could also be uniquely the Son of God, which is evidenced by their inability to answer the question.[142] Using this question and lack of response by the Pharisees reinforces the development of Matthew's narrative to explain and intensify the balance between the human and transcendent identity of Jesus.

After Jesus silences the Pharisees,[143] Matthew presents Jesus's final discourse (Matt 23:1—25:46). Maintaining Mark's storyline, Matthew expands Mark's short warning to the crowds regarding the need to be aware of the religious leaders and turns it into a harsh and lengthy condemnation of the scribes and Pharisees (Matt 23:1–36 // Mark 12:37b–40).[144] Due to its harshness, this woe section raises questions regarding the use of the humanity of Jesus in Matthew's Gospel, especially in light of Jesus's Sermon on the Mount teaching on anger and derogatory name calling.[145] Since Jesus is Matthew's archetype, one may wonder why the number of times Jesus calls the scribes and Pharisees hypocrites, blind fools, brood of vipers, and blind guides increases (Matt 23:1–36).

While these names are unsettling, the negative term used most to describe the Pharisees is ὑποκριτής ("hypocrite").[146] The term ὑποκριτής ("hypocrite") is the failure of deeds to match words.[147] For Matthew, hypocrites seek human recognition rather than divine approval (Matt 6:2, 5, 16).[148] Jesus calls out the Pharisee and tells the crowds and the disciples, "[D]o not

141. Only Matthew phrases the question of Jesus's identity this way (Matt 26:63 // Mark 14:61 // Luke 22:67). As will be seen below, Matthew later addresses the identity question by changing Jesus's response from Mark's ἐγώ εἰμι ("I am") to σὺ εἶπας ("you have said so," Matt 22:64 // Mark 14:62).

142. Hagner, *Matthew 14–28*, 651.

143. Keener, *Commentary*, 534.

144. Luke's Gospel contains six of the seven woes depicted in Matthew (Luke 11:39–52). For further discussion, see Newport, *Sources*.

145. Luz, *Theology of the Gospel of Matthew*, 124.

146. Matt 22:18; 23:13, 15, 23, 25, 27, 29.

147. Luz, *Theology of the Gospel of Matthew*, 122. Bauer, "ὑποκριτής," BDAG, 1038, translates the term as "pretender, dissembler."

148. Turner, *Matthew*, 554.

do as they do, for they do not practice what they preach" (23:3). The Pharisees are examples of how not to behave.[149] Why would Matthew portray his
exemplar in a manner that fails to connect word and deed at this point of
the story? Even though Luz observes Jesus's exemplar status elsewhere,[150] he
reasonably questions the consistency of Jesus's words and deeds in light of
the Sermon on the Mount.[151] How can Matthew maintain Jesus's exemplar
status in light of a tirade in which he calls the Pharisees hypocrites? If Jesus's
actions contradict, then Matthew betrays the high ethical nature of his main
character from a narrative critical perspective.

Within the Sermon on the Mount and Matthew's Gospel, the heart
matters.[152] Is it possible that in the context of the *Sitz im Leben* the words
Matthew portrays Jesus speaking neither contradict loving one's enemy nor
incorrectly apply the word ὑποκριτής ("hypocrite")? Is it possible that Matthew's Jesus accurately describes the hypocritical character of the Pharisees?
If Jesus speaks the truth, then is Matthew's Jesus actually a hypocrite and
failure as an exemplar in this moment from a narrative critical perspective?

In light of the readers' *Sitz im Leben*, the answer is "no" for three primary reasons. First, while some shudder at Jesus calling the Pharisees and
scribes seemingly derogatory names,[153] the rebuke of hypocrisy reflects not
only Matthew's source material (Mark 7:6), but also the Second Temple
period rebuke literature reflecting conventional accusations of the time.[154]
They reflect normal verbal conflict during the time of Christ that portrays
the intense struggle between the followers of Jesus, the scribes, and the
Pharisees after 70 CE.[155] Second, Luke T. Johnson indicates that the rhetoric
in this discourse reflects the Jewish polemic,[156] and, according to Steven

149. Allison, *Studies in Matthew*, 153.

150. Luz, *Matthew 21–28*, 419, considers Jesus a moral model especially in the Garden as he does not resist the evil doer to demonstrate that pacifism should prevail (Matt
5:39; 26:50–56).

151. Luz, *Theology of the Gospel of Matthew*, 124.

152. Matt 5:8, 28; 9:4; 12:34; 13:15; 15:8; 18:35; 22:37. Jesus indicates that the mouth
speaks what is in the heart (12:34). Lawful outward behavior does not necessarily indicate that the heart is with the Lord (7:22–23; 12:34; 15:7–9, 19; 18:35; 22:37; 24:12).

153. Luz, *Theology of the Gospel of Matthew*, 123, Hagner, *Matthew 14–28*, 673, and
Davies and Allison, *Matthew 19–28*, 260–61, suggest that categorizing all of the Pharisees and scribes as hypocrites is unjust.

154. Garland, *Intention of Matthew 23*, 91–123. Sir 1:29; 32:15. Saldarini, "Delegitimization of Leaders," 659–80 (659). Davies and Allison, *Matthew 19–28*, 260.

155. Saldarini, "Delegitimization of Leaders," 659. Cohen, *From the Maccabees*, 150;
Saldarini, *Matthew's Christian-Jewish Community*, 44–47; Overman, *Church and Community*, 13–16.

156. See Johnson, "New Testament's Anti-Jewish Slander," 419–44. He provides

Saldarini, even though the "rhetoric is harsh, the argument is Jewish and serious."[157] The setting is that Jesus lives as a Jew in a Jewish context,[158] and Matthew's Jesus would possess awareness of the rhetoric of the period. Just as Jesus uses language and examples people recognize in parables and teaching, the Jewish Christian readers could understand Jesus's argument as the language of the day. Third, the rhetoric is a warning. The Jewish community needs to heed the message of Jesus or face judgment just as the religious leaders will face it according to the story (Matt 23:1–39).[159] If there is an obligation to love others (5:44; 22:39), there is also an obligation to save them even if it means offending them when necessary (15:12–14; 18:17).[160] Therefore, Matthew's portrayal of Jesus, using the rhetoric of his time, reaches the crowds, both present and the ones reading the text. For the readers, there is no disconnect between Matthew's Sermon on the Mount and Woe Discourse. The Matthean Jesus maintains his status as the moral model even in the woe pronouncements because the Jewish Christian community reading this passage would not consider the words of Jesus an affront.

The woes pronounced by Jesus reflect the prophetic nature of impending judgment both in the OT and NT.[161] Jesus reserves the judgment pronouncements for the Pharisees and scribes (Matt 23:1–36), yet the following pericope predicts judgment on all of Israel in Jesus's Jerusalem lament. The people will face judgment if they follow the religious leaders (23:37–39).[162] This section is apocalyptic in nature, and Matthew's Christology maintains the humanity of Jesus in light of the developing clarity that Jesus is both human and transcendent.

Two aspects of this section of the fourth discourse reinforce the developing clarity of Jesus's dual identity (Matt 24:1–51). First, Matthew alters the description of the false christs and prophets (Matt 24:23–24 // Mark 13:21–22). While both Matthew and Mark indicate false christs and false prophets will demonstrate signs and wonders, Matthew adds μεγάλα ("great") to the description.[163] He has already broached the subject of evildoers

---

examples from Josephus (*Ag. Ap.* 2.6 §68; 2.14 §148; 1.11 §59). Garland, *Intention of Matthew 23*, 92.

157. Saldarini, "Delegitimization of Leaders in Matthew 23," 680.

158. See ch. 1, n2 above.

159. Newport, *Sources*, 70.

160. Allison, *Studies in Matthew*, 249.

161. Isa 3:11; 5:8, 11, 18, 20–22; 10:5; 29:1; 31:1; Jer 48:1, 46; Amos 5:18; 6:1; Hab 2:6, 9, 12, 15, 19; Zeph 2:5; 3:1; Zech 11:17; Jude 11; Rev 8:13.

162. Luz, *Studies in Matthew*, 52.

163. Scripture provides examples of the miraculous being counterfeited. See Exod 7:11–12, 22; Acts 8:9–11; 2 Thess 2:9; Rev 13:13–14; 16:14.

accomplishing δυνάμεις πολλὰς ("many deeds of power")[164] in the Sermon on the Mount (Matt 7:21–23). The narrative reinforces that Matthew's Jesus is capable of a δύναμις ("deed of power" or "miracle," 11:20–23; 13:54; 13:58), not only by Matthew's use of the term δύναμις ("deed of power") but also through the numerous miraculous deeds depicted in the Gospel. Matthew's Jesus teaches that other human beings can perform a δύναμις ("deed of power") within the first, second, and fifth discourses (7:21–23; 10:1, 8; 24:24). Both the true Christ and true prophet and the false messiahs and false prophets can use their deeds and wonders to influence people (4:23–25; 24:23–24). Matthew's human Jesus does not have to be transcendent in order to accomplish a δύναμις ("deed of power"). The possibility of false christs and false prophets leads Matthew to use the humanity of Jesus to demonstrate comparatively that he is a true prophet and the real Messiah.

The second way Matthew preserves the human identity in this discourse is his willingness to maintain Mark's description of Jesus's lack of knowledge (Matt 24:36 // Mark 13:32),[165] an aspect Luke removes from his narrative (Luke 21:33–34).[166] Here, in Matthew's portrayal, Jesus admits that only the Father knows the day and hour of the Son of Man's return. Mark Goodacre observes that Matthew and Luke reluctantly retain accounts that limit Jesus's power.[167] One example includes Matthew and Luke removing a scene where Jesus fails to heal a blind man on his initial attempt (Mark 8:22–25). Another opportunity arises in this pericope for Matthew to remove a limitation for Jesus,[168] his knowledge. Unlike Luke, Matthew reinforces the limitation by adding that μόνος ("only") the Father knew the day and the hour.[169] Even though Matthew has the opportunity

164. Bauer, "δύναμις," BDAG, 263, classifies this term as "a deed that exhibits ability to function powerfully."

165. Vermes, *Religion of Jesus*, 160, shows that this is an authentic statement of Jesus as a "Jewish saying with a Christian ending." While this affirmation suggests that Jesus considers himself the Son of God, it also implies that Matthew willingly maintains the limitations of Jesus as part of his narrative.

166. Other possible passages suggest Jesus's lack of knowledge (Matt 13:51–52; 14:12–13; 27:34, 46). For a fuller discussion, see Brown, "How Much Did Jesus Know," 315–45.

167. Only Mark's Jesus desires to leave the crowd in case they θλίβωσιν ("might crush") him (Matt 12:15–16 // Mark 3:9 // Luke 6:17–19). Goodacre, "Criticizing the Criterion," 167, states: "Matthew's and Luke's reluctance to relate Markan material that limits Jesus's power illustrates the possibility that the same kind of thing happened in the earliest decades."

168. Davies and Allison, *Matthew 19–28*, 377, indicate this passage suggests a "real limitation" to Jesus's knowledge.

169. While a textual criticism issue exists here, Metzger, *Textual Commentary*, 62, correctly suggests that εἰ μή ὁ πατὴρ μόνος ("but the father only") is the original phrase

to remove Jesus's lack of foreknowledge, he chooses to retain his source material and reinforce the distinction between Jesus and the Father. Raymond Brown points out the remarkable nature of Jesus's admission by stating, "It is curious that the very passage that speaks of Jesus absolutely as the Son of God is the most famous passage in the Gospels for indicating that [Jesus's] knowledge was limited."[170] As another passage that can cause us to consider Jesus's "genuine humanity,"[171] the question is why Matthew retains language that limits Jesus's knowledge?

First, Matthew embraces the humanity of Jesus to tell his story.[172] As Brown points out, retaining Jesus's lack of knowledge effectively connects the transcendent vertical and human horizontal aspects of Jesus's identity. Second, Matthew's choice to maintain Jesus's lack of knowledge fits well with the development of not only Jesus's lack of knowledge in the narrative,[173] but also his interest in the humanity of his main character. This interest fits well with other first-century writings regarding Jesus's human limitations written from a Hebrew perspective (Phil 2:6–8; Heb 2:18; 4:15).[174] Third, omniscience is not a condition of Matthew's Christology.[175] Luke removes Jesus's explicit unawareness, but Matthew's interest in the humanity of Jesus influences his portrayal in a different way. It is an imperfect, but adequate way to describe Matthew's view of Jesus's transcendent status in light of his

---

composed by Matthew. Gundry, *Matthew*, 492, states: "Theologically, we may say that just as Jesus did not exercise his omnipotence except to further the kingdom (cf. his refusal to make stones into bread), so he did not exercise his omniscience except to further the kingdom . . . The incarnation did not destroy divine potencies, but it did limit actualities." While it does limit, could the limit have to do more with Jesus's reliance on the Holy Spirit rather than Jesus having access to "omni" powers and not using them (Matt 12:15–21, 28)? Matthew's interests in the humanity of Jesus suggests the former.

170. Brown, "How Much Did Jesus Know," 338.

171. Turner, *Matthew*, 589.

172. Hagner, *Matthew 14–28*, 716.

173. Matt 13:51–52; 14:12–13; 24:36; 27:34, 46.

174. Sim, *Gospel of Matthew*, 188–213, argues that theological conflict exists not only between Matthean and Pauline theology but also Matthean and Pauline Christianity. If that is the case, Matthew had access to Pauline thought, making it reasonable for him to retain Jesus's knowledge limitations. Silva, *Philippians*, 92–93, considers the importance of whether the poem in Philippians is originally Paul's or an early church doctrine. See the seminal work of Lohmeyer, *Kyrios Jesus*, as he discusses the passage to be an early hymn with which early believers are familiar. Whether it is a hymn or poem, based on the evidence above, it is reasonable to postulate that Matthew is aware of this and other thinking that demonstrates an understanding that Jesus is transcendent in status but practically human (Heb 2:18; 4:15). Matthew balances and attempts to develop Jesus's dual identity throughout the story. For a fuller discussion of the multiple views on the status of this hymn, see Martin, *Hymn of Christ*.

175. Hagner, *Matthew 14–28*, 716.

human existence. Fourth, understood pedagogically, the humanity of Jesus serves as an example that if Jesus remains faithful without all knowledge, then the disciples and the Jewish Christian community can also follow God's will.[176] Matthean Christology intentionally prioritizes Jesus's human identity to present an adequate understanding of his transcendent status in the midst of a human depiction.

Before Matthew describes the end of Jesus's human life, he finishes the fifth and final discourse with a section unique to Matthew that brings the eschatological discourse to its pinnacle (Matt 25:31–46).[177] The readers may assume that Matthew's intent is to establish Jesus's transcendence once and for all with this final section, but Davies and Allison provide evidence that the motif of a "human being" serving as judge in an eschatological context exists in Jewish texts elsewhere.[178] For example, the Testament of Abraham envisions a "man" sitting on a heavenly throne to "judge all creation" (T. Ab. 12:4—13:4). Another example, the OT figure Melchizedek in the Qumran Scrolls will "carry out the vengeance of God's judgments" (11QMelch 2:13).[179] In Baruch, God's Messiah will call all nations in judgment, some to spare and some to remove (2 Bar. 72:2–6). This final parable not only speaks to the identity of Jesus, it also illustrates the earthly preparation, watchfulness, and faithfulness necessary for the reader to meet the Son of Man in judgment.[180]

Jesus's conflict in Jerusalem assists the readers to recall the reasons he experiences difficulty with the religious authorities in preparation for Jesus's death. Jesus's entrance into Jerusalem as a Messianic figure fulfills another OT prophecy (Zech 9:9; Matt 21:4–5), but the roars of the crowd and Jesus's temple tantrum rouse suspicion (21:12–17). In the midst of the surrounding conflict, Jesus teaches about the power of faith (21:18–22), condemns hypocrisy (23:1–36), predicts the future in spite of his limitations (24:1–44), and identifies what needs to be considered in preparation for the return of the Son of Man (24:42—25:46). Continuing to portray Jesus as the exemplar who lives what he teaches, Matthew depicts Jesus as the one who, even though he knows he will be crucified, resolutely journeys into Jerusalem in accordance with his Father's will. However, while in Jerusalem, Matthew's

176. Luz, *Matthew 21–28*, 213–14, briefly overviews the history of interpretation and comments that it is not until the modern period that a positive meaning of this passage develops.

177. Davies and Allison, *Matthew 19–28*, 416.

178. Davies and Allison, *Matthew 19–28*, 421.

179. Davies and Allison, *Matthew 19–28*, 421n23, indicate that the Melchizedek figure may have been an angelic being.

180. France, *Gospel of Matthew*, 957.

portrayal of Jesus solidifies the balance between the transcendent status of Jesus with the practicality of his humanity. In spite of Jesus's humility (21:4–6), anger (21:12–13; 23), hunger (21:28), and ignorance (24:36), Matthew shifts Jesus's self-disclosure to include his transcendent position as the Son of God publicly (21:28–46; 22:41–45).[181] Even though Matthew follows much of Mark's progression, the importance of Matthew's maintenance of the human story becomes even more apparent as he does so in contrast to the public's growing awareness of his claims to a transcendent status which will contribute to his death.

4.5 PREPARING FOR A HUMAN DEATH (MATT 26:1–35)

As Matthew provides a final prediction of Jesus's crucifixion (Matt 26:2), Matthew has already communicated events that will lead to the cross. Matthew's narrative methodically guides the reader through the teachings and life of Jesus, explaining his ministry and mission. As he does, he maintains Jesus's dual identity all the while preparing the reader for his suffering, death, and resurrection. This section clearly reminds the reader of Jesus's human existence.

After Matthew's Jesus completes his eschatological discourse (Matt 24:1–25:46), the narrative shifts to fulfilling Jesus's predictions, the crucifixion of the Son of Man (26:2). With the confirmation that all four predictions are set in motion,[182] Matthew depicts the scenario for the plot to arrest and kill Jesus. The scenario includes the chief priests and elders while they are in the palace of Caiaphas, the high priest (26:3–5).

Leaving the house of Caiaphas, the readers are taken to Bethany and into the house of Simon the Leper (Matt 26:6). There, a woman anoints Jesus with expensive oil (26:7). The disciples are indignant at the waste of this costly act, yet Matthew adds Jesus's awareness of their anger (26:8–10).[183] Responding, Jesus makes clear not only the beauty of her act but also the reality that the oil prepares him for his burial (26:10–12). While Jesus knows he will die and be buried, both reflect Matthew's christological interest in Jesus's human story.

After the episode at Simon's house in Bethany, part of the plot to arrest Jesus comes from within the ranks of his disciples. Judas Iscariot approaches the chief priests and agrees to betray Jesus for thirty pieces of silver (Matt 26:14–16). As a detail only provided by Matthew, again, the human

181. Kingsbury, *Matthew as Story*, 80–93.
182. Matt 16:21–23; 17:22–23; 20:17–19; 26:1–2.
183. See ch. 3.1.2 above for Matthew's use of γινώσκω ("know").

story serves as another means to demonstrate the fulfillment of Zechariah's prophecy (Zech 11:12–13).

After Judas's betrayal is planned, Matthew's Jesus prepares for the Passover (Matt 26:17–20). Matthew maintains the story of the Last Supper with alterations that reinforce the balance between the practical reality of Jesus's humanity in combination with his transcendent status. At this Last Supper, Jesus establishes a new Passover meal. He will be the "eschatological Passover lamb" replacement.[184] This becomes possible through the sacrifice of his body and shedding of his blood,[185] two elements of a human existence.[186] Jesus's physical death provides a new way for a vicarious atonement.[187] Only Matthew's Jesus adds that his blood is "for the forgiveness of sins" (Matt 26:28 // Mark 14:24 // Luke 22:20). Jesus's human body and blood serve as the means to establish a new covenant,[188] a component of the story the First Evangelist chooses to emphasize because the literal death of Jesus serves to complete his role as the one who will save people from their sins (Matt 1:21; 19:25–26; 26:28).[189] The clear predictions of his death and the symbolism of his body and blood at the Last Supper make it clear that these forecasts will now be physically fulfilled.[190]

However, Matthew again strengthens Jesus's transcendent status in the midst of maintaining his humanity. In Mark, Jesus vows to avoid wine until the kingdom of God arrives (Mark 14:25). Only Matthew alters the statement as Jesus states he will drink the fruit of the vine ἐν τῇ βασιλείᾳ τοῦ πατρός μου ("in my Father's kingdom," Matt 26:29 // Mark 14:25). Matthew continues to connect Jesus with πατρός μου ("my Father").[191] This prediction links Jesus to his Father but foretells an imminent death. Even at the Last

---

184. Hagner, *Matthew 14–28*, 774, refers to Paul's passage for support (1 Cor 5:7).

185. The terms themselves identify Jesus's humanity. Luz, *Matthew 21–28*, 379, 384, points out the literal nature of the body and blood of Jesus when referencing the Last Supper (Matt 26:26–28). The σῶμα ("body") is something concrete one can clothe or anoint (6:25; 26:12). The αἷμά ("blood") being shed suggests a violent death. There is "no possibility of making the saving significance of this ritual independent of the death of Jesus." Consequently, Matthew's maintenance and use of the humanity of Jesus continues to be important to the narrative in light of the growing awareness of Jesus's transcendent identity in Jerusalem.

186. Davies and Allison, *Matthew 19–28*, 471, state the body and the blood are "the two elements making up a person."

187. Blomberg, *Matthew*, 391.

188. Luz, *Matthew 21–28*, 380.

189. Heil, *Death and Resurrection of Jesus*, 8.

190. France, *Gospel of Matthew*, 992.

191. See ch. 3, n35 above.

Supper, Matthew's redactions purposely balance the human and transcendent identity for the reader.

Finishing the Last Supper with a song, Jesus and the disciples head to the Mount of Olives (Matt 26:30). The Matthean Jesus approaches his journey to the cross with an awareness of what is to occur.[192] Jesus predicts the disciples falling away and Peter's denials (26:31–35). Quoting another prophecy from Zechariah (Zech 13:7 // Matt 26:31 // Mark 14:27), Jesus, the shepherd, will be struck and the sheep, the disciples, will scatter. With another resurrection prediction, both Matthew and Mark use a passive ἐγερθῆναί ("to be raised," Matt 26:32 // Mark 14:28).[193] Jesus's declaration demonstrates his dependence on something other than himself to be raised from the dead. Believing something will raise him from the dead, he informs the disciples that in spite of their falling away, he will meet them in Galilee (Matt 26:32). In spite of physical death, connecting Jesus to God as his Father in combination with his human struggle, death, and dependent resurrection highlights the balance that Matthean Christology addresses because of his focus on the dual nature of Jesus's identity.

4.6 HUMAN EMOTION IN THE GARDEN (MATT 26:36–44)

Prior to the fulfillment of Jesus's suffering, death, and resurrection predictions, Matthew portrays an emotional Jesus who confesses a will that is contrary to the Father's (Matt 26:36–44).[194] Besides the physical death of Jesus, no other scene in the Gospel of Matthew depicts as clearly the reality of Jesus's humanity.[195] Matthew describes Jesus as sorrowful, troubled, and grieving (Matt 26:37–38).[196] John Paul Heil describes the scene as Jesus

192. As Jesus and the disciples eat, Jesus foretells his betrayal (Matt 26:21). As the disciples question one another, only Matthew provides a brief interaction between Judas and Jesus (Matt 26:25 // Mark 14:21–22 // Luke 22:22–23). Judas asks whether he is the betrayer and Jesus responds, "You have said so" (26:25). Alterations to the portrayal demonstrate Jesus's awareness of his own death.

193. See discussion in ch. 4, n21 above.

194. Luz, *Matthew 21–28*, 394, points out that for the ancient church the Gethsemane scene is "one of the most difficult episodes."

195. Brown, *Death of the Messiah*, 1:12, indicates that tradition is probably aware of Jesus crying out to God in the face of death (Heb 5:7). Harrington, "Man Christ Jesus," 9, describes Jesus as most human in this scene.

196. Williams, "Gospel of Matthew," 97, states that "the struggle between the divine and human within the Savior was mostly a pretense for our benefit." While this reinforces Jesus as a model, if Matthew has and will continue to prioritize the human portrayal of Christ in the narrative, then the struggle in the Garden is real for Matthew's

experiencing "human trepidation at approaching death."[197] Davies and Allison indicate that Jesus seems to be "at war with himself."[198] While these are current perceptions of the main character's emotional state, comparing the Synoptic portrayals of the emotions in Gethsemane and defining the words selected to describe Jesus's feelings demonstrate that Matthew depicts Jesus's struggles as real in three ways.

First, Mark portrays Jesus ἐκθαμβεῖσθαι ("to be greatly distressed") καὶ ἀδημονεῖν ("and to be troubled") in addition to being περίλυπός ἕως θανάτου ("very sorrowful even to death," Mark 14:33–34). Examination of the terms assists to understand why Matthew prioritizes the humanity of Jesus's story, especially in light of Luke's removal of Jesus's emotions (Matt 26:37–38 // Mark 14:33–34 // Luke 22:40).[199] The descriptors Matthew keeps are ἀδημονεῖν ("to be troubled") and περίλυπός ("very sorrowful). Bauer defines ἀδημονεω as "to be in anxiety, be distressed, troubled,"[200] and περίλυπός as "very sad, deeply grieved."[201] Examining the pericope, Jesus experiences these emotions because of the cup which he desires to be passed from him (Matt 26:39, 42). Matthew presents Jesus as a normal human being who experiences anxiety and fear.[202] Why would someone as aware of what is about to occur experience distress, trouble, or anxiety? The storyline suggests that the prospect of his physical suffering and impending death looms, causing Jesus anguish.[203] While Luke removes these emotions, Matthew chooses to maintain, yet modify Mark's tradition of what Jesus felt. Being truly human, Jesus experiences the dread of suffering and death.[204]

---

main character.

197. Heil, *Death and Resurrection of Jesus*, 43.

198. Davies and Allison, *Matthew 19–28*, 502.

199. While Luke removes the specifics of Jesus's emotional state, there is a textual criticism issue with Luke's garden scene (Luke 22:43–44). This variant suggests that an angel comes to Jesus to strengthen him and his prayers are so intense that sweat like drops of blood falls. Metzger, *Textual Commentary*, 177, suggests that while this text is not part of Luke's original Gospel due to the textual witnesses, the testimony of church Fathers such as Justin, Irenaeus, and Eusebius provide evidence within antiquity for support of the account. Whichever the case, Luke removes Jesus's self-described emotional turmoil reported in Mark and altered in Matthew.

200. Bauer, "ἀδημονεω," BDAG, 19. This term describes an emotion of Epaphroditus (Phil 2:26), but is never used to describe God in the LXX or NT.

201. Bauer, "περίλυπός," BDAG, 802.

202. Hare, *Matthew*, 301.

203. France, *Gospel of Matthew*, 1004.

204. Keener, *Commentary*, 639, n90. Hagner, *Matthew 14–28*, 782. See Cullmann, *Immortality of the Soul*.

Second, Matthew changes Mark's ἐκθαμβεῖσθαι ("to be greatly distressed") to λυπεῖσθαι ("to grieve," Matt 26:37 // Mark 14:33). With this
switch, Matthew chooses a term that is not limited to Jesus's emotional
experience. Matthew uses forms of λυπέω ("grieve") in the parable of the
unforgiving servant and to describe the emotion of a young man (Matt
18:31; 19:22). Twice, Matthew's disciples are said to experience this emotion. First, the disciples ἐλθπήθησαν ("grieved," 17:23), an emotion that is
only located in Matthew's second prediction of his death. Second, the disciples feel λυπούμενοι ("sorrow") as Jesus foretells his betrayal at the Last
Supper (26:22). Matthew could either remove Jesus's emotions as Luke did
or maintain language to describe emotions that are unique to Jesus. Instead,
he alters at least one emotion in Gethsemane that is similar to the emotions
of other human beings in his narrative. Davies and Allison point out that
Matthew "softened" Jesus's struggle in comparison to Mark.[205] However, as
the exemplar who experiences the emotions of his disciples, it is reasonable
to conclude that even though he softens the struggle, Matthew selects a term
that identifies Jesus with not only the reader but also other humans in his
narrative. In spite of the softening, Matthew still chooses λυπέω, a term that
Bauer defines as to "be sad, be distressed, grieve."[206] Unlike Luke's complete
removal of Jesus's emotional state in the Garden of Gethsemane, Matthew
maintains the humanity of Jesus to demonstrate a genuine struggle with
drinking the cup of God's wrath and following his Father's will.

Third, Matthew edits Jesus's imperative in Mark from γρηγοπεῖτε ("you
all watch") to γρηγοπεῖτε μετ' ἐμοῦ ("you all watch with me," Matt 26:38 //
Mark 14:34). The Jesus in Matthew is so distraught that Matthew wants to
make clear that Jesus does not desire to be alone (Matt 26:38). In light of
Matthew's redaction, Hagner correctly states: "It is only natural that Jesus
would want the emotional support of his closest friends."[207] This natural
status of Jesus's desire for emotional support is only natural if the character
Matthew portrays is human. As John P. Meier points out, the "more Jesus
feels distant from God, the more he seeks the closeness of his followers."[208]
Once again, in spite of Matthew's presentation of Jesus's seemingly transcendent awareness of what will happen, he is portrayed as a human in distress
who does not want to be alone (26:38).[209]

205. Davies and Allison, *Matthew 19–28*, 492.

206. Bauer, "λυπέω," BDAG, 604, lists λυπέω ("grieve") as an emotion assigned to a
human being (Matt 19:22; 26:22).

207. Hagner, *Matthew 14–28*, 782–83, also suggests that Jesus lacks the desire to
face this troublesome time alone.

208. Meier, *Matthew*, 324.

209. Davies and Allison, *Matthew 19–28*, 496.

In spite of distress, Matthew's human Jesus has a will of his own that will submit to his Father's. Jesus opens his prayer: "My Father, if it is possible, let this cup pass from me; yet not what I want but what you want" (Matt 26:39). The adversative ἀλλα ("but") in combination with pronouns ἐγω ("I") and σύ ("your") point out it is the Father's and not the Son's will that should be done.[210] Douglas Hare says that Jesus is "free to rebel against God's will."[211] As we consider the prayers of Jesus in the Garden of Gethsemane, it should be kept in mind that Jesus prays elsewhere in the narrative (14:23). Although Matthew's Jesus does not pray as much as Luke's,[212] as the exemplar, prayer serves as an act consistent with human existence.[213]

Matthew's Jesus prays, but the portrayal is not the same among the Synoptics. Matthew shifts Mark's language from αββα ὁ πατήρ ("Abba Father") to πάτερ μου ("My Father") while Luke simply portrays Jesus saying, πάτερ ("Father," Matt 26:39 // Mark 14:36 // Luke 22:42).[214] In the garden, the Jesus of Matthew communicates the filial relationship of a Son explicitly pleading with his Father in two of the three prayers (Matt 26:39, 42). The relationship between the Father and the Son is being tested and confirmed.[215] This holds the practicality of the main character's humanity in balance with his transcendent status through the prayer in the garden, especially with the prayer's alteration.[216]

The process of testing and confirming the relationship is demonstrated in the three prayers. Through the narrative, Matthew demonstrates that Jesus possesses a level of awareness of what will occur. Each Synoptic author depicts Jesus possessing a will contrary to the Father's (Matt 26:39 // Mark 14:36 // Luke 22:42), but due to Matthew's alterations and previous familial connections between Jesus and "my Father,"[217] the difference in wills is more pronounced. In Matthew, Jesus says, οὐχ ὡς ἐγω θέλω ἀλλ' ὡς σύ ("not as I will, but as you [will]," 26:39). Just as the reader can observe how Jesus deals

210. Luz, *Matthew 21–28*, 396, suggests this could remind the readers of how Jesus models the prayer in the Sermon on the Mount as he exemplifies, "Thy will be done" (Matt 6:10).

211. Hare, *Matthew*, 300.

212. Luke 3:21; 5:16; 6:12; 9:18, 28–29; 11:1; 22:41–45.

213. Matt 5:44; 6:5–13; 9:38; 14:23; 19:13; 21:13, 22; 24:20; 26:36–44.

214. See ch. 3, n35 above.

215. France, *Gospel of Matthew*, 1004.

216. Turner, *Matthew*, 633, correctly assesses that this scene demonstrates that Jesus is "truly divine and truly human." It should be noted that Jesus's prayers are heard (Heb 5:7), but even the prayers of Jesus, the exemplar, are not answered with a change in his Father's will.

217. See ch. 4, n191 above.

with temptation elsewhere in the narrative (4:1–11; 16:22–23), Matthew's portrayal serves as a model. As a model, Jesus displays the ability to go to the Father with one's deepest struggles and fears yet ultimately submit to the will of the Father.[218]

As a human, Matthew's Jesus can choose to follow his will or his Father's.[219] While in Judaism there is a struggle to understand the role between humankind's will and divine sovereignty,[220] a Jewish notion exists that God can and potentially will change his mind in response to a prayerful and repentant heart.[221] The will of human existence involves a choice even for Jesus. While Jesus does not question God's will,[222] his love for his Father does not always result in a desire to face what his Father places before him. While that is true for the human experience,[223] the exemplar demonstrates his love for God with the choice to follow his Father's will in spite of the feelings of distress and grief.

When Matthew's Jesus prays a second time, the prayer portrays an indication that Jesus has submitted to the Father. Jesus says, "My Father, if this cannot pass unless I drink it, your will be done" (Matt 26:42). It appears that Jesus has received his answer and aligns his will to his Father's. The shift in the second prayer clarifies for the reader that although a will contrary to the Father exists, just as the exemplar submits, so can they. Even though Matthew does not record the words of the third prayer, he indicates that the prayer is εἰπών πάλιν ("spoken again," 26:44).

These prayers serve as a testimony to what Jesus asserts to the disciples. The spirit is willing but the flesh is weak (Matt 26:41). In spite of the weakness of the flesh, the prayers of Jesus model the challenge to be alert and follow the Father's will.[224] As Jesus commands them with γρηγορεῖτε καὶ προσεύχεσθε ("you all watch and pray," 26:41), the purpose is so that they may not enter into temptation (26:41). As the exemplar prays more than once to submit to the will of God,[225] one can submit to the Father even though it may mean suffering and death.[226]

---

218. Heil, *Death and Resurrection of Jesus*, 45.

219. Keener, *Commentary*, 639.

220. McKnight, *Letter of James*, 375.

221. Judg 2:1–3; 1 Sam 2:27–36; 2 Kgs 20:1–6; Jer 18:5–11. Davies and Allison, *Matthew 19–28*, 497.

222. Davies and Allison, *Matthew 19–28*, 491.

223. Keener, *Commentary*, 639.

224. Turner, *Matthew*, 632.

225. Hagner, *Matthew 14–28*, 783.

226. Turner, *Matthew*, 633.

Matthew's use of the prayers of Jesus in the Garden show the struggle between the will of the human Jesus in tension with his status as a transcendent Son. Since Matthew, in contrast to Luke, maintains the emotional turmoil of Jesus and expands the prayer scene, it leads to the conclusion that Jesus is, in the words of Davies and Allison, the "model of faithful discipleship."[227] As a result, emotions such as sorrow, grief, and trouble are part of a righteous life before God.[228] Unlike the disciples, these emotions keep Jesus awake as he prays and submits to the will of God in the midst of his own demise (Matt 26:45).

4.7 ARREST AND TRIALS (MATT 26:45—27:26)

After the prayerful struggle in the Garden of Gethsemane, Matthew's Jesus stands ready for betrayal, arrest, and trials (Matt 26:45—27:26). Balancing the humanity and transcendence of Jesus again plays out in Matthew's narrative. Explaining that his arrest is part of the plan so that the scriptures might be fulfilled (26:54, 56), Matthew's Jesus allows the arrest to occur. Adding to the scene, only Matthew reinforces Jesus's filial relationship with God using μου πατέρα ("my Father"), and because of that relationship, only Matthew's Jesus has legions of angels at his disposal (Matt 26:53 // Mark 14:47–48 // Luke 22:51–52). Matthew's alteration continues to demonstrate Jesus as a "moral model," as Davies and Allison put it.[229] In the Sermon on the Mount, Jesus proclaimed, "Do not resist an evildoer" (Matt 5:39), and with the angels at his disposal, he chooses the will of God over a holy war. In the Garden of Gethsemane, Jesus's life illustrates the reality of what he proclaims in the Sermon, pacifism triumphs self-defense.[230]

After Jesus's arrest, a trial with false witnesses provides an opportunity for Matthew to remind the readers of the human and transcendent identity of Jesus through two alterations (Matt 26:57–67). First, each Synoptic depicts the interaction between Jesus and the chief priest differently. Mark's chief priest asks, "Are you the Christ, the Son of the Blessed?" (Mark 14:61). Luke's question comes from the council, "Are you the Son of God?" (Luke 22:70). Matthew's chief priest asks, "[T]ell us if you are the Christ, the Son of God" (Matt 26:63). Matthew's alteration reinforces two of his primary

---

227. Davies and Allison, *Matthew 19–28*, 503.

228. Luz, *Matthew 21–28*, 408.

229. Davies and Allison, *Matthew 19–28*, 513.

230. Luz, *Matthew 21–28*, 419, stresses that the pacifism is uncompromising, but it should be kept in mind that Matthew's Jesus is portrayed as knowing the arrest, suffering, and crucifixion are all the Father's will for his life.

christological interests (16:16). Jesus is both the Christ and the Son of God, which balances the humanity and transcendent status.[231] Second, Matthew backs away from another opportunity to identify Jesus's transcendence. When asked about his identity, Mark's Jesus responds to the question with ἐγώ εἰμι ("I am," Mark 14:62).[232] Luke's Jesus responds to the question from the council, "You say that I am" (Luke 22:70). Even though Matthew does not repeat Mark's ἐγώ εἰμι ("I am"),[233] Matthew's Jesus responds by replying, "You have said so" (Matt 26:64). Matthew's shift to "You have said so" puts the onus on the high priest who correctly states Jesus's identity.[234]

The shift away from the ἐγώ εἰμι ("I am") is another indicator of Matthew's interest in Jesus's humanity. Even though ἐγώ εἰμι ("I am") develops into an expression for divine claims by the time of the Gospel of John,[235] the divine claim associated with ἐγώ εἰμι ("I am") according to Brown is "not totally foreign to the Synoptic tradition."[236] Matthew forgoes using ἐγώ εἰμι ("I am")[237] and reinforces Jesus's claim to be the Son of Man who will sit at the right hand of power (Matt 26:64). The claim to sit at the right hand, in combination with Jesus's admission that he is the Christ, the Son of God, leads the high priest to claim he speaks blasphemy, which sets up Jesus's physical suffering and the plot for Jesus's execution (26:64–65; 27:1–2).[238]

---

231. While the reader of the narrative will understand the significance of the titles, it is probable that Caiaphas's character understands Son of God as a messianic rather than transcendent term. Turner, *Matthew*, 639, provides 2 Sam 7:14; Pss 2:7; 89:26–27, as evidence. At the time of Jesus's trial, Caiaphas did not consider the Son of God a transcendent being. See Hagner, *Matthew 14–28*, 799.

232. In spite of the variant, both Hooker, *Gospel According to Saint Mark*, 361, and Brown, *Death of the Messiah*, 2:489, argue that the original reading of Mark is ἐγώ εἰμι ("I am").

233. Hagner, *Matthew 14–28*, 800. Brown, *Gospel According to John*, 1:538, suggests that Matthew's use of ἐγώ εἰμι ("I am") at the scene of walking on the water indicates not only that Jesus is present but also elicits a response from the disciples regarding his status as Son of God (Matt 14:33).

234. Hooker, *Gospel According to Saint Mark*, 2:361. Keener, *Commentary*, 649.

235. John 6:48; 8:12, 58; 9:5; 10:9, 11; 11:25; 14:6; 15:1.

236. Brown, *Death of the Messiah*, 2:261–62. See Brown, *Gospel According to John*, 1:538, for a summary of the Synoptic usage of ἐγώ εἰμι ("I am," Mark 14:62 // Luke 22:70; Matt 14:27 // Mark 6:50; Luke 23:36 in some manuscripts).

237. Matthew's Jesus does use ἐγώ εἰμι ("I am") when he walks on the water. In that case, he maintains the response of Mark's Jesus (Matt 14:27 // Mark 6:50).

238. Mocking Jesus, the religious leaders spit in his face, slap him, and strike him (Matt 26:67). In the midst of admitting that he is the Son of God and that he will sit at the right hand of power, Matthew's human Jesus begins to face the cup that causes him ἀδημονεῖν ("to be troubled"), λυπεῖσθαι ("to grieve"), and to be περίλυπός ("very sorrowful") in Gethsemane (26:36–38).

Prior to Jesus's trial before Pilate, only Matthew returns to the end of Judas's story (Matt 27:3–10). Within that pericope, Matthew's human christological interests are observable in two primary ways.[239] First, Matthew structures the human story of Jesus to be able to demonstrate that his life fulfills prophecy again.[240] Second, Matthew characterizes Judas betraying αἷμα ἀθῷον ("innocent blood," 27:4).[241] The First Evangelist reinforces the idea of Jesus's innocence in other scenes. Matthew retains Mark's Pilate asking the crowds what evil has Jesus done (Matt 27:23 // Mark 15:14).[242] As a result of a dream, Pilate's wife informs him that Jesus is δικαίῳ ("righteous," Matt 27:19). In the first Gospel narrative reliable dreams come from God (1:20; 2:12).[243] With Matthew's interest to present Jesus as the transcendent Son of God, he could have used the dream from Pilate's wife to communicate that Jesus is God's Son.[244] Instead of highlighting the transcendent status of Jesus, Matthew's use of the dream ends with an understanding of Jesus's exemplar status that Pilate is dealing with an individual who is δικαίῳ ("righteous").[245]

Reinforcing Jesus's innocence, Matthew revises the story to place the responsibility of Jesus's death on the Jews. Pilate, wanting to avoid culpability for the innocent Jesus, washes his hands of Jesus's innocent blood before the crowd (Matt 27:24). In response, only Matthew's crowd takes ownership for the death of Jesus by declaring that they and their children take full responsibility for his blood (Matt 27:25 // Mark 15:15 // Luke 23:24).[246] While

239. Jesus is delivered by Judas to the Jewish authorities (Matt 26:45), then the authorities deliver Jesus to Pilate (27:2), and then Pilate delivers Jesus to be crucified (27:26). Heil, *Death and Resurrection of Jesus*, 67, points out this not only fulfills what Jesus predicts (20:18–19), but also, according to Davies and Allison, *Matthew 19–28*, 555, connects Jesus with the fates of John the Baptist and other Christians with his repeated use of forms of παραδίδωμι ("deliver," 4:12; 10:17, 19, 21; 24:9–10).

240. Matt 27:8–10; Zech 11:12–13; Jer 19:1–13; 32:6–9. Considered the last of the fulfillment prophecies, Davies and Allison, *Matthew 19–28*, 573–77, provide an overview of the issues involved in this fulfillment prophecy.

241. Hagner, *Matthew 14–28*, 812, explains this is a common expression in the OT that warns against shedding innocent blood (Deut 19:10, 13; 21:8–9; 27:25; 1 Sam 25:31; 2 Kgs 21:16; 24:4; Isa 59:7). Luz, *Matthew 21–28*, 470n33, specifies the phrase is in the LXX 19 times.

242. France, *Gospel of Matthew*, 1050.

243. Davies and Allison, *Matthew 19–28*, 587. Angels bring messages from God in the OT. For example, Daniel and Joseph interpret dreams that are understood to come from YHWH (Gen 40:1—41:40; Dan 1:17; 2:19–45).

244. In light of Matthew's use of dreams in the birth narratives, he understands them to be a means for the divine to communicate with humanity.

245. See ch. 2, n72 above.

246. Heil, *Death and Resurrection of Jesus*, 8.

interpretation of "[Jesus's] blood be on us and on our children!" has had tragic consequences (Matt 27:25),[247] the repetition of Matthew's attention to Jesus's blood and innocence in these final few scenes is of interest to this project.

Matthew's portrayal of Jesus begins with a mission to fulfill all righteousness (Matt 3:15), and as the moral exemplar throughout his life, his righteousness is confirmed by describing him as innocent and righteous prior to his death (27:4; 19, 24). As the narrative of Jesus's life draws to a close, some of the comments added by Matthew regarding the blood of Jesus assume something about the status of this human character that Matthew prioritizes.[248] While the statements may have been colloquial, Matthew uses the blood of Jesus for his own purposes. He highlights Jesus's righteous innocence to remind the reader that Jesus suffers unjustly so his blood can be shed for the forgiveness of sins (1:21; 26:28), both unique additions to Matthew's Gospel narrative.

4.8 THE SUFFERING, CRUCIFIXION, AND DEATH OF THE HUMAN SON OF GOD (MATT 27:27-66)

As a result of Pilate's execution order, the soldiers take Jesus away (Matt 27:27). To emphasize the extent of unjust suffering the Christ endures, Matthew describes the events that lead to the cross. In the evening he is spit on, hit, slapped, and mocked by the religious leaders (26:67–68). The Roman soldiers flog Jesus (27:26). The form of flogging included a flesh-tearing instrument that accelerated the death of its subject.[249] A crown of thorns is put on his head and a reed in his right hand to symbolize the king they mock (27:29–30). The extent of beating results in the cross being carried not by Jesus but by Simon the Cyrene to Golgotha (27:32–33). The most logical explanation concerning the beating of Jesus described by Matthew is that Jesus is too weak to carry the cross himself.[250] Matthew's explanation of the suffering that Jesus endures as a human is believable and his need for help remains in the story.[251]

---

247. Beare, *Gospel According to Matthew*, 531, states: "It is appalling for a Christian to think how suffering has been inflicted upon the Jews throughout the ages." For further discussion of this scene, see Cargal, "'His Blood,'" 101–12; Heil, "Blood of Jesus," 117–24.

248. Matt 26:28; 27:4, 6, 8, 24, 25.

249. See Josephus, *J.W.* 2.306, 308; 5.449; 6.304; 7.200–209.

250. Luz, *Matthew 21–28*, 527.

251. Keener, *Commentary*, 676; Davies and Allison, *Matthew 19–28*, 610.

At Golgotha, the soldiers offer Jesus wine mixed with gall, a change from Mark's wine and myrrh combination (Matt 27:33–34 // Mark 15:22–23). The combination of wine and myrrh may have been a sedative (*b. Sanh.* 43a), but Matthew's redaction of wine and gall more likely echoes a Psalm as a sign (Ps 69:21 // Matt 27:34). The Jewish reader could understand that Matthew symbolizes a just man being abused by his enemies with the wine and gall redaction.[252] Whether Matthew's redaction communicates a sedative or a symbol, Proverbs specifies giving strong drink to assist to alleviate pain (Prov 31:6–7).[253] Only the Jesus in Matthew tastes the drink (Matt 27:34 // Mark 15:23 // Luke 23:33). The portrayal of Jesus's willingness to taste the mixture suggests that Jesus is thirsty and unaware of what he could drink.[254] Through becoming aware of the mixture through taste, Jesus keeps his promise and does not drink the mixture, which included wine, until he is with the disciples in his Father's kingdom (Matt 26:29). With abstaining, Matthew also portrays Jesus choosing to remain cognizant of his pain.[255] Consequently, the Matthean Jesus endures the suffering of the cross unaffected by whatever the wine mixture contains.

With Jesus hanging on the cross and his death, Matthew balances the humanity and transcendence more than Mark and Luke through the words and activities of those at Golgotha. While each Synoptic author depicts guards casting lots and a sign declaring Jesus is the King of the Jews (Matt 27:35–37 // Mark 15:24–26 // Luke 23:34, 38), Matthew describes the jeering differently (Matt 27:38–43 // Mark 15:27–32 // Luke 23:35–38). Using the snide comments as an opportunity to remind the reader of the argument Matthew has been making throughout the narrative, the First Evangelist adds the title Son of God to the bystander ridicule twice (Matt 27:40, 43 // Mark 15:30, 32 // Luke 23:35). Through the human story, the author consistently builds the argument that Jesus's identity consists of more than humanity and a general assumption that Son of God means "specially favored by God or pleasing to God," as Dunn puts it.[256] For Matthew, in spite of the physical brutality, thirst, and impending death, Jesus remains the transcendent Son of God. Only Matthean chief priests, scribes, and elders challenge Jesus to prove his sonship by saving himself (Matt 27:43 // Mark 15:32 // Luke 23:38). Of the Synoptic authors, only Matthew portrays the mockers

---

252. Brown, *Death of Messiah*, 2:942–43.

253. Keener, *Commentary*, 677–78.

254. Davies and Allison, *Matthew 19–28*, 613.

255. Keener, *Commentary*, 678. Davies and Allison, *Matthew 19–28*, 613, specify that both understandings are possible and reflect that Jesus either recognizes the mockery or avoids a "shortcut to death."

256. Dunn, *Christology in the Making*, 16.

claiming Jesus said, "I am God's Son" (Matt 27:43 // Mark 15:32 // Luke 23:35). Matthew's alterations emphasize the tension of a human Son of God crucified to set up the death scene.

After a darkness covers the land,[257] Jesus finally speaks, "Θεέ μου θεέ μου, ἱνατί με ἐγκατέλιπες;" ("My God, my God, why have you forsaken me?," Matt 27:46 // Mark 15:34).[258] Hagner describes this scene as "something about which the reader and the exegete can only wonder . . . of the most impenetrable mysteries of the entire Gospel narrative."[259] Even though Luke removes this cry from the cross (Luke 23:44–48), Matthew maintains Mark's, θεέ μου θεέ μου ("my God, my God"). Instead of Matthew's regular shift to μου πατρός ("my father"),[260] Matthew avoids the filial language and portrays Jesus as forsaken. Matthew does not explain how this is possible in regards to Jesus's transcendent status and human existence, but the portrayal depicts that Jesus experiences the feeling the Psalmist faced (Ps 22:1). The repetition of phraseology suggests that this does not represent a temporary loss of faith but rather a loss of connection between the Father and the Son.[261] As Matthew's righteous human character physically suffers,[262] Jesus feels forsaken and suffers for the rest of humankind.[263]

In the midst of feeling forsaken by God, Matthew's alterations surrounding the death of the human Jesus occur alongside an "explosion of the supernatural," as Davies and Allison put it.[264] While Matthew and Mark depict the temple veil being torn in two (Matt 27:51 // Mark 15:38),[265] Mat-

257. Hagner, *Matthew 14–28*, 844 states: "Darkness is, of course, also a common metaphor for judgment that will come on 'the Day of the Lord' (cf. such passages as Joel 2:2, 31; Zeph 1:15)." The implication is that the darkness communicates the importance of this character who dies on the cross.

258. For a history of interpretation, see Luz, *Matthew 21–28*, 545–49.

259. Hagner, *Matthew 14–28*, 843–45, describes the death scene of the Son of God as involving an "impenetrable mystery." That mystery only intensifies as Matthew maintains and reinforces the human story of Jesus all the while building the case for his transcendent identity. However, Matthew initiates his Gospel with a similar mystery, a virgin birth (Matt 1:18–25).

260. Matt 7:21; 10:32–33; 11:27; 12:50; 15:13; 16:17; 18:10, 19, 35; 20:23; 25:34; 26:29, 39, 42, 53.

261. France, *Gospel of Matthew*, 1077.

262. Matt 3:15; 26:67–68; 27:4, 19, 24, 27–31. Luz, *Matthew 21–28*, 554.

263. Matt 1:21; 19:25–26; 24:22; 26:36–45; 27:46.

264. Davies and Allison, *Matthew 19–28*, 639.

265. While the tearing of the temple veil is depicted in Mark and Matthew (Matt 27:51 // Mark 15:38), the symbolic significance of the event should not be ignored because of the balance that Matthew's inclusion of this event maintains. Collins, *Mark*, 760, designates the tearing of the veil symbolizes the removal of the "barrier between humanity and God." Hagner, *Matthew 14–28*, 853, reinforces that humankind can be in

thew's Jesus breathes his last and the earth shakes,[266] tombs open, and saints resurrect (Matt 27:50–53). Through theologically accurate mocking, miraculous signs such as the darkness (27:45), the earth shaking (27:51), opened tombs (27:52), and resurrected saints (27:52–53), the readers understand that the explosion of the supernatural announces an important figure has died.[267]

These events are depicted to occur after Jesus dies, yet each of the descriptions of Jesus's dying words differ among the Synoptic authors. Matthew's description differs from Mark and Luke, which reinforces a Matthean purpose to portray Jesus as human and transcendent. Mark describes Jesus breathing his last as he gives a loud cry (Mark 15:37). Luke keeps Mark's description but adds that Jesus commits his spirit to the Father (Luke 23:46). Matthew's death description of Jesus is more ambiguous. His Jesus cries with a loud voice and ἀφῆκεν τὸ πνεῦμα ("gave up his spirit," Matt 27:50). While Matthew does not provide what Jesus says or cries with a loud voice, the ambiguous nature of ἀφῆκεν τὸ πνεῦμα ("gave up his spirit") deserves attention.

While both Matthew and Mark use ἀφίμι ("give up"), Mark's ἀφίμι ("give up") refers to a loud cry and Matthew's ἀφίμι ("give up") refers to his πνεῦμα ("spirit").[268] Ἀφῆκεν τὸ πνεῦμα ("Gave up his spirit," Matt 27:50) serves as another way for Jesus to demonstrate his power in a situation.[269] Jesus has demonstrated power throughout the Matthean narrative. He has healed illness (4:23; 9:35), cast out demons (8:28–34; 12:22–28), and calmed the seas (8:23–27; 14:22–33). Matthew's Jesus teaches with authority (7:28–29), has the authority to forgive sins (9:6), transfers authority to the disciples (10:1), and performs the aforementioned miracles. Describing the idiomatic expression ἀφῆκεν τὸ πνεῦμα ("gave up his spirit," 27:50),[270] Robert Gundry correctly argues: "The revision has the purpose and result of making Jesus, who is a majestic and authoritative figure throughout the

---

fellowship with God as a result of Jesus's death as signified through the torn temple veil symbolizing that God's presence is available to everyone.

266. Matthew presents earthquakes in apocalyptic language (Matt 24:7; 28:2). Hagner, *Matthew 14–28*, 849, points to the OT background for further support (Isa 24:19; 29:6; Jer 10:10; Amos 8:8).

267. Brown, *Death of the Messiah*, 2:1113–114. E.g., 4 Macc 9:20; Josephus, *Ant.* 17.6.4.

268. Bauer, "ἀφίμι," 156. Bauer, "πνεῦμα," BDAG, 832–36.

269. Davies and Allison, *Matthew 19–28*, 627–28.

270. E.g., Gen 35:18 LXX; 1 Esd 4:21; Josephus, *Ant.* 1.218; 5.147; 12.430; 14.369. Turner, *Matthew*, 669.

first gospel, die of his own accord. He does not die with a last gasp, but by an act of the will."[271]

Could Matthew's redaction suggest a double entendre?[272] With authority expressed by giving up his spirit yet a human life's end, Hagner points out that Matthew's redaction meets in the middle of Mark, Luke, and John's final expressions from Jesus on the cross.[273] Matthew's alteration allows the Jewish Christian reader to observe the balance between the human and transcendent identity in Jesus's death. Jesus breathes his final physical breath and dies. That, in conjunction with the authority to give up his spirit, the supernatural events, and the next declaration of his identity, Matthew continues to keep the balance between the human and transcendent before the reader.

Jesus's death marks the initiation of miraculous events for Matthew (Matt 27:51–53), and he uses these events to set up the centurion's statement that Jesus is the Son of God (27:54). Each of the Synoptic authors has a centurion on the scene to verify the identity of Jesus. Mark's centurion indicates that this ἄνθρωπος ("man") was the Son of God (Mark 15:39). Luke's centurion specifies that this ἄνθρωπος ("man") is innocent (Luke 23:47). Of the three, Matthew is the only one to remove the ἄνθρωπος ("man") descriptor by his centurion, stating that Jesus is the Son of God (Matt 27:54). In light of Matthew's persistence in portraying the human story of Jesus in conjunction with building his argument for the transcendence of Jesus,[274] Matthew wanted to emphasize for the reader Jesus's transcendent status in the midst of Jesus's death as a human.

After portraying the end of Jesus's life, Matthew develops the story to strengthen the believability of Jesus's physical death and placement in the tomb.[275] Matthew adds an account of a request and approval for extra security to guard the tomb to counter any claim that the body was stolen

271. Gundry, *Matthew*, 575.

272. Cargal, "'His Blood,'" 110, provides the suggestion that with a double entendre the reader is not asked to decide which meaning the author intends. Consequently, the reader will be asked to "recognize both levels of meaning in a fashion congruous with the understanding of the narrator." With Matthew's balance between the human and transcendent and somewhat ambiguous expression ἀφῆκεν τὸ πνεῦμα ("gave up his spirit," 27:50), especially in light of its description in comparison with other Gospel writers, it is possible that Matthew intends another double entendre here. One that identifies Jesus as both human and transcendent.

273. Hagner, *Matthew 14–28*, 845. See Mark 15:37; Luke 23:46; John 19:30.

274. Matt 3:17; 4:3, 6; 8:29; 11:25–27; 14:33; 16:16; 17:5; 21:37–39; 22:42–45; 26:63; 27:40, 43.

275. Each Synoptic author includes information regarding the burial account of Jesus (Matt 27:57–61 // Mark 15:42–47 // Luke 23:50–56).

(Matt 27:62–66; 28:11–15).[276] In this additional scene, Matthew's narrative increases the credibility of Jesus's literal, physical death with the addition of τὸ σῶμα ("the body," 27:59)[277] in preparation for the bodily resurrection of Jesus.

4.9 THE RESURRECTED, AUTHORITATIVE HUMAN (MATT 28:1–20)

Shifting the scene from the death and burial of Jesus to the first day of the week, Matthew focuses on an empty tomb and resurrection. Even the tomb and resurrection reinforce Matthew's interest in the human portrayal of Jesus. Two Marys proceed to the tomb where the soldiers guard his body (Matt 28:1). While each of the Synoptic authors indicate that the stone is rolled away, only Matthew describes how (Matt 28:2 // Mark 16:4 // Luke 24:2). One might think the Son of God rolls away the stone on his own, but there is a μέγας σεισμός ("great earthquake") and an angel rolls back the stone (Matt 28:2). Matthew attributes the stone's movement to a cause other than Jesus. As the women at the scene are told of the crucified Jesus's resurrection,[278] the angel informs them ἠγέρθη ("he has been raised," Matt 28:6 // Mark 16:6). As has been consistent throughout Matthew's narrative,[279] he has selected the passive forms of ἐγείρω ("rise") to describe the resurrection.[280] Jesus is a recipient of the resurrection (Matt 28:6).[281] In spite of the guards at the tomb and the seal on the tomb, the angel rolls away the stone and proclaims that Jesus has been raised (27:66; 28:2–6). The assumption is that both events occur on behalf of the human Son of God.

276. Hagner, *Matthew 14–28*, 857, 861.

277. Matthean addition. It is implied in Mark, but Matthew desires to remove any doubt that the body was stolen, was never dead, or was not buried (Matt 27:59 // Mark 15:46).

278. France, *Gospel of Matthew*, 1100, indicates that Matthew's statement that Jesus was crucified reaffirms the "real death" of the resurrected Jesus.

279. Matt 16:21; 17:23; 20:19; 26:32. Matthew uses ἐγείρω ("rise") to refer to Jesus rising from the dead in other parts of the narrative (17:9; 26:32). Matthew consistently selects passive forms of ἐγείρω ("rise") in terms of the resurrection of others (9:25; 10:8; 11:5; 14:2; 27:52).

280. See ch. 4, n21 above for the discussion regarding the passive use of ἐγείρω ("raised").

281. Kirk, *Man Attested by God*, 379, points out that "resurrection does not carry connotations that a being is divine, but that the eschatological vindication of the humans who are the people of God has occurred."

Witnessing the empty tomb, the Marys leave full of joy and fear after being commanded to tell the disciples (Matt 28:7–8), and the First Evangelist adds their encounter with the resurrected Jesus (Matt 28:8–9 // Mark 16:1–8). As readers recall supernatural encounters in Matthew, each result in fear. An angel of the Lord meets Joseph in a dream, the angels tell him to not be afraid (Matt 1:20). After Peter, James, and John observe the transfiguration of Jesus, he tells them to not be afraid (17:7). The guards fear when they encounter the angel at Jesus's tomb, and when the angel encounters the women, he tells them to not be afraid (28:3–5). In this scene, even with an extraordinary encounter with the risen Jesus, Matthew's description is quite ordinary.[282] With a simple Ἰησοῦς ὑπήντησεν αὐταῖς ("Jesus met them," 28:9), the initial interaction and reaction between Jesus and the Marys is not only not what one might expect but also completely unlike those other extraordinary situations because Matthew portrays Jesus as a resurrected human with transcendent status.

As Jesus encounters them, his first words are not "do not be afraid" (Matt 28:5) but rather an ordinary χαίρετε ("Greetings!" 28:9).[283] Seeing Jesus, the women's response is neither fear nor inability to recognize him. Knowing Jesus by sight,[284] they worship and ἐκράτησαν αὐτοῦ τοὺς πόδας ("grasped his feet," 28:9). As Matthew has developed the transcendent status of Jesus throughout his narrative, the response of worship reflects the transcendent status as Son of God. However, why does Matthew add that they ἐκράτησαν ("held" or "grasped") his feet? The implied response is that Matthew's Jesus possesses a resurrected body. The ability to touch his feet suggests a physical reality of Jesus's tangible, resurrected state.[285] In spite of the supernatural events surrounding his resurrection, Matthew's Jesus appears with a simple greeting, feet that are able to be held, and women who respond in worship (28:9).[286]

After the women's response, Jesus commands them to communicate to the disciples to meet in Galilee (Matt 28:10). Rather than calling them disciples, Jesus addresses them as ἀδελφοῖς ("brothers," 28:10). Matthew upholds a distinction between the familial relationship God the Father has

282. Hagner, *Matthew 14–28*, 874.

283. Hagner, *Matthew 14–28*, 874.

284. Kirk, *Man Attested by God*, 379, adds that the ability to recognize him by sight suggests that his appearance before and after death are similar.

285. France, *Gospel of Matthew*, 1102. Hagner, *Matthew 14–28*, 874.

286. Luz, *Matthew 21–28*, 606.

with his children[287] and the Son of God has with his brothers.[288] In spite of their desertion of him in the Garden of Gethsemane (26:56), Jesus refers to his disciples as ἀδελφοῖς ("brothers," 28:10). Nowhere in Matthew's narrative does Jesus communicate with the Israelites or others that they are brothers or sisters of God. Matthew makes it possible for people to understand they can be called children of God.[289] However, Matthew considers Jesus a literal brother of Mary's children (12:46–47; 13:55) and a brother to those who are disciples (12:48–50; 25:40; 28:10). In contrast to the Father's relationship, Matthew's resurrected, human, and transcendent Jesus maintains a brotherly view of his relationships with his disciples as he also establishes Jesus as one with all authority (28:18).

Matthew portrays Jesus's final meeting with the disciples in order to convey his final commission (Matt 28:16). Unlike Luke who describes the disciples as startled and frightened when Jesus appears to them after the resurrection (Luke 24:36–37), Matthew's portrayal of their meeting the resurrected Jesus is neither connected with fear, a command to not be afraid, any dazzling clothes, nor natural disasters. Even though Luke portrays Jesus eating after the resurrection (Matt 24:41), Luke's Jesus opens the minds of his disciples to understand the Scriptures and ascends into heaven before the disciple's eyes (24:45, 51). Matthew does not describe the resurrected Jesus with any unique physical or visibly transcendent qualities. Here, Matthew depicts mixed responses to Jesus in his final meeting with the disciples. Some worship while others doubt (28:17). The human leader of the disciples has now become an object of worship and doubt.[290]

In the midst of worship and doubt, Matthew's Jesus claims that he has been given πᾶσα ἐξουσία ("all authority," Matt 28:16–18). The authority is granted once he fulfills the Father's will as the exemplar, submits in being crucified, and is raised from the dead. While these do not occur without Matthew conveying the human component of Jesus, receiving and delegating authority maintains a distinction between himself and the Father not only here but also in the command itself. [291]

Ending the Gospel with a commission (Matt 28:18–20), Jesus commands his followers to make disciples of all nations, baptizing them in the name of the Father, Son, and Holy Spirit, and teaching them to obey his commands (28:19–20). The human story of Jesus Matthew presents provides the

---

287. Matt 5:9, 45; 6:1–8, 14–18, 32; 7:7–10.

288. Kirk, *Man Attested by God*, 380.

289. Matt 3:9; 5:9; 6:9; 7:11.

290. France, *Gospel of Matthew*, 1118.

291. Blomberg, *Matthew*, 431.

example to follow and how it is possible through Jesus's presence (28:20). Jesus promises that he will always be with his disciples to the end of the age (28:20).[292] Matthew demonstrates how the moral exemplar lives a life with the presence and power of God with him. The First Evangelist's narrative portrays the life of the human Jesus in a manner that encourages the Jewish Christian readers to believe in and imitate Jesus Christ's character and priorities.

CONCLUSION

This final section of Matthew's Gospel is set apart by his last use of the structural marker ἀπὸ τότε ἤρξατο ("from that time he began," Matt 16:21). Peter's confession is the turning point in the Matthean narrative (16:16).[293] Marking the beginning of the end, the death predictions in this final section inform the disciples of Jesus's impending suffering, death, and resurrection (16:21—28:20).[294] As Matthew draws his Jesus story to a close, Matthean interest in the humanity of Jesus drives the story to fulfill Jesus's predictions that start after ἀπὸ τότε ἤρξατο ("from that time he began," 16:21). Matthew leads the audience through the end of his main character's life and prioritizes the human story of Jesus through many examples. Jesus is angry (21:12–13), hungry (21:18), and displays a lack of knowledge (24:36). Sorrowful and troubled (26:37–38), he confesses a will contrary to his Father (26:39). Jesus suffers (26:67; 27:27–54), dies (27:45–54), and depends on God to rise bodily from the dead (28:9). While each of these can be located in Mark, as has been seen, Matthew adds to and emphasizes the role the humanity of Jesus plays in Matthew's narrative because Matthew wants to accentuate different aspects of Jesus's humanity.

Matthew emphasizes the human story of Jesus as an instrument for prophetic fulfillment. Only Matthew adds fulfillment to the triumphal entry and Judas's betrayal (Matt 21:4–5; 27:3–10). As an apologetic for belief, the story of Jesus's humanity not only reinforces belief in him as the Messiah but also as an exemplar. Only Matthew adds Jesus paying a temple tax

---

292. France, *Gospel of Matthew*, 1108, observes that Matthew brackets the Gospel by echoing the concept that God is with us (1:23; 28:20). Hagner, *Matthew 14–28*, 888, also points out the recall of the promise that Jesus will be with the church during the confrontation of sin (18:20). In light of OT passages, several indicate that YHWH is immanent with his people (Gen 28:15; Exod 3:12; Josh 1:5, 9; Isa 41:10). Luz, *Matthew 21–28*, 620, reminds the reader of other assurances of God's presence from OT prophecies (Hag 1:13; 2:4; Jer 49:11).

293. Hagner, *Matthew 14–28*, 476–77.

294. Matt 16:21–23; 17:22–23; 20:17–19; 26:1–2.

to avoid offense (17:24–27). Only Matthew portrays Jesus being tempted to sin after Peter's confession (16:23), but Jesus obediently submits to the Father's will in spite of his own (26:39–44). Jesus verifies his status as a transcendent Son through obedience, which models a life of obedience for the disciples.[295] Only Matthew's Jesus expressly gives his life so others can experience forgiveness through the shedding of his own blood (26:26–29). Prior to shedding his blood, only Matthew emphasizes Jesus' innocence and righteousness (27:4, 19). In this Gospel, the storyline serves as a means to imitate Christ not only through the story but also in light of Jesus's presence with them (28:20). Finally, Matthew purposely balances the humanity and transcendence of Jesus. Providing the evidence that Jesus is the human Son of God, Matthew prioritizes and develops the human story of Jesus to accomplish the necessary prophetic fulfillments and apologetic for belief in a manner that resonates with his Jewish Christian audience so that they can believe in and submit to the moral exemplar who is both human and transcendent.

While the portrait of Jesus's human journey displays transcendence through his life, the Jesus story ends with a human death, burial, and also dependent resurrection. All the while balancing the human and transcendent identity for the audience, Matthew continues to display an interest in the humanity of Jesus even at the resurrection. Again, as an apologetic for Jewish Christian belief, the story of the end of Jesus's life resonates with the audience's knowledge of the end and new beginning in spite of the lie that has been spread that the disciples stole the body of Jesus (Matt 28:11–15). Matthew prioritizes a post-resurrected human with an ordinary description of Jesus and the ability of the women to grasp his feet (28:8–10). The purposeful balance between the humanity and transcendent identity of Jesus remains intact as the one who possesses all authority, yet that authority is given to him after being raised from the dead (28:5–6, 18). The one who lives as the moral exemplar throughout Matthew's narrative perspective now provides not only the final command to make disciples but also the promise that he will be with them (28:19–20). For Matthew's character to proclaim and to promise these things, Matthew chooses to maintain and develop that balance between the human and transcendent as he ends the story of Jesus's earthly existence.

295. Luz, *Studies in Matthew*, 93.

5

Jesus the Man and the Model

JOHN P. MEIER STATES, "Jesus was a man and a Jew of his times."[1] While Matthew's portrayal depicts Jesus as a Jewish man living in the first century, the focus on his transcendence in scholarship has clouded the discussion of Jesus's humanity. Dale C. Allison Jr. states, "Again and again Jesus' deity has all but liquidated his humanity, making him a historically impossible figure. He has been a simulacrum, his humanity merely a doctrine to be believed, not a fact to be felt."[2] As has been seen, in spite of Jesus being a Jewish man,[3] few studies explore the humanity of Jesus in the Gospels.[4] J. R. Daniel Kirk uses "thin" to describe the work done on the humanity of Jesus in the Gospels.[5] However, this narrative critical study of Matthew gives voice to Matthew's portrait of Jesus's humanity. Through this project it has become clear that Matthew's Jesus is regularly described in a manner that is similar to the rest of humankind.[6] Indeed, prima facie, of the Gospel writers, Matthew appears most preoccupied with depicting the human element of Jesus's identity throughout the Gospel.

This, then, is the first *et seriatim* study of the humanity of Jesus in Matthew. Examining Matthew through the lens of narrative criticism provides the opportunity to examine Jesus as the main character of the narrative.

1. Meier, *Mentor, Message, and Miracles*, 407.
2. Allison, *Historical Christ*, 82.
3. Meier, *Mentor, Message, and Miracles*, 407.
4. See ch. 1.3 above.
5. Kirk, *Man Attested by God*, 16.
6. Allison, *Historical Christ*, 80, indicates that the Gospel "texts present [Jesus] as a human being like the rest of us, a person of flesh and blood and of human psychology."

As the primary tool in this study, application of narrative criticism demonstrates Matthew's intentional interest in the human element of the Jesus portrait. With the additional implementation of redaction criticism, Matthew's interest in the human portrait of Jesus is apparent. These two tools have enabled this study to answer questions that help define and develop our understanding of the Matthean concern for the human portrait of Jesus.

In this study, it has become clear that attention to the First Evangelist's human portrayal of Jesus is of academic and pastoral value. Academically, in the midst of growing interest in the humanity of Jesus,[7] this study gives voice to Matthew's depiction of Jesus's humanity. Pastorally, giving voice to Matthew's portrayal of the humanity of Jesus encourages his followers to imitate their master and teacher in order to be disciple makers (Matt 10:24–25; 28:18–20). As has been seen, Matthew structures and develops his narrative to show that Matthew's Jesus expects his followers to imitate him.

This project confirms what Irenaeus points out: Matthew's Gospel "is the Gospel of [h]is humanity; for which reason it is, too, that a humble and meek man is kept up through the whole Gospel."[8] We have seen in the portrait of the human beginning (chapter 2), the portrait of the human life with transcendent status (chapter 3), and the portrait of the human end (chapter 4), that Matthew develops the significance of the humanity of Jesus and its role in his Christology in these sections of Matthew in three primary ways. These conclusions point out the priority, purpose, and perspective of Matthew's portrayal of the human Jesus.

5.1 THE PRIORITY OF JESUS'S HUMANITY

Through narrative and redaction criticisms, this project demonstrates that Matthew's interest in Jesus as a human is greater than the other Gospel authors. Matthew prioritizes the human story to encourage his audience to believe Matthew's perspective on the human identity of Jesus. He initiates his Gospel connecting Jesus's human lineage with David and Abraham (Matt 1:1–17). That portrayal authenticates him as a Jew and royal descendent.[9] As the only Gospel to initiate the story with Jesus's genealogy and birth,[10]

---

7. See ch. 1, n41 above.

8. Irenaeus, *Haer.* 3.11.8.

9. Luz, *Matthew 1–7*, 81–82. Bock and Simpson, *Jesus According to Scripture*, 123–24.

10. See ch. 1, n146 above. Comparing the Gospels, John begins with the deity of Jesus (John 1:1). Luke initiates his Gospel with John the Baptist (Luke 1:1–25). Mark does

it is evident that Matthew's Gospel prioritizes the human origin story. W. D. Davies and Allison suggest that Christology evolves from lesser to greater "because [Matthew] lacks certain details which make Jesus more human,"[11] yet as has been seen, prioritizing the humanity of Jesus is a recurring motif for Matthew. Matthew preserves, elaborates, and uses the humanity of Jesus more than the other Gospel authors throughout his portrait.

We began comparing the different levels of interest in the humanity of Jesus with John's Gospel. John's Gospel explicitly encourages readers to believe that Jesus is the Christ, the Son of God so that people can experience life (John 20:31). Even though the climactic confession of Peter in Matthew is that Jesus is the Christ, the Son of the living God (Matt 16:16), John's portrayal does not include Matthean emphases that reinforce Jesus's humanity. For example, John does not include Jesus's human genealogy, temptation, transfiguration, or agony in Gethsemane. Marianne Meye Thompson has dedicated a monograph to the humanity of Jesus in John's Gospel,[12] yet the author of John is the least interested in the humanity of Jesus particularly in light of the prologue and the proclamation of unity with the Father, both uniquely Johannine (John 1:1–18; 10:30).

Initially, one might balk at the idea that Mark's Jesus is less human than Matthew's due to multiple instances where Matthew modifies Mark's portrayal seemingly to reduce the human element. For instance, Matthew removes the Markan scene where Jesus fails to heal the blind man on the initial attempt (Mark 8:22–25). Matthew alters Jesus's inability to heal in his hometown (Matt 13:58 // Mark 6:5). Matthew lessens the depiction of the emotional stress at the Garden of Gethsemane (Matt 26:37–38 // Mark 14:33–34). However, Matthew's portrayal of Jesus includes much more of the human story of Jesus than Mark.

We have seen that Matthew provides the origin story and birth narratives of Jesus, connecting his genealogical descent from David and Abraham (Matt 1:1—2:23). Only Matthew's portrayal of Peter's rebuke proves to be σκάωδαλον ("a stumbling block") for Jesus (Matt 16:23 // Mark 8:33).[13] At first, it appears that Mark's Jesus expresses more emotions than Matthew's Jesus. R. T. France, describing the removal of ἐθαύμαζεν ("he marveled") in Nazareth (Matt 13:58 // Mark 6:6), suggests that Matthew "typically omits"

not provide Jesus's birth narratives and opens with the good news and John the Baptist (Mark 1:1–8).

11. Davies and Allison, *Matthew 1–7*, 104–5.

12. Thompson, *Humanity of Jesus*.

13. Bauer, "σκάωδαλον," BDAG, 926, defines σκάωδαλον as "an action or circumstance that leads one to act contrary to a proper course of action or set of beliefs."

matters that are considered "unessential" to the story.[14] Richard Burridge also suggests Matthew has a tendency to omit Mark's references to Jesus's human feelings.[15] However, both fail to note that the Matthean Jesus at some point in the narrative expresses each of the redacted Markan emotions in the story except indignance and love (Mark 10:14, 20–21).[16] It has been demonstrated that Matthew redacts the human element for storytelling and theological purposes.[17] This is reinforced by activities that emphasize Jesus's humanity. Mark does not indicate the source of Jesus's ability when casting out demons, but Matthew's Jesus casts out demons by the Spirit of God (Matt 12:28 // Mark 3:22–27 // Luke 11:20).[18] Matthew makes clear Jesus's passivity in being raised from the dead.[19] Finally, the women at the tomb hold Jesus's feet after the resurrection (Matt 28:9).[20] If Jesus has feet pre-resurrection and touchable feet after (4:6; 15:30; 28:9), then the pre- and post-Easter body is similar.[21] These prime examples in light of this work as a whole suggest that Matthew is more interested in the human element of the portrayal than Mark.

Even though Luke includes a lengthy birth narrative and is the only Gospel author to incorporate pre-ministry activities at the temple for Jesus such as an eight-day-old baby and twelve-year-old child (Luke 1:26—2:52), Matthew is more interested in the humanity of Jesus. Five examples make this point. First, Luke removes the angels ministering to Jesus after the temptation scene (Matt 4:11 // Mark 1:13 // Luke 4:13). Second, only Luke's Jesus inexplicably passes through the midst of an angry crowd in Nazareth (Luke

14. France, *Gospel of Matthew*, 309.

15. Burridge, *Four Gospels*, 78.

16. "Sternly charged" (Matt 9:30 and Matt 8:4 // Mark 1:43). "Compassion" (Matt 20:34 // Mark 10:51–52 and Matt 8:3 // Mark 1:41). "Marvel" (Matt 8:10 and Matt 13:58 // Mark 6:6).

17. See ch. 3.1.1 above.

18. Luke's language for the source of Jesus's power differs from Matthew's (Matt 12:28 // Luke 11:20). Luke portrays that the power to cast out demons is due to the "finger of God" (Luke 11:20). In Jewish literature, the "finger of God" indicates the "active power of God." See, ch. 3, n168 above.

19. Matt 16:21 // Mark 8:31 // Luke 9:22. Matt 17:23 // Mark 9:31 // Luke 9:44. Matt 20:19 // Mark 10:34 // Luke 18:33. See ch. 4, n21 above.

20. Grasping Jesus's feet may be accomplishing more than one thing in the narrative. Luz, *Das Evangelium nach Matthäus*, 4:418, contends grasping the feet of Jesus does not emphasize the physical body of Jesus but acts as homage. Allison, *Studies in Matthew*, 115, correctly points out that Luz assumes the interpreter must choose between the two. In light of Matthew's interest in the humanity of Jesus and balancing the transcendent and human identity, Matthew's addition reinforces the portrayal of both.

21. Allison, *Studies in Matthew*, 111.

4:29–30). Third, unlike Matthew, Luke removes Jesus's lack of knowledge regarding his return (Matt 24:36 // Mark 13:32 // Luke 21:33–34) and being forsaken (Matt 27:46 // Mark 15:34 // Luke 23:46). Fourth, Luke vacillates on whether or not Jesus was a passive recipient of the power to be raised from the dead in the prediction descriptions. In the one prediction, Mark uses ἀναστῆναι ("to rise"), and Matthew and Luke select ἐγερθῆναι ("to be raised," Matt 16:21 // Mark 8:31 // Luke 9:22). In another, Luke omits the prediction that Jesus will be raised (Matt 17:23 // Mark 9:31 // Luke 9:44). In the last prediction, Luke follows Mark's use of ἀναστήσεται ("he will rise"), while Matthew employs ἐγερθήσεται ("he will be raised," Matt 20:19 // Mark 10:34 // Luke 18:33).[22] Matthew consistently depicts Jesus as dependent on something other than himself to be raised from the dead. Fifth, Luke's portrayal in the Garden of Gethsemane removes Jesus's emotional struggle with grief and distress due to the imminent suffering (Matt 26:37–38 // Mark 14:33–34 // Luke 22:40–42).[23] These five examples demonstrate Matthew is more interested in the human portrayal than Luke.

In light of this evidence, Matthew's portrayal turns out to be the most human of the Gospels followed by Mark, Luke, and then John. If Matthew prioritizes Jesus's humanity as more human than Mark, Luke, or John, then Matthew's purpose for and perspective on the humanity of Jesus deserves attention by those who read his narrative and describe the portrayal of Matthew's main character. The following two conclusions, in light of this project, suggest why.

5.2 THE PURPOSE OF JESUS'S HUMANITY

Matthew's purpose in the portrayal is to encourage belief in the human element of the Jesus story. For example, Matthew's Jesus has a mother, brothers, and sisters (1:18—2:1; 13:55). Jesus needs protection (2:13–23), encounters temptation (4:1–11; 16:21–23), gets hungry (4:2; 21:18), displays emotions,[24] experiences a lack of knowledge (24:36; 27:46), suffers,[25]

---

22. See ch. 4, n21 above.

23. Luke 22:43–44 is regarded as a later tradition. These verses describe angels ministering to Jesus as he prays to the Father so intensely that he sweats drops of blood. See Metzger, *Textual Commentary*, 177; Ehrman and Plunkett, "Angel and the Agony," 401–16; Green, "Jesus on the Mount of Olives," 29–48.

24. Ἐθαύμασεν ("He marveled," Matt 8:10); ἐνεβριμήθη ("he sternly charged," 9:30); forms of σπλαγχνίζομαι ("to have compassion," 9:36; 14:14; 15:32; 20:34); λυπεῖσθαι ("to be grieved," 26:37) and ἀδημονεῖν (" to be troubled," 26:37); περίλυπός ("very sorrowful," 26:38).

25. Matt 16:21; 17:12. Matt 26:67–68 // Mark 14:65 // Luke 22:63–65. Matt 27:26 //

depends on God,[26] dies (27:45–54), and rises bodily from the dead (28:9). In spite of a resurrection from the dead, Jesus's physical body remains intact as he is touchable and recognizable to those who interact with him (28:9, 17). The human element of the story assists to develop the believability of Matthew's main character.

Customizing the story to strengthen belief in Jesus as a fulfiller of prophecy,[27] Matthew uses the life activities of the human Jesus to present him as a human, genealogical descendant of David. Each phase of life depicted contains sections that connect the human existence of Jesus with prophetic fulfillment. In the portrait of the human beginning, Matthew connects Jesus not only to David and Abraham (Matt 1:1–17) but also specifically to a virgin birth (1:22–23), a birth in Bethlehem (2:5–6), a call out of Egypt (2:15), a cry for children (2:17–18), and life as a Nazarene (2:23). Prior to the beginning of his ministry, only Matthew geographically connects a prophetic utterance to the earthly location of Jesus's ministry beginnings (4:14–16). In the portrait of the human life with transcendent status, Jesus would bear the infirmities and sickness of others (8:16–17),[28] and the Spirit rests on him (12:17–21). Even Jesus teaching in parables fulfills prophetic expectations (13:14–15, 35).[29] In the final phase of the portrait of the human end, only Matthew points out that the triumphal entry and betrayal for thirty pieces of silver fulfill messianic expectations (21:4–5; 27:9–10). Birger Gerhardsson claims that "practically every page of the New Testament witnesses to the early Christians' eagerness to show that the ministry of Jesus took place 'according to the scriptures' . . . The efforts are most strikingly evident in the Gospel of Matthew, especially in the eleven so-called formula quotations."[30] While Gerhardsson's assertion is correct, he does not address the way the life activities of the human portrayal make the Matthean efforts feasible. Each of these prophetic fulfillments are made possible through Matthew's intentional use of the human portrayal of Jesus.

Even though Matthew preserves and elaborates his human depiction, it has been seen that he balances the human and transcendent existence of Jesus. In response to Peter's confession (Matt 16:16), Allison and Davies point out, "As Jewish messianism had anticipated, the Messiah in Matthew

---

Mark 15:15. Matt 27:27–31 // Mark 15:17–20 // Luke 19:1–3.

26. See ch. 4, n21 above.

27. Matt 1:22–23; 2:5–6, 15, 17–18, 23; 4:14–16; 8:17; 12:17–20; 13:14–15, 35; 21:4–5; 27:9–10.

28. See ch. 3.1.1 above.

29. Isa 6:9–10; Ps 78:2; Matt 13:14–15, 35.

30. Gerhardsson, "Christology of Matthew," 28.

is certainly a human figure. But he also stands in a special relation to God, as God's Son."[31] This study shows that Matthew's depiction intentionally provides a description of Jesus that makes the human and transcendent identity believable. Harry Boer argues that the Christian community tended to protect the transcendent at the expense of the humanity of Jesus.[32] Even though Matthew builds the argument for Jesus's transcendence, he does not do so at the expense of the human portrayal. For example, rather than elevating Jesus's transcendence at the healing of the paralytic, Matthew alters the story to demonstrate authority to forgive sins is not limited to Jesus.[33] In the scene describing the young man who desires to obtain eternal life, Matthew emphasizes the human portrayal to draw out the attitude of the young man (Matt 19:16–22 // Mark 10:17–22 // Luke 18:18–23). Matthew's Jesus still struggles at the Garden of Gethsemane and feels forsaken by God (Matt 26:37–38; 27:46). At the resurrection, Matthew's Jesus possesses all authority, yet that authority is given to him after being raised from the dead (28:5–6, 18). Matthew does protect Jesus's transcendence but he accomplishes this in light of and not at the expense of the humanity of Jesus.

As has been seen, Matthew preserves the human story to distinguish Jesus and God in a manner that anticipates the dogma of two natures in the church.[34] Matthew purposely writes so that the community can be expected to maintain belief in Jesus's transcendent and human identity. In light of Matthew's interest in telling the human story and establishing Jesus with transcendent status, Matthew keeps the human identity intact for the reader. Even though Ulrich Luz states: "While he is human, he is not only and not primarily human,"[35] this project suggests it may be more appropriate to say that Jesus is the human person in whom God is wholly present.[36]

5.3 THE PERSPECTIVE ON JESUS'S HUMANITY

It has been shown that Matthew develops the human portrayal of Jesus so that his readers will imitate him. The form and function of Matthew's narrative reflects a Greco-Roman biography,[37] and according to David E. Aune, one purpose of this genre is to portray the main character as a moral

31. Davies and Allison, *Matthew 8–18*, 642.

32. Boer, "Rich Young Ruler," 16.

33. Matt 16:19; 18:18. Matt 9:8 // Mark 2:12 // Luke 5:26.

34. Luz, *Studies in Matthew*, 96.

35. Luz, *Matthew 21–28*, 91.

36. Harrington, "Jesus Our Brother," 118.

37. Aune, "Greco-Roman Biography," 107–26.

model.[38] For Paul, other early Christian authors, and Origen, Jesus is a model for emulation.[39] As Matthew portrays Jesus, it is clear that the perspective on the portrayal of Jesus's human story is the *imitatio Christi*.[40]

Matthew's human portrayal connects the humanity of Jesus with the humanity of the disciples. Even though Aune remarks that Matthew fails explicitly to "emphasize the *imitation* of Jesus,"[41] Allison indicates Matthew portrays Jesus as "a real human being and therefore as a real ethical model."[42] Only Matthew's Jesus desires "to fulfill all righteousness" (Matt 3:15). We have seen that the Matthean Sermon on the Mount connects multiple principles of the sermon with the human activities of Jesus.[43] Commissioning his disciples, Matthew's Jesus expands its instructions (Matt 10:1, 5–16 // Mark 6:8–11 // Luke 9:2–5). While Luke's Jesus commissions the disciples to heal and preach, Matthew details the instructions to the twelve disciples to heal the sick, raise the dead, cleanse lepers, and cast out demons (Matt 10:8 // Luke 9:2). Only Matthew's narrative leading up to the mission shows Jesus performing each of these seemingly transcendent activities. Jesus heals the sick Centurion's servant (Matt 8:5–13). A daughter is raised from the dead (9:18–26). He cleanses a leper and drives out the Gadarene demons (8:1–4; 28–34). After the miracles within the second discourse, Matthew and Luke portray Jesus saying the disciple may be like his teacher (Matt 10:24–25 // Luke 6:40), but only Matthew reinforces the imitation motif that portrays servants are to be like their master (10:24–25). If Matthew completely removes the believability of the humanity of Jesus, it undermines his attempt not only to maintain the credibility of the story of Jesus but also betrays the goal to portray Jesus as one the disciples are capable of imitating.

The pragmatic side of Jesus's human life as the moral exemplar has been somewhat lost in the midst of our social milieu. R. H. Culpepper states that when "the genuine humanity of Jesus is taken seriously, it has revolutionary effects in both the personal and social dimensions."[44] Those dimensions encourage humankind to engage the world in a manner that is necessary for human flourishing, and one way human flourishing occurs is

38. Aune, *New Testament*, 62 (emphasis original).

39. 1 Cor. 11:1; Rom 15:1–7. Allison, *Studies in Matthew*, 148–49n43–45. Sim, "Pacifist Jesus," 2, emphasizes that Jesus is "the definitive role model."

40. Allison, *Studies in Matthew*, 135–57.

41. Aune, *New Testament*, 62 (emphasis original), remarks that Matthew and Luke "do not explicitly emphasize the *imitation* of Jesus" because the exemplar status is "implicitly understood."

42. Allison, *Studies in Matthew*, 149.

43. See ch. 3, n24 above.

44. Culpepper, "Humanity of Jesus," 26.

through emulating Jesus, Matthew's moral exemplar. The *imitatio Christi* motif is made possible because of the Matthean perspective on the humanity of Jesus in the narrative.

5.4 THE HUMANITY OF JESUS IN MATTHEW

This project serves as a launching pad to take the human portrayal of Jesus seriously enough that it becomes a part of the conversation for the advanced study of Matthean theology. As David C. Sim specifies, there is a "desperate need" for an advanced study of Matthean theology.[45] Indeed, christological studies are giving us too narrow a view of Jesus. To this point, our perception of and interest in his transcendence eclipses Jesus's humanity in christological studies. However, Matthew wrote a Gospel that shows clear interest in Jesus's humanity. We have seen that Matthew's portrayal of the humanity of Jesus gives rise to our three conclusions. First, along the Gospel spectrum of interest in the humanity of Jesus, Matthew prioritizes the humanity of Jesus because he had the greatest interest. Second, Matthew, purposely balancing the human and transcendent identity of Jesus, encourages belief in both the humanity and transcendent status. Third, providing the perspective that Jesus is the exemplar to imitate, Matthew preserves and develops the human story of Jesus.

Imitation of the exemplar is possible because of Jesus's human existence. Matthew's depiction of Jesus as a man is not only a doctrine to be believed but also a reality to be experienced.[46] Through a narrative critical approach, Matthew's portrait makes clear that Jesus's identity includes his humanity, and Matthew's Jesus lived a model life that can be emulated. The question, at a pastoral level, is whether people will examine Matthew's Gospel and believe so they will obey the command to be like their master and teacher in order to be disciple makers.

---

45. Sim, "Matthew," 34–35.

46. Allison, *Historical Christ*, 82. This is a modification of Allison's assertion that Jesus's humanity is a "doctrine to be believed, not a fact to be felt."

Bibliography

Abegg, Martin G., and Craig A. Evans. "Messianic Passages in the Dead Sea Scrolls." In *Qumran-Messianism: Studies on the Messianic Expectations in the Dead Sea Scrolls.* Edited by James H. Charlesworth et al., 191–203. Tübingen: Mohr Siebeck, 1998.

Aland, Kurt, ed. *Synopsis of the Four Gospels: Greek-English Edition of the Synopsis Quattuor Evangeliorum.* 9th ed. Germany: Biblia-Druck Stuttgart, 1989.

Albright, W. F., and C. S. Mann. *Matthew.* AB 26. Garden City, NY: Doubleday, 1971.

Allen, W. C. *Critical and Exegetical Commentary on the Gospel According to S. Matthew.* New York: Charles Scribner's Sons, 1925.

Allison, Dale C., Jr. *Constructing Jesus: Memory, Imagination, and History.* Grand Rapids: Baker Academic, 2010.

———. *The Historical Christ and the Theological Jesus.* Grand Rapids: Eerdmans, 2009.

———. *The New Moses: A Matthean Typology.* Minneapolis: Fortress, 1993. Repr. Eugene, OR: Wipf & Stock, 2013.

———. "The Structure of the Sermon on the Mount." *JBL* 106 (1987) 423–45.

———. *Studies in Matthew: Interpretation Past and Present.* Grand Rapids: Baker Academic, 2005.

Anderson, Janice Capel. "Double and Triple Stories, the Implied Reader, and Redundancy in Matthew." *Semeia* 31 (1985) 71–89.

Aune, David E. "Greco-Roman Biography." In *Greco-Roman Literature and the New Testament: Selected Forms and Genres*, edited by David E. Aune, 107–26. Atlanta: Scholars, 1988.

———. *The New Testament in Its Literary Environment.* LEC. Philadelphia: Westminster, 1987.

Bakke, O. M. *When Children Became People.* Minneapolis: Fortress, 2005.

Baltes, Guido. *Hebräisches Evangelium und synoptische Überlieferung: Untersuchungen zum hebräischen Hintergrund der Evangelien.* WUNT 2/312. Tübingen: Mohr Siebeck, 2011.

Barrett, C. K. "The Background of Mark 10:45." *New Testament Essays* (1959) 1–18.

Barton, Stephen C., ed. *The Family in Theological Perspective.* Edinburgh: T. & T. Clark, 1996.

———. "The Transfiguration of Christ according to Mark and Matthew: Christology and Anthropology." In *Auferstehung—Resurrection*, edited by Friedrich Avemarie and Hermann Lichtenberger, 231–46. WUNT 135. Tübingen: Mohr Siebeck, 2001.

Basser, Herbert W. "Derrett's 'Binding' Reopened." *JBL* 104 (1985) 297–300.

Batto, Bernard. "The Sleeping God: An Ancient Near Eastern Motif in Divine Sovereignty." *Biblica* 68 (1987) 153–77.

Bauckham, Richard, ed. *The Gospels for All Christians: Rethinking the Gospel Audiences.* Grand Rapids: Eerdmans, 1997.

———. *Jesus and the Eyewitnesses: The Gospels as Eyewitness Testimony.* Grand Rapids: Eerdmans, 2006.

Bauer, Walter, et al. *Greek-English Lexicon of the New Testament and Other Early Christian Literature.* 3rd ed. Chicago: University of Chicago Press, 2000.

Bayer, Hans F. *Jesus' Predictions of Vindication and Resurrection.* WUNT 20. Tübingen: Mohr Siebeck, 1986.

Beare, F. W. *The Gospel According to Matthew: Translation, Introduction, and Commentary.* New York: Harper & Row, 1982.

Becker, Eve-Marie. *Das Markus-Evangelium im Rahmen antiker Historiographie.* WUNT 194. Tübingen: Mohr Siebeck, 2006.

Berger, Klaus. "Jesus als Nasoräer/Nasiräer." *NovT* 38 (1996) 323–35.

Betz, Hans Dieter. "The Portrait of Jesus in the Sermon on the Mount." *CurTM* 25 (1998) 165–75.

Black, C. Clifton. "The Quest of Mark the Redactor: Why Has It Been Pursued, and What Has It Taught Us?" *JSNT* 33 (1988) 19–39.

Blomberg, Craig L. *Matthew.* NAC 22. Nashville: Broadman, 1992.

Bock, Darrell L. "Son of Man." In *DJG* 894–900.

Bock, Darrell L., and Benjamin Simpson. *Jesus According to Scripture: Restoring the Portrait from the Gospels.* 2nd ed. Grand Rapids: Baker Academic, 2017.

———. *Jesus the God-Man: The Unity and Diversity of the Gospel Portrayals.* Grand Rapids: Baker Academic, 2016.

Boer, Harry R. "The Rich Young Ruler." *Reformed Journal* 26 (1976) 15–18.

Bressler, Charles E. *Literary Criticism: An Introduction to Theory and Practice.* 2nd ed. Upper Saddle River, NJ: Prentice-Hall, 1999.

Bromley, Donald Howard. "The Healing of the Hemorrhaging Woman: Miracle or Magic?" *Proceedings* 25 (2005) 15–27.

Brown, Raymond E. *The Birth of the Messiah: A Commentary on the Infancy Narratives in the Gospels of Matthew and Luke.* Rev. ed. ABRL. New York: Doubleday, 1993.

———. *Death of the Messiah: From Gethsemane to the Grave.* ABRL. 2 vols. New York: Doubleday, 1994.

———. *The Gospel According to John 1–12.* AB 29. Garden City, NY: Doubleday, 1966.

———. "How Much Did Jesus Know: A Survey of the Biblical Evidence." *CBQ* 29 (1967) 315–45.

———. *An Introduction to New Testament Christology.* New York: Paulist, 1994.

———. *Jesus God and Man: Modern Biblical Reflections.* New York: Macmillan, 1967.

Brown, Raymond E., and John P. Meier. *Antioch and Rome: New Testament Cradles of Catholic Christianity.* New York: Paulist, 1983.

Burkett, Delbert. *The Son of Man Debate: A History and Evaluation.* SNTSMS 107. Cambridge: Cambridge University, 1999.

Burridge, Richard A. *Four Gospels, One Jesus? A Symbolic Reading.* 3rd ed. Grand Rapids: Eerdmans, 2014.

———. *What are the Gospels? A Comparison with Graeco-Roman Biography.* 2nd ed. Grand Rapids: Eerdmans, 2004.

Cargal, Timothy B. "'His Blood Be Upon Us and Upon Our Children': A Matthean Double Entendre?" *NTS* 37 (1991) 101–12.

Carson, D. A. "Redaction Criticism: On the Legitimacy and Illegitimacy of a Literary Tool." Pages 119–46 in *Scripture and Truth*. Edited by D. A. Carson and John D. Woodbridge. Repr. Eugene, OR: Wipf & Stock, 2002.

Carter, Warren. "Paying the Tax to Rome as Subversive Praxis." *JSNT* 76 (1991) 3–31.

Clarke, Howard. *The Gospel of Matthew and Its Readers: A Historical Introduction to the First Gospel*. Bloomington: Indiana University Press, 2003.

Cohen, Shaye J. D. *From the Maccabees to the Mishnah*. LEC 7. Philadelphia: Westminster, 1987.

Collins, Adela Yarbro. "Establishing the Text: Mark 1:1." In *Texts and Contexts: Biblical Texts in Their Textual and Situational Contexts*, edited by Tord Fronberg and David Hellholm, 111–27. Oslo: Scandinavian University Press, 1995.

———. *Mark*. Hermeneia—A Critical and Historical Commentary on the Bible. Philadelphia: Fortress, 2007.

Compton, Todd. "Was Jesus a Feminist?" *Di* 32 (1999) 1–17.

Conzelmann, Hans. *Die Mitte der Zeit: Studien zur Theologie des Lukas*. BHT 17. Tübingen: Mohr Siebeck, 1954.

Cox, Patricia. *Biography in Late Antiquity: A Quest for the Holy Man*. Berkeley: University of California Press, 1983.

Crisp, Oliver D. *Divinity and Humanity: The Incarnation Reconsidered*. Current Issues in Theology. Cambridge: Cambridge University Press, 2007.

Crossan, John Dominic, et al. *The Jesus Controversy: Perspectives in Conflict*. The Rockwell Lecture Series. Harrisburg, PA: Trinity, 1999.

Cullmann, Oscar. *The Christology of the New Testament*. Rev. ed. Translated by Shirley C. Guthrie and Charles A. M. Hall. NTL. Philadelphia: Westminster, 1963.

———. *Immortality of the Soul or Resurrection of the Dead: The Witness of the New Testament*. London: Epworth, 1958.

Culpepper, R. H. "The Humanity of Jesus the Christ: An Overview." *Faith and Mission* 5 (1988) 14–27.

Dahood, Mitchell. *Psalms I: 1–50*. AB 16. Garden City, NY: Doubleday, 1965.

Davies, W. D., and Dale C. Allison Jr. *A Critical and Exegetical Commentary on the Gospel According to Saint Matthew 1–7*. ICC. Edinburgh: T. & T. Clark, 1988.

———. *A Critical and Exegetical Commentary on the Gospel According to Saint Matthew 8–18*. ICC. Edinburgh: T. & T. Clark, 1988.

———. *A Critical and Exegetical Commentary on the Gospel According to Saint Matthew 19–28*. ICC. Edinburgh: T. & T. Clark, 1997.

Denaux, Adelbert, ed. *John and the Synoptics*. BETL. Leuven: Leuven University Press, 1992.

Donaldson, Terence L. "The Vindicated Son: A Narrative Approach to Matthean Christology." In *Contours of Christology in the New Testament*, edited by Richard N. Longenecker, 100–21. Grand Rapids: Eerdmans, 2005.

Dorman, T. M. "Oscar Cullman (1902–1999)." In *DMBI* 333–38.

Duling, Dennis C. "Binding and Loosing: Matthew 16:19; Matthew 18:18; John 20:23." *Forum* 3 (1987) 3–31.

Dunn, James D. G. *Christology in the Making: A New Testament Inquiry into the Origins of the Doctrine of the Incarnation*. Philadelphia: Westminster, 1980.

―――. *Jesus Remembered*. Vol. 1 of *Christianity in the Making*. Grand Rapids: Eerdmans, 2003.

Dunn, James D. G., and James P. Mackey. *New Testament Theology in Dialogue: Christology and Ministry*. Philadelphia: Westminster, 1987.

Durham, John I. *Exodus*. WBC 3. Nashville: Thomas Nelson, 1987.

Edwards, James R. *The Hebrew Gospel and the Development of the Synoptic Tradition*. Grand Rapids: Eerdmans, 2009.

Ehrman, Bart D., and Mark A. Plunkett. "The Angel and the Agony: The Textual Problem of Luke 22:43–44." *CBQ* 45 (1983) 401–16.

Ennulat, Andreas. *Die Minor Agreements: Untersuchungen zu einer offenen Frage des synoptischen Problems*. WUNT 62. Tübingen: Mohr Siebeck, 1994.

France, R. T. *The Gospel of Matthew*. NICNT. Grand Rapids: Eerdmans, 2007.

―――. "Herod and the Children of Bethlehem." *NovT* 21 (1979) 98–120.

―――. *The Intention of Matthew 23*. NovTSup 52. Leiden: Brill, 1979.

―――. *Matthew: Evangelist and Teacher*. Repr. Eugene, OR: Wipf & Stock, 2004.

Garland, David E. *Reading Matthew: A Literary and Theological Commentary*. Reading the New Testament. Macon, GA: Smyth & Helwys, 2001.

―――. "The Temple Tax in Matthew 17:24–25 and the Principle of not Causing Offense." In *Treasures New and Old: Recent Contributions to Matthean Studies*, edited by David R. Bauer and Mark Allen Powell, 69–98. Atlanta: Scholars, 1996.

Gerhardsson, Birger. "The Christology of Matthew." In *Who Do You Say That I Am?: Essays on Christology*, edited by Mark Allan Powell and David R. Bauer, 14–32. Louisville: Westminster John Knox, 1999.

―――. *The Testing of God's Son (Matt 4:1–11 and Par): An Analysis of an Early Christian Midrash*. ConBNT 2.1. Lund: Gleerup, 1966.

Gibson, Jeffrey. "Jesus' Refusal to Produce a 'Sign' (MK 8.11–13)." *JSNT* 38 (1990) 37–66.

Goldingay, John. *Isaiah*. NIBCOT 13. Peabody, MA: Hendrickson, 2001.

Goodacre, Mark. "Criticizing the Criterion of Multiple Attestation: The Historical Jesus and the Question of Sources." In *Jesus, Criteria, and the Demise of Authenticity*, edited by Chris Keith and Anthony Le Donne, 152–72. New York: T. & T. Clark, 2012.

―――. *The Synoptic Problem: A Way Through the Maze*. BibSem 80. Sheffield: Sheffield Academic, 2001.

Green, Joel B. *The Gospel of Luke*. NICNT. Grand Rapids: Eerdmans, 1997.

―――. "Jesus on the Mount of Olives (Luke 22:39–46): Tradition and Theology." *JSNT* 26 (1986) 29–48.

―――, ed. *Hearing the New Testament: Strategies for Interpretation*. 2nd ed. Grand Rapids: Eerdmans, 2010.

Grün, Anselm. *Jesus, The Image of Humanity: Luke's Account*. Translated by John Bowden. New York: Continuum, 2003.

Gundry, Robert. *Matthew: A Commentary on His Literary and Theological Art*. Grand Rapids: Eerdmans, 1982.

―――. *The Old Is Better*. WUNT 178. Tübingen: Mohr Siebeck, 2005.

―――. *The Use of the Old Testament in St. Matthew's Gospel: With Special Reference to the Messianic Hope*. NovTSup 18. Leiden: Brill, 1975.

Hagner, Donald A. *Matthew 1–13*. WBC 33A. Nashville: Nelson, 1993.

―――. *Matthew 14–28*. WBC 33B. Grand Rapids: Zondervan, 2015.

Hallman, Joseph M. "The Seed of Fire: Divine Suffering in the Christology of Cyril of Alexandria and Nestorius of Constantinople." *JECS* 5 (1997) 369–91.

Hare, Douglas R. A. *Matthew*. IBC. Louisville: John Knox, 1993.

Harrington, Daniel J. *The Gospel of Matthew*. SP 1. Collegeville, MN: Liturgical, 1991.

Harrington, Wilfrid J. "Jesus Our Brother: The Humanity of the Lord." *ScrC* 39 (2009) 118–28.

———. "The Man Christ Jesus." Text presented at the Eighth Annual Flannery Lecture at Gonzaga University. Spokane, WA, April 1984.

Hawthorne, Gerald F. *The Presence and the Power: The Significance of the Holy Spirit in the Life and Ministry of Jesus*. Dallas: Word, 1991.

Hayes, John H., ed. *Dictionary of Biblical Interpretation*. 2 vols. Nashville: Abingdon, 1998.

Heil, John Paul. "The Blood of Jesus in Matthew: A Narrative-Critical Perspective." *PRSt* 18 (1991) 117–24.

———. *The Death and Resurrection of Jesus: A Narrative-Critical Reading of Matthew 26–28*. Repr. Eugene, OR: Wipf & Stock, 2003.

———. *Jesus Walking on the Sea: Meaning and Gospel Functions of Matt 14:22–33, Mark 6:45–52, and John 6:15b–21*. AnBib 87. Rome: Biblical Institute Press, 1981.

Hengel, Martin. *The Charismatic Leader and His Followers*. Translated by James Greig. SNTW. New York: Crossroad, 1981.

———. *The Four Gospels and One Gospel of Jesus Christ: An Investigation of the Collection and Origin of the Canonical Gospels*. Translated by John Bowden. Harrisburg, PA: Trinity, 2000.

Hill, David. "In Quest of Matthean Christology." *IBS* 9 (1986)135–42.

Hooker, Morna. *The Gospel According to St Mark*. BNTC 2. Peabody, MA: Hendrickson, 1991.

———. *Jesus and the Servant: The Influence of the Servant Concept of Deutero-Isaiah in the New Testament*. Repr. Eugene, OR: Wipf & Stock, 2010.

Horbury, Williams. "The Temple Tax." *Jesus and the Politics of His Day*. Edited by Ernst Bammel and C. F. D. Moule, 265–86. Cambridge: Cambridge University Press, 1984.

Horn, Cornelia B., and John W. Martens. *"Let the Little Children Come to Me": Childhood and Children in Early Christianity*. Washington, DC: Catholic University Press of America, 2009.

Hull, John M. *Hellenistic Magic and the Synoptic Tradition*. SBT 28. Naperville, IL: Allenson, 1974.

Hummel, Reinhart. *Die Auseinandersetzung zwischen Kirche und Judentum im Mattäusevangelium*. BEvT 33. Munich: Kaiser, 1963.

Hurtado, Larry W., and Paul L. Owen, eds. *'Who Is This Son of Man?': The Latest Scholarship on a Puzzling Expression of the Historical Jesus*. LNTS. New York: Bloomsbury, 2012.

Instone-Brewer, David. "The Two Asses of Zechariah 9:9 in Matthew 21." *TynBul* 54 (2003) 87–98.

Jeremias, Joachim. "Das Lösegeld für Viele (Mk 10,45)." In *Abba*, 216–29. Göttingen: Vandenhoeck & Ruprecht, 1966.

———. *The Eucharistic Words of Jesus*. Translated by Norman Perrin. NTL. 4th ed. London: SCM, 1976.

Johnson, Luke Timothy. "Learning the Human Jesus: Historical Criticism and Literary Criticism." Pages 153–77 in *The Historical Jesus: Five Views*. Edited by James K. Beilby and Paul Rhodes Eddy. Downers Grove, IL: InterVarsity Press, 2009.

————. "The New Testament's Anti-Jewish Slander and the Convention of Ancient Polemic." *JBL* 108 (1989) 419–44.

Josipovici, Gabriel. *Touch*. New Haven, CT: Yale University Press, 1996.

Kalin, Everett R. "Matthew 9:18–26: An Exercise in Redaction Criticism." *CurTM* 15 (1988) 39–47.

Kee, Howard Clark. "Jesus: A Glutton and a Drunkard." *NTS* 42 (1996) 374–93.

Keener, Craig S. *A Commentary on the Gospel of Matthew*. Grand Rapids: Eerdmans, 1999.

————. *Miracles: The Credibility of the New Testament Accounts*. 2 vols. Grand Rapids: Baker, 2011.

Keith, John M. *Complete Humanity in Jesus: A Theological Memoir*. Montgomery, AL: NewSouth, 2009.

Kilpatrick, G. D. *The Origins of the Gospel According to St. Matthew*. Repr. Wauconda, IL: Bolchazy-Carducci, 2007.

Kingsbury, Jack Dean. *Matthew as Story*. 2nd ed. Philadelphia: Fortress, 1988.

————. *Matthew: Structure, Christology, Kingdom*. Minneapolis: Fortress, 1975.

————. "Observations on the 'Miracle Chapters' of Matthew 8–9." *CBQ* 40 (1978) 559–73.

————. "The Significance of the Earthly Jesus in the Gospel of Matthew." *ExAud* 14 (1998) 59–65.

Kirk, J. R. Daniel. *A Man Attested by God: The Human Jesus of the Synoptic Gospels*. Grand Rapids: Eerdmans, 2016.

Klink, Edward W., III, ed. *The Audience of the Gospels: Further Conversations about the Origin and Function of the Gospels in Early Christianity*. LNTS. London: T. & T. Clark, 2010.

Knox, John. *The Humanity and Divinity of Christ: A Study of Pattern in Christology*. New York: Cambridge University Press, 1967.

Kupp, David D. *Matthew's Emmanuel: Divine Presence and God's People in the First Gospel*. SNTSMS 90. Cambridge: Cambridge University Press, 1996.

Law, David R. *The Historical-Critical Method: A Guide for the Perplexed*. Guides for the Perplexed. New York: T. & T. Clark, 2012.

————. "Redaction Criticism." In *The Historical-Critical Method: A Guide for the Perplexed*, 181–215. Guides for the Perplexed. New York: T. & T. Clark, 2012.

Leim, Joshua. *Matthew's Theological Grammar: The Father and the Son*. WUNT 2/402. Tübingen: Mohr Siebeck, 2015.

————. "Worshiping the Father, Worshiping the Son: Cultic Language and the Identity of God in the Gospel of Matthew." *Journal of Theological Interpretation* 9 (2015) 65–84.

Lichtenberger, Hermann. "Messianic Expectations and Messianic Figures in the Second Temple Period." Pages 9–20 in *Qumran-Messianism: Studies on the Messianic Expectations in the Dead Sea Scrolls*. Edited by James H. Charlesworth et al. Tübingen: Mohr Siebeck, 1998.

Lindars, Barnabas. *Jesus Son of Man: A Fresh Examination of the Son of Man Sayings in the Gospels in the Light of Recent Research*. Grand Rapids: Eerdmans, 1984.

Loader, William R. G. "Son of David, Blindness, Possession, and Duality in Matthew." *CBQ* 44 (1982) 570–85.

Lohmeyer, Ernst. *Kyrios Jesus: Eine Untersuchung zu Phil. 2, 5–11*. Darmstadt: Wissenschaftliche Buchgesellschaft, 1961.

Longenecker, Richard N. "Christological Materials in the Early Christian Communities." In *Contours of Christology in the New Testament*, edited by Richard N. Longenecker, 47–76. Grand Rapids: Eerdmans, 2005.

———. *The Christology of Early Jewish Christianity*. Repr. Vancouver: Regent College, 2001.

Longman, Tremper, III. *Literary Approaches to Biblical Interpretation*. Edited by Moisés Silva. Foundations of Contemporary Interpretation 3. Grand Rapids: Academic Books, 1987.

Luz, Ulrich. *Matthew 1–7*. Hermeneia—A Critical and Historical Commentary on the Bible. Rev. ed. Philadelphia: Fortress, 2007.

———. *Matthew 8–20*. Hermeneia—A Critical and Historical Commentary on the Bible. Philadelphia: Fortress, 2001.

———. *Matthew 21–28*. Hermeneia—A Critical and Historical Commentary on the Bible. Philadelphia: Fortress, 2005.

———. *Studies in Matthew*. Translated by Rosemary Selle. Grand Rapids: Eerdmans, 2005.

———. *The Theology of the Gospel of Matthew*. New Testament Theology. Edited by James D. G. Dunn. Translated by J. Bradford Robinson. Cambridge: Cambridge University Press, 2000.

Macquarrie, John. "The Humanity of Christ." *Theology* 74 (1971) 243–50.

Manson, T. W. *The Sayings of Jesus*. Repr. Grand Rapids: Eerdmans, 1979.

Mantey, J. R. "The Causal Use of Eis in the New Testament." *JBL* 70 (1952) 45–58.

Marcos, Natalio Fernández. *The Septuagint in Context: Introduction to the Greek Version of the Bible*. Translated by Wilfred G. E. Watson. Leiden: Brill, 2000.

Marcus, Ralph. "On Causal Eis." *JBL* 70 (1952) 129–30.

Martin, Martina E. "It's My Prerogative: Jesus' Authority to Grant Forgiveness and Healing on Earth." *JRT* 59–60 (2006–2007) 67–74.

Martin, Ralph P. *A Hymn of Christ: Philippians 2:5–11 in Recent Interpretation and in the Setting of Early Christian Worship*. 2nd ed. Downers Grove, IL: InterVarsity, 1997.

Marxsen, Willi. *Der Evangelist Marcus: Studien zur Redaktionsgeschichte des Evangeliums*. Göttingen: Vandenhoeck & Ruprecht, 1959.

McCartney, Dan. "*Ecce Homo*: The Coming of the Kingdom as the Restoration of Human Vicegerency." *WTJ* 56 (1994) 1–21.

McDonnell, Kilian. *The Baptism of Jesus in the Jordan: The Trinitarian and Cosmic Order of Salvation*. Collegeville, MN: Liturgical, 1996.

McKnight, Scot. *The Letter of James*. NICNT. Grand Rapids: Eerdmans, 2011.

Meeks, Wayne A., and Robert L. Wilken. *Jews and Christians in Antioch: In the First Four Centuries of the Common Era*. SBL Sources for Biblical Study 13. Missoula, MT: Scholars, 1978.

Meier, John P. *Matthew*. NTM. Wilmington, DE: Glazier, 1980.

———. *Mentor, Message, and Miracles*. Vol. 2 of *A Marginal Jew: Rethinking the Historical Jesus*. New York: Doubleday, 1994.

———. *The Roots of the Problem and the Person.* Vol. 1 of *A Marginal Jew: Rethinking the Historical Jesus.* New York: Doubleday, 1991.

———. *The Vision of Matthew: Christ, Church, and Morality in the First Gospel.* New York: Paulist, 1979.

Mendez-Moratalla, F. "Repentance." In *DJG* 771–74.

Menken, Martinus J. J. "The Sources of the Old Testament Quotation in Matthew 2:23." *JBL* 120 (2001) 451–68.

Metzger, Bruce M. *A Textual Commentary on the Greek New Testament.* 3rd ed. Stuttgart: United Bible Societies, 1975.

Michaels, J. Ramsey. *The Gospel of John.* NICNT. Grand Rapids: Eerdmans, 2010.

Milton, Helen. "Structure of the Prologue to St Matthew's Gospel." *JBL* 81 (1962) 175–81.

Moiser, Jeremy. "The Structure of Matthew 8–9: A Suggestion." *ZNW* 76 (1985) 117–18.

Moloney, Francis J. "Constructing Jesus and the Son of Man." *CBQ* 75 (2013) 719–38.

Morris, Michael. "Deuteronomy in the Matthean and Lucan Temptation in Light of Early Jewish Antidemonic Tradition." *CBQ* 78 (2016) 290–301.

Muller, Mogens. *Der Ausdruck "Menschensohn" in den Evangelien.* Leiden: E. J. Brill, 1984.

Myllykoski, Matti. "'Christian Jews' and 'Jewish Christians': The Jewish Origins of Christianity in English Literature from Elizabeth I to Toland's *Nazarenus*." In *The Rediscovery of Jewish Christianity: From Toland to Baur*, edited by F. Stanley Jones, 3–44. HHBS 5. Atlanta: Society of Biblical Literature, 2012.

Neusner, Jacob. *Genesis Rabbah the Judaic Commentary on the Book of Genesis: A New American Translation Volume I Parashiyyot One through Thirty-Three on Genesis 1:1 to 8:4.* BJS 104. Atlanta: Scholars, 1985.

———. *Questions and Answers: Intellectual Foundations of Judaism.* Peabody, MA: Hendrickson, 2005.

Newport, Kenneth G. C. *The Sources and Sitz Im Leben of Matthew.* JSNTSup 117. Sheffield: Sheffield Academic, 1995.

Novakovic, Lidija. "Jesus as the Davidic Messiah in Matthew." *HBT* 19 (1997) 148–91.

Olivares, Carlos. "The Term ὀλιγόπιστος (Little Faith) in Matthew's Gospel: Narrative and Thematic Connections." *Colloq* 47 (2015) 274–91.

Oppenheim, A. Leo. *Ancient Mesopotamia: Portrait of a Dead Civilization.* Revised edition by Erica Reiner. Chicago: University of Chicago Press, 1977.

Osborne, Grant R. "Redaction Criticism." In *Dictionary for Theological Interpretation of the Bible*, edited by Kevin J. Vanhoozer, 663–66. Grand Rapids: Baker, 2005.

Oswalt, John N. *The Book of Isaiah 1–39.* NICOT. Grand Rapids: Eerdmans, 1986.

———. *The Book of Isaiah 40–66.* NICOT. Grand Rapids: Eerdmans, 1998.

Overman, John Andrew. *Church and Community in Crisis: The Gospel according to Matthew.* The New Testament in Context. Valley Forge, PA: Trinity, 1996.

———. *Matthew's Gospel and Formative Judaism: The Social World of the Matthean Community.* Minneapolis: Fortress, 1990.

Oyen, Geert van. "The Doublets in the 19th-Century Gospel Study." *ETL* 73 (1997) 277–306.

Page, Sydney H. T. "The Authenticity of the Ransom Logion (Mark 10:45b)." Pages 137–62 in *Gospel Perspectives: Studies of History and Tradition in the Four Gospels.* Edited by R. T. France and David Wenham. Repr. Eugene, OR: Wipf & Stock, 2003.

Pamment, Margaret. "The Son of Man in the First Gospel." *NTS* 29 (1983) 116–29.

Pannenberg, Wolfhart. *Jesus-God and Man.* Translated by Lewis L. Wilkins and Duane A. Priebe. 2nd ed. Philadelphia: Westminster, 1977.

Parry, Robin. "Narrative Criticism." In *Dictionary for Theological Interpretation of the Bible,* edited by Kevin J. Vanhoozer, 528–31. Grand Rapids: Baker Academic, 2005.

Perrin, Norman. *What is Redaction Criticism?* Edited by Dan O. Via Jr. Repr. Eugene, OR: Wipf & Stock, 2002.

Porter, Stanley E., and Bryan R. Dyer, eds. *The Synoptic Problem: Four Views.* Grand Rapids: Baker Academic, 2016.

Powell, Mark Allen. "Narrative Criticism." In *DBI* 2:201–4.

———. "Narrative Criticism." Pages 240–58 in *Hearing the New Testament: Strategies for Interpretation.* Edited by Joel B. Green. 2nd ed. Grand Rapids: Eerdmans, 2010.

———. *What is Narrative Criticism? A New Approach to the Bible.* Repr. London: SPCK, 1993.

Przybylski, Benno. *Righteousness in Matthew and His World of Thought.* SNTSMS 41. Cambridge: Cambridge University Press, 1980.

Reed, Jonathan L. "Nazareth." In *EDB* 951.

Repschinki, Boris. *The Controversy Stories in the Gospel of Matthew: Their Redaction, Form and Relevance for the Relationship between the Matthean Community and Formative Judaism.* Göttingen: Vandenhoeck & Ruprecht, 2000.

Resseguie, James L. *Narrative Criticism of the New Testament: An Introduction.* Grand Rapids: Baker Academic, 2005.

Rhoads, David, et al. *Mark as Story: An Introduction to the Narrative of a Gospel.* 3rd ed. Minneapolis: Fortress, 2012.

Robertson, A. T. *A Grammar of the Greek New Testament in Light of the Historical Research.* Nashville: Broadman, 1934.

Saldarini, Anthony J. "Delegitimization of Leaders in Matthew 23." *CBQ* 54 (1992) 659–80.

———. *Matthew's Christian-Jewish Community.* CSHJ. Chicago: University of Chicago Press, 1994.

Schnackenburg, Rudolf. "Jesus ist (von den Toten) auferstanden." *BZ* 13 (1969) 1–17.

Schottroff, Luise, and Wolfgang Stegemann. *Jesus and the Hope of the Poor.* Translated by Matthew J. O'Connell. Maryknoll, NY: Orbis, 1986.

Scott, J. Martin C. "Matthew 15.21–28: A Test-Case for Jesus' Manners." *JSNT* 63 (1996) 21–44.

Silva, Moisés. *Philippians.* BECNT. 2nd ed. Grand Rapids: Baker Academic, 2005.

Sim, David C. *The Gospel of Matthew and Christian Judaism: The History and Social Setting of the Matthean Community.* SNTW. Edinburgh: T. & T. Clark, 1998.

———. "Matthew: The Current State of Research." In *Mark and Matthew I: Comparative Readings: Understanding the Earliest Gospels in their First-Century Settings,* edited by Eve-Marie Becker and Anders Runesson, 33–54. WUNT 271. Tübingen: Mohr Siebeck, 2011.

———. "The Pacifist Jesus and the Violent Jesus in the Gospel of Matthew." *HvTSt* 67 (2011) 1–6.

Smith, Mahlon H. "No Place for a Son of Man." FF 4 (1988) 83–107.

Stanton, Graham. *A Gospel for a New People: Studies in Matthew.* Repr. Louisville: Westminster John Knox, 1993.

———. "The Origin and Purpose of Matthew's Gospel: Matthean Scholarship from 1945 to 1980." *ANRW* 2: 1889–951.

Stegner, William Richard. "The Temptation Narrative: A Study in the Use of Scripture by Early Jewish Christians." *BR* 35 (1990) 5–17.

Stein, Robert H. *Studying the Synoptic Gospels: Origin and Interpretation.* 3rd ed. Grand Rapids: Baker Academic, 2004.

Strecker, Georg. *Der Weg der Gerechtigkeit: Untersuchung zur Theologie des Matthäus.* FRLANT 82. Göttingen: Vandenhoeck & Ruprecht, 1971.

Streeter, Burnett Hillman. *The Four Gospels: A Study of Origins.* London: Macmillan, 1924.

Stronstad, Roger. *The Charismatic Theology of St. Luke: Trajectories from the Old Testament to Luke-Acts.* 2nd ed. Grand Rapids: Baker Academic, 2012.

Swanson, Reuben, ed. *New Testament Greek Manuscripts: Variant Readings Arranged in Horizontal Lines Against Codex Vaticanus, Matthew.* Sheffield: Sheffield Academic, 1995.

Taylor, Vincent. *The Gospel According to St. Mark: The Greek Text with Introduction, Notes, and Indexes.* 2nd ed. New York: St. Martin's, 1974.

Theissen, Gerd. *The Miracle Stories of the Early Christian Tradition.* Translated by Francis McDonagh. SNTW. Edinburgh: T. & T. Clark, 1983.

Theological Dictionary of the New Testament. 10 vols. Edited by Gerhard Kittel and Gerhard Friedrich. Translated by Geoffrey W. Bromiley. Grand Rapids: Eerdmans, 1964–1976.

Thompson, Marianne Meye. *The Humanity of Jesus in the Fourth Gospel.* Philadelphia: Fortress, 1988.

Thompson, William G. "Reflections on the Composition of Mt 8:1–9:34." *CBQ* 33 (1971) 365–88.

Toland, John. *Nazarenus: Or, Jewish, Gentile, and Mahometan Christianity.* 2nd ed. London: J. Brotherton, 1718.

Turner, David L. *Matthew.* BECNT. Grand Rapids: Baker Academic, 2008.

Twelftree, Graham. *Jesus the Exorcist: A Contribution to the Study of the Historical Jesus.* Tübingen: Mohr Siebeck, 1993. Repr. Eugene, OR: Wipf & Stock, 2010.

———. *Jesus the Miracle Worker: A Historical and Theological Study.* Downers Grove, IL: InterVarsity, 1999.

Van Beek, Gus W. "Frankincense and Myrrh." *BA* 23 (1960) 70–95.

Vermes, Geza. *Jesus the Jew: A Historian's Reading of the Gospels.* London: Collins, 1973.

———. *The Religion of Jesus the Jew.* Minneapolis: Fortress, 1993.

Viljoen, Francois P. "Jesus Healing the Leper and the Purity Law in the Gospel of Matthew." *IDS* 48 (2014) 1–7.

Vine, Cedric E. W. *The Audience of Matthew: An Appraisal of the Local Audience Thesis.* LNTS. London: Bloomsbury, 2015.

Viviano, Benedict Thomas. "God in the Gospel According to Matthew." *Int* 64 (2010) 341–54.

Voorwinde, Stephen. *Jesus' Emotions in the Gospels.* New York: T. & T. Clark, 2011.

Ware, Bruce A. *The Man Christ Jesus: Theological Reflections on the Humanity of Christ.* Wheaton, IL: Crossway, 2012.

Watts, John D. W. *Isaiah 1–33.* WBC 24. Nashville: Thomas Nelson, 2006.

Watts, Rikki E. "Messianic Servant or the End of Israel's Exilic Crisis? Isaiah 53.4 in Matthew 8.17." *JSNT* 38 (2015) 81–95.

Williams, D. H. "The Gospel of Matthew in Service of the Early Fathers." *ProEccl* 23 (2014) 81–98.

Wilson, Alistair I. *When Will These Things Happen? A Study of Jesus as Judge in Matthew 21–25.* Paternoster Biblical Monographs. Milton Keynes: Paternoster, 2004.

Witherington, Ben, III. *Matthew.* SHBC. Macon, GA: Smith & Helwys, 2006.

Zerwick, Max. *A Grammatical Analysis of the Greek New Testament.* 5th ed. Translated by Mary Grosvenor. Rome: Pontifical Biblical Institute, 1996.

Index of Ancient Sources

Matthew *(cont.)*

Matthew (cont.)

Mark

Luke